Praise for *Untethered*

"When life falls apart, it's easy to assun ~~...~~
Or worse, that you're stuck there. *Unt.* ~~.....~~ ~~...~~
of life's disorienting darkness punctuat~~ed~~ ~~b~~y lightning strikes of hope.
Laura forces readers to confront the vulnerability of being human
while offering a rousing call to more abundant life. If you've ever felt
blindsided by disappointment and disillusionment, Laura's journey of
faith amid failure is not to be missed. Highly recommend!"

–Jonathan Merritt, contributing writer for *The Atlantic*
and author of *Learning to Speak God from Scratch*

"*Untethered* is a breathtaking glimpse into the unraveling of a life
after death. With winsome prose, Whitfield's poignant coming-of-
age narrative takes the reader on a journey of what happens when
we come undone. This is a timely memoir of loss, sex, beauty, family, and the courage it takes to regain our footing amid chaos."

–J. Dana Trent, author of *Dessert First:*
Preparing for Death While Savoring Life

"*Untethered* is about learning to forgive yourself and deal with the
unresolved grief from compounded traumas that so many of us
as women carry, believing that burden to be our cross to bear in
silence and shame. A deep and satisfying read."

–Echo Montgomery Garrett, author of *My Orange Duffel Bag:*
A Journey to Radical Change and cofounder of
the Orange Duffel Bag Initiative

"With radiant honesty, Whitfield tells the story of losing her beloved brother, which set her on a quest to find emotional and spiritual sanctuary. We follow her wild years in the Outer Banks, New York City, and Chapel Hill, where she seeks solace in men, jobs, and her writing. What she must learn is how to find a way 'for my faith and my life to line up.' Whitfield's frank, vibrant memoir reads with the page-turning urgency of a novel you can't put down. Fans of Mary Karr's *Lit* and Anne Lamott's *Traveling Mercies* will want to read this book."

—Marianne Gingher, professor of English
and creative writing, UNC, and author of *A Girl's Life*
and *Adventures in Pen Land*

"*Untethered* is a page-turning read for anyone who has dared to follow a dream, suffered tragic loss, and longed for redemption."

—Michael Morris, author of *A Place Called Wiregrass*,
Slow Way Home, and *Man in the Blue Moon*

"It's not easy to reach into our darkest truths. In *Untethered*, Whitfield takes the deep dive into faith, family, love, loss, and the longing to find oneself."

—Cheryl Sharp, CEO of Sharp Change Consulting
and former head of the National Council for
Behavioral Health's Trauma-Informed Care initiatives

"Whitfield's memoir is an engrossing coming-of-age tale. Marked by deep grief and aspiration, broken relationships and restoration, her story moves from a quiet beginning in North Carolina, to New York City and back again, all in pursuit of a defined sense of self.

In her generous telling, Whitfield reminds us that humility, grace, and deep gratitude can yield the richest rewards, and that this life's greatest fulfillment comes in relationship with others."

—Rebecca Brewster Stevenson,
author of *Healing Maddie Brees* and *Wait*

"*Untethered* is an exciting journey of a dynamic woman—and while it represents her life, there are so many moments of "Oh, I know that feeling" that she could be writing about me and my life, only with different names! So many of us have gone through the journey of finding ourselves while thinking it takes a man to get there—Whitfield's story shows us that we need ourselves to find ourselves—and along the way, we might also find love. A great read for women of all ages."

—Jen Oleniczak Brown, founder of The Engaging Educator
and author of *Think on Your Feet*

Untethered

Untethered

Faith, Failure, and Finding Solid Ground

Laura Whitfield

SHE WRITES PRESS

Copyright © 2022 Laura Whitfield

All rights reserved. No part of this publication may be reproduced, distributed, or transmitted in any form or by any means, including photocopying, recording, digital scanning, or other electronic or mechanical methods, without the prior written permission of the publisher, except in the case of brief quotations embodied in critical reviews and certain other noncommercial uses permitted by copyright law. For permission requests, please address She Writes Press.

Published 2022

Printed in the United States of America

Print ISBN: 978-1-64742-221-9
E-ISBN: 978-1-64742-319-3
Library of Congress Control Number: 2021914307

For information, address:
She Writes Press
1569 Solano Ave #546
Berkeley, CA 94707

She Writes Press is a division of SparkPoint Studio, LLC.

All company and/or product names may be trade names, logos, trademarks, and/or registered trademarks and are the property of their respective owners.

NAMES AND IDENTIFYING CHARACTERISTICS
HAVE BEEN CHANGED TO PROTECT THE PRIVACY
OF CERTAIN INDIVIDUALS.

To Mama, Daddy,

Lawrence, and Horace.

Because of you, I am.

Author's Note

This is my story the way I remember it. If other people were to tell this story from their perspective, it would be different. But that would be their story to tell. This is mine.

All of the events presented here did happen as told through the filter of memory. It is my best recollection of what took place long ago. Some of it is mined from newspapers, journals, and conversations. The dialogue—and there is quite a bit—is what I recall being said. When I was unable to remember a conversation verbatim, I captured its essence and intent.

Finally, I meant no harm to anyone in the writing of my story. I simply needed to get it down. Most of the names and some identifying details were changed to protect the privacy of those I wrote about. To those who have passed away, I hope this honors your memory.

I am inclined to believe that God's chief purpose in giving us memory is to enable us to go back in time so that if we didn't play those roles right the first time round, we can still have another go at it now.

—Frederick Buechner, author of *Telling Secrets*

~ᴈ·ᴄ~

Chapter One

I remember driving down a highway in 1990 and seeing a sign that read, "Lane ends in 2,000 feet." I counted the seconds as I drove to where the lane ran out. It seemed endless. My brother, Lawrence, had fallen half that distance as he was climbing Ben Nevis. Almost twenty years had passed, and the same questions still haunted me: *What was he thinking as he plummeted? Was it about his fiancée, Julie? Horace? My parents? Me?*

It was a Sunday in late February of 1971, and Mama and I had just returned home from seeing the movie *Love Story*. As I'd watched Ryan O'Neal and Ali MacGraw playing in the snow, I'd thought of Lawrence, who was now living in Scotland, working on a master's in English at the University of Edinburgh. It had been six months since I'd seen him, and I missed him terribly.

"It was so sad," I told Daddy. "They fell in love and then she died."

I looked out the den window. It was starting to get dark. The phone rang, and Daddy went to answer it. He returned a few minutes later.

"That was Claude," he said to Mama. "He told me he needs to stop by for a few minutes."

His mood was somber. Claude Sitton was Daddy's editor at the *News & Observer*. He had never been to our house. A Sunday afternoon visit from someone at the paper was certainly unusual.

Mama went into the kitchen to brew a pot of coffee. She seemed anxious, so I asked if I could help. I knelt on the yellowed linoleum and searched in the cabinet for the percolator we used when company came.

"Do you think Daddy's gonna lose his job?" I asked.

"I don't think so," she replied tentatively.

When the doorbell rang half an hour later, Daddy answered it and I helped Mama arrange a few slices of pound cake on a fancy glass plate.

Mama and I waited in the den so Mr. Sitton could tell Daddy whatever news he'd come to deliver. A few minutes later, Daddy walked into the den alone, his face ashen.

"Lawrence has been in a fatal mountain climbing accident," he said in a tone that was unfamiliar. "It came across the wire service. AP—Claude saw it."

He faltered. I looked at Mama. She glanced down, her lips parted. Nothing. Daddy's words hung in the air like poison. *"Somebody say something!"* I wanted to shout.

"At least he's not . . ." I offered, breaking the silence. Then I stopped short. The word *fatal* sank in. That was the moment my life changed forever.

Lawrence was climbing Scotland's tallest mountain, Ben Nevis, when an unexpected storm blew up. The wind was fierce, the face icy, his equipment inadequate, and the outcome tragic.

He had graduated from the University of North Carolina at Chapel Hill the previous May with highest honors in English. He'd won a George C. Marshall Fellowship to study William Blake at Edinburgh. He had dreams of writing, teaching at a university, and marrying Julie, the girl he loved. Lawrence had met Julie over spring break his junior year. She had gone to Edinburgh just before Christmas, and they'd decided to get married when he finished his studies.

Julie was sweet and warm, the sister I'd always longed for.

Lawrence had joined the University Mountaineering Club when he arrived in Edinburgh the previous fall. Never especially athletic, he soon wrote home to share his love of climbing. There were several outings that winter in preparation for Ben Nevis, the most challenging climb of the semester. He was with a small band of climbers when he lost his footing and fell one thousand feet.

I would read years later about what individuals experience as they fall, taken from testimonies of people who had fallen great distances and survived. The first few seconds are panic, followed by a sense of euphoria, and then one's life flashing before one's eyes.

The State Department told Daddy that it was too dark to send out a rescue team; they would have to wait until morning to search for Lawrence's body. Hours later, we got the news that he'd been found.

For twenty-three years, Lawrence embraced life. He read everything from Dietrich Bonhoeffer to Malcolm X. He had a brilliant mind and a passion for social justice. At UNC, he was chairman of the Judicial Reform Committee and participated in protests to help African American students and campus cafeteria workers gain equal rights. The fall of his junior year, he called to tell my parents he was in Washington, DC, protesting the Vietnam War.

Everyone knew that Lawrence had a profound faith in God. He was thinking of becoming a pastor; he had a full scholarship to Yale Divinity School when he returned from Edinburgh. Not one to accept faith blindly, however, he asked hard questions and sought the answers in books and through experiences like climbing. I'd never thought much about Lawrence's interest in climbing until I read this excerpt from a letter he wrote to my parents a few months before his death. Then I understood. Climbing made him feel closer to God. It made sense.

I haven't figured out yet what is so compelling about climbing a mountain.

The long wet walks, the wind, the cold, the rain, or the thought of doing it? Perhaps it's because one discovers that the spiritual world is more real, more enduring than the physical—which may explain why climbers seldom talk about what they see.

The minutes and hours following that devastating news remain a blur. I believe my mother said something about calling my brother Horace, who was attending East Carolina University, an hour and a half away. The next thing I remember is that my aunt Karen arrived. She was Mama's baby sister and lived across town.

"There'll be people here soon," she said. "I'll help you make your bed."

We pulled up the pink chenille bedspread, and I looked at her and said with newfound wisdom, "Life is short. You have to make every moment count." That revelation was way beyond my experience or understanding; I was just fourteen. How could I know those words would alter the course of my life?

It was late when Horace got home. I was standing in the bedroom he'd always shared with Lawrence. He walked through the door, his face tearstained and swollen.

"Hey," I said, walking over to him. Without saying a word, he put his arms around me and pulled me close. We had spent most of our childhood fighting, but that ended at that moment. He sat down on the antique rocker by the window and I sat on his lap, and we held each other and sobbed. I don't know how long we were there, rocking. It felt like hours, and maybe it was. What I do know is that the creaking of that gooseneck rocker and the sound of our sobs was like a healing balm. All those years of bickering just fell away and revealed a new truth: we were all each other had.

It took a week for Lawrence's remains to be shipped home from Scotland. That word—*remains*—struck me. In Lawrence's case it was probably accurate, since he was certainly a bunch of body parts after having been hurled against rock and snow. What could possibly be left of my brother? I wasn't sure, but I couldn't stop thinking about it.

That week we had lots of visitors. Mama chatted with them while Daddy just walked around with a sad smile. He took care of Mama while Horace and I took care of each other. Our days were filled with flowers (I especially remember a fragrant purple hyacinth), casseroles, and Lawrence's friends. Many of them had left the area after graduation, and they came from all over: Boston, California, and, of course, Chapel Hill. Phone calls, cards, and telegrams flooded in. Mama saved every keepsake—a large cardboard box filled with almost two thousand items. How could someone so young be loved so much?

Classes in the English department at UNC were canceled. Memorial services were held at our church, the Wesley Foundation (the Methodist campus organization where Lawrence had been president), and at the University of Edinburgh. Some of Lawrence's friends sat down with my parents and discussed starting the James Lawrence Whitfield Jr. Traveling Fellowship at UNC. The idea was to award a small stipend each year to a student scholar who was interested in studying abroad. Someone from Edinburgh called to say that the English department was hanging a plaque in Lawrence's honor on the wall outside the university library, while the mountain climbing club was raising funds to place a stone memorial at the bottom of Ben Nevis.

Lawrence's remains finally came, and Daddy went to the funeral home to receive them. We now had something tangible; there was no more denying that this terrible thing had really happened.

"The casket will have to be closed for the funeral," Daddy announced when he got home.

Mama and I stood in the kitchen, listening raptly. Open caskets were commonplace in the South.

"They had to nail it shut," he added with finality.

We all knew why. Mama's face froze.

"But . . ." she started, and then her eyes went hazy. This is a look I'd come to recognize in the months and years to follow as Mama began to slip into a deep depression. Never getting a last glimpse of her firstborn surely made her grief more impossible to bear.

My parents picked out a burial plot at one of Raleigh's newest cemeteries, away from the highway, and took Horace and me to see it. They found a spot on a hill, which my mother felt was appropriate, with a pine tree nearby. She liked the tree because the rest of the hill was bare except for grave markers and plastic flowers in brass vases.

"If I park the car directly in front of this tree and walk up the hill," she explained, "Lawrence will be easy to find." That idea seemed to bring her comfort, and it brought me comfort too. I could go there any time, especially when I needed to talk, and Lawrence would be there. Right in front of that tree. I could count on it.

The day we lowered Lawrence into the ground, the temperature dropped to freezing and the wind was bitter. It was March 8, 1971. I wore a dress that I'd sewn out of brown polyester. My legs were bare except for the nylon stockings I'd just recently been allowed to wear. Even though I was wrapped up in a winter coat, the wind passed through me as though I was hollow, which I was.

I remember standing on that hill, looking around at Mama, Daddy, Horace, Julie, and the friends and relatives gathered, wondering how we would all go on. Lawrence had been my whole life—I was lost without him. He had always protected me when Horace went on the offensive; he'd swoop me up onto his shoulders, and I knew nothing could touch me there. He'd taught me how to play chess. He'd taken me to see *Lawrence of Arabia* and *2001: A Space*

Odyssey when I was just eleven. I remember sitting in the Cardinal Theatre, feeling important because he'd brought me to a movie that only grown-ups could understand.

For my thirteenth birthday, he gave me a Gordon Lightfoot album and a copy of *The Diary of a Young Girl* by Anne Frank. I still have the book—it is the only thing from him I still possess.

As the weeks passed, I searched for clues as to how this could have happened. Surely if I thought back through my life to date, I could find an answer. At least I could try.

My parents moved into our house on Valentine's Day of 1956, and they said I was conceived that night. That's the most sexual reference they ever made in my presence. Even though Lawrence and Horace were ten and six years older than me, I never felt that I was a "mistake"—and if I was, no one ever let on. I was the long-awaited girl, but I don't think Mama knew what to do with me. I always had short, boyish hair when I was little because she didn't know how to braid. My best friend, Donna Dixon, had long, wavy hair to her waist. I sat in the back seat of her parents' car on the way to church many Sundays and watched with envy as Mrs. Dixon worked her hands through her daughter's hair with great love.

My parents liked to tell the story of how, when they brought me home from the hospital, Lawrence sat by my crib all afternoon and held my hand while Horace went out to play. Whether it was our early bond or shared disposition, Lawrence became the brother I adored and the model by which I measured every other man. God heaped every good gift on Lawrence—looks, intellect, talent. In my eyes he was perfect, and I adored him.

The other person I adored was Daddy. I was a "Daddy's girl," and everyone knew it, especially me. Daddy was gentle, sweet, and witty—the complete opposite of Mama, who was beautiful but serious, and hard to get close to. I know because I spent my entire life trying.

Horace was the middle child. He pushed boundaries, tested limits, and picked on me relentlessly. Why couldn't he just be nice to me, like Lawrence? Horace also had gifts. Girls found him charming. The prettiest ones at Tanglewood Swimming Pool played with me just to get his attention.

He fooled those girls and everyone with that charm, especially Mama and our piano teacher, Mrs. Sutter. Horace got through almost every piano lesson without ever playing a note. I would sit there in her living room waiting for my lesson, which followed his. Listening through the accordion partition, I was amazed at how adept he was at keeping Mrs. Sutter distracted. "Is that a new dress?" he'd gush to our plump, matronly teacher. Then he'd go on and on about his drum major audition or about the boat he was building in our basement. By the time my lesson started, Mrs. Sutter was tired of small talk and ready to get down to business.

"He did it again!" I'd complain to Mama as we slid into the car to go home.

"Did what?" Horace would ask slyly.

"You know!" I'd fume, rolling my eyes. "You talked and talked and didn't play a thing!"

"Now, Laura," Mama would reply, amused. "It can't be as bad as you say."

Mama always seemed to take the boys' side. They were older and knew how to manipulate her to get their way, but she was more at ease around the boys too. Her eyes lit up when they talked, and she laughed like a schoolgirl. She was especially that way with Lawrence. He had her piercing brown eyes and angular face, and when she looked at him, I believe she saw herself. "Lawrence just made honor roll," she'd brag to her friends. "And he's going to Boys State this year."

Mama was different around me. She was often demanding. I never felt like I could do anything right. When I was twelve, two years before we lost Lawrence, Mama was out shopping one Saturday, so I decided to surprise her and make a cake. When the cake came out of the oven, it wasn't quite done, so I put toothpicks between the layers to hold them together. It seemed like a good idea to me. After the cake cooled, I iced it and hid it on the steps going up to the attic.

After supper, I retrieved the cake and proudly placed it in front of Mama.

"I made it all by myself," I said, beaming.

"Why are there so many toothpicks?" she asked as she cut into the first piece.

"It was falling apart," I said.

"If you'd cooked it longer, you wouldn't have needed them," she announced.

I stopped making cakes after that and spent less and less time in the kitchen with Mama.

During the week, Daddy would go to the paper while we went to school. On Saturdays, there was no playing until we finished our chores. So the boys and I scrubbed the bathrooms while Mama put up pickles or sewed dresses and Daddy worked in the yard. After chores, Lawrence and Horace would go hunting or frog gigging; squirrel and frog legs were common fare at our house. I was happy just wandering through the fields surrounding our neighborhood, picking bachelor's buttons, tossing stones into a nearby pond, and looking for shapes in the clouds.

We went to Longview Methodist Church on Sundays and took an occasional vacation to the mountains or the beach. We never went to exotic places like Florida or California or even Charlotte. It never crossed our minds. We were always hanging out with our cousins, aunts, and uncles—they were as much a part of our life as our nuclear family. For the most part, life was simple and good.

Daddy was an editor at the *News & Observer* and worked the evening shift, so when I was young, we spent most mornings together. We'd hang out in the kitchen, and I'd play with dolls or look at books while Daddy worked at his typewriter. I especially looked forward to lunch. Daddy would turn on *Love of Life* or *Sky King*, and we'd eat Campbell's soup and peanut butter and jelly sandwiches on TV trays.

Every spring, I'd help Daddy put in a vegetable garden. As soon as the weather got warm, we'd make our annual trip to the hardware store. We'd come home with rope and a small board, and Daddy would fashion them into a swing and hang it from a branch of the huge sycamore that shaded our backyard. Every fall, Daddy and I would go to the State Fair, where we rode the Tilt-A-Whirl and ate cotton candy. Those were the best times because I had Daddy all to myself. The boys weren't so lucky. Daddy wasn't around for the things that were important to them, like band concerts and prom night, and his absence left a hole, especially for Horace.

It seemed Mama was always in the kitchen or working in her flower gardens or volunteering at church, and she needed help running the house. So, like many other families in the 1960s South, we had a maid. There were several over the years—Mary Washington, Viola Neil, Berlene Lee. I remember Viola the best because she practically raised me from the time I was five until I was about twelve.

I sometimes wondered why our maids were Black, and not white like us. I also wondered about their families. Did they have husbands? Or children like me? If they did, why weren't they home taking care of them instead of looking after me? Then I'd realize that Mama was busy doing other things too, and that made me sad.

Mama went back to teaching first grade when I was in kindergarten.

"I heard Mama tell Daddy she's tired of being at home," Horace offered one day. "She wants to go back to work."

Daddy was supportive; he just wanted Mama to be happy. So Mama started teaching, Daddy did his part, and our maids helped. Time passed. Lawrence grew up and went off to college, and Horace followed. I was the only one left at home.

I was in junior high now and going through what people call that "awkward stage." I wore glasses and braces, and my hair was cut in an unstylish bob. While my friends' chests blossomed, my own body remained dormant, like an eternal winter. I was sure that I would never get a boyfriend, much less find a husband or ever have children. I was deeply insecure and desperate to be like everyone else. I lamented my plight in a diary and shed secret tears. I would have given anything to confide in Mama, but I didn't dare.

Despite my misery, I knew Daddy loved me and so did Lawrence, and because of that, I believed everything would be okay. Once Mama said to me when Daddy was standing there, "Your father loves you more than he loves me." That was the most hurtful thing she ever said to me, and I never forgot it. I knew it came from a deep place of pain, but it would be years before I'd discover why my close relationship with Daddy grieved her so.

Lawrence returned almost every weekend since he was just down the road at UNC. I lived for those visits. Lawrence treated me like an adult. We would hang out and talk and listen to music together. He loved Wagner and knew how to play "Moonlight Sonata" on the piano. On Sundays, I would mope through church just thinking about Lawrence heading back to school. After church, our family would have a formal, sit-down dinner—usually a pot roast or Mama's famous fried chicken. There was white linen on the table, our best silver, and our Haviland china. Mama was all smiles as she made the foods Lawrence loved most.

After lunch, Daddy would drive Lawrence down to the highway to hitchhike a ride, or we'd make the thirty-minute drive up

Highway 54 to Chapel Hill. I used to dread Sunday afternoons. Everyone was happier and our life went more smoothly when Lawrence was home. He was the glue that held our family together, and things just didn't feel normal when he was away.

After he died, it sometimes felt like he was still simply away. Then I'd realize there would be no weekend visits, no dinners with all of us around the table. Those things were now in the past.

In early spring, five weeks after that fateful phone call, a large wooden crate arrived at our house, the kind once used to ship medical supplies overseas. Daddy pried back the wood, and we opened the top and began to go through the contents. In the crate was everything belonging to Lawrence at the time of his death: his suitcases, clothes, books, and letters. Mama reached in and pulled out three gray composition books—Lawrence's journals. She sat down and opened them and began thumbing through the pages filled with his familiar scrawl. Lawrence was a prolific writer; he always wrote with a black Flair pen, and his handwriting looked like a doctor's, almost impossible to decipher.

Moments later, a page fell open and Mama's face went pale.

"What's wrong?" I asked.

I walked over and looked down at the open book on her lap. The letters were clear and unmistakable.

"I have had a premonition of my death," she read aloud.

What does one do with such a revelation? She didn't speak about the journal entry much after that. Maybe she was asking herself the same questions we were: *Did he know how he was going to die? Did he know it was going to be that day? If so, why did he go?*

Several months later, I was home alone. Mama and Daddy were out running errands, and the house was quiet. I wandered up to the attic, as I often did, to poke around objects and through boxes, hoping to find some unexpected treasure. As I made my way past the brick chimney, I noticed the large wooden crate. I walked over and opened the lid. Everything was just the way we'd left it the day we discovered Lawrence's journals. On top was a small box filled with the things Lawrence had in his pocket the day he fell—a lapel pin with a white dove holding an olive branch, a silver whistle, and a few British coins. Under the box were several Oxford cloth shirts, like the ones he used to pay me a quarter to iron. I picked up a blue one, held it to my face, and breathed in.

After all this time, it still smelled like Lawrence and English Leather, his favorite cologne. I'd barely been holding it together, and now the tears began to flow.

"Laura?" I heard Daddy call from downstairs.

My parents were back. I lifted my face, knowing I should answer, but I didn't. I didn't want to break the spell.

I left the attic door cracked. They'll figure it out. I pressed my face into the cloth and breathed in deeply, desperate to bring Lawrence back to life. Wasn't this lingering scent a sign that he was still here? That he'd left the room and would soon return?

I felt a hand on my shoulder and looked up, hopeful. It was Daddy.

"You okay?" he asked gently.

I didn't answer. I just pulled Lawrence's shirt to my face and cried.

~⁀◦⁀~

Chapter Two

"I want to move to the beach and live with Horace," I announced to my parents over spring break my freshman year of college. It was March; summer was approaching, my friends were making plans, and the last thing I wanted to do was spend my summer at home.

"And what are you going to do for a job?" Mama asked.

"I can wait tables or get a job at The Christmas Shop," I told her, knowing I'd already made up my mind. The Christmas Shop, filled year-round with Christmas trees and knickknacks, as well as local pottery, leather goods, and art, was Roanoke Island's most novel attraction. It seemed like a fun place to work.

"I'll call your brother and see how he feels," Daddy said.

What Daddy didn't know was I'd already run the idea by Horace. While he hadn't said yes, he'd at least agreed to think about it.

Daddy walked into the kitchen, picked up the phone, and dialed Horace's number.

"Your sister wants to come live with you for the summer," he said in his usual upbeat way. They chatted for a few minutes, and I stood there listening, anxiously watching Daddy's face for a sign. What if Horace said no? I couldn't imagine waking up every morning in my blue-and-lime-green childhood room and going to work at the mall.

"Your brother wants to talk to you," Daddy said, handing me the phone.

"Hey," I said nervously.

"Promise not to drive me crazy?" Horace teased.

"Promise." I passed the phone back to Daddy, relieved.

"Keep an eye on her," I heard him say before hanging up.

I called The Christmas Shop and they told me they were hiring. I asked if they would mail me an application, and when it came I promptly filled it out and sent it back. In early April, one of the owners, Edward Greene, called to tell me he'd like me to come and work as a sales clerk beginning the middle of May. Now everything was in place. I was elated. Back at school, I finished up classes, studied for finals, and counted the days until I could leave for the Outer Banks.

The Outer Banks are as remote as an island chain can be. Until Horace moved there after graduating from college, our family had only visited once. On that trip, we drove the five and a half hours to Manteo and stayed at the Duke of Dare Motor Lodge. We ate at the Polar Bear Drive-in, the only restaurant in town, and rode the Roanoke Island ferry across the sound to get to the beach. Daddy stopped at a shell shop called Shipwreck, and I picked out a box of exotic conchs and cowries housed in a pale green box to bring home as a souvenir.

On the way home, I sat in the back seat, rubbing my fingers across those colorful shells. Something about this place had slipped into my heart. It would remain there the rest of my life.

May finally arrived. When exams were over, I packed my suitcase and a few boxes into the '68 Camaro I'd inherited from Horace and headed to the beach.

My freshman year had been a huge disappointment. UNC

Greensboro had just turned coed, and there were only a handful of guys on campus. I certainly hadn't signed up for an all-girls school, and this felt like one. I liked my classes and some of my professors, but campus life was boring. I wasn't sure I wanted to go back in the fall, and the beach seemed like a good place to go and figure it out.

After hours of driving past greening farmland and dilapidated tobacco barns, I arrived in Manteo, a quiet, waterfront town with a courthouse, small post office, and several docks jutting out into the creek leading to Shallowbag Bay. Eleven years had passed since our family vacation there, and nothing seemed to have changed.

I was moving into the old two-story house on Sir Walter Raleigh Street that Horace shared with his friend Tommy, who had been one of Horace's fraternity brothers in college. Tommy lived in a separate apartment in the back of the house with his three Persian cats. He was from eastern North Carolina, and he called me "darlin'" and "sugar." He felt like another brother, and I was used to having guys around. Our living arrangement felt safe and familiar.

The house was rambling and rickety and had vines growing up along the chimney. There was a parlor with a woodstove. The windowpanes rattled when the wind blew. My room was on the second floor at the top of the stairs. It was sparsely furnished with a bed and a cardboard box that I used for a bedside table. It was far from fancy, but I didn't care. I was finally on my own, away from college and, for the first time, away from my parents' watchful eyes. I sensed that something exciting was about to happen, something life altering, though I didn't know for sure what it was. What I did know was that nothing had been the same since Lawrence died.

The fall after his accident, I'd started high school. I'd made new friends, studied hard, and stayed busy working on the yearbook and singing in the mixed ensemble. But in the afternoons I'd come home to an empty house, and that's when it hit me: Lawrence was never coming back. I'd sit in Daddy's La-Z-Boy and do my homework, and tears would come to my eyes. I pushed down the pain by watching TV and stuffing potato chips into my mouth, but nothing helped. What I didn't know was that grief is caustic. That it corrodes you from the inside out.

Now four years had passed, and only Mama spoke about Lawrence. In those four years, Mama had changed. After Lawrence died, she'd started complaining about not having any energy. One day, a pill bottle appeared on her dresser. I picked it up to see what it was. Valium. I didn't know why she was taking it, but Mama was always complaining about one ailment or another, so I brushed it off. I noticed that during the week she'd go to school, then come home, lie down on the sofa, and nap. Just before Daddy got home from work, she would lift herself up as though she weighed four hundred pounds, put her feet on the floor, and say, flatly, "Well, I guess I'd better go make supper." Then she'd stand up, walk into the kitchen, and do just that.

I didn't understand that Mama was depressed. People didn't talk about depression back then, especially with their children. All I knew was that she was sad and missed Lawrence—and that I understood. It occurred to me that this might be one of the few things we still had in common.

Daddy, Horace, and I knew Mama wasn't herself, but I wasn't sure the rest of us were either. I could look at Daddy's face and tell he was worried about Mama. Horace had become president of his fraternity at East Carolina, and I guessed that he was trying to get Mama and Daddy's attention and somehow fill Lawrence's shoes. I was fragile, but no one knew it because I never said a word. I just kept on doing what was expected of me, so they all thought I was fine. Nobody ever said to me, "Laura, are you okay? I know losing your brother must have been hard. Would you like to talk about it?" If they had, perhaps I would have been able to articulate my feelings—but maybe not. My big brother was gone. My life didn't make sense anymore. I felt empty, and I just wanted the sadness to go away.

Instead of talking to a therapist about all of this, which of course was never even considered, I wrote poems. When I was sitting with my composition book in my lap, wrapping words around my pain, I wasn't sad. Books were my other escape. I could open the pages of a book and let my eyes fall on one word and then another until I was lost in sentences and paragraphs and transported to a place where there was no pain, or if there was, at least I had the comfort of knowing I wasn't alone.

I had only one friend I could talk to about Lawrence. Her name was Teresa. She understood what I was going through because she'd lost her brother in a drowning accident ten months after Lawrence died.

The day I heard the news about her brother, Wayne, Mama dropped me off at Teresa's house on St. George Road.

"Come in, honey," her mom said, giving me a hug. Mrs. Fogleman had lost her only son, and she had the same sad eyes as Mama. She knew why I was there and pointed to the hallway and Teresa's room. I knocked, then walked in to find Teresa sitting on her bed, staring. I knew that look. It was the look of someone who was lost. I was still lost, and now Teresa and I had found each other. She looked up and smiled.

"I knew you'd come," she said, and I sat down beside her on the bed, and we put our arms around each other and cried.

It wasn't long before my life revolved around The Christmas Shop. I loved the owners, Edward and Richard, and quickly made friends: Katie Stewart from Suffolk, Virginia, and Kelly Cole, who we called by her last name, from Swan Quarter, North Carolina. Cole's daddy owned a bank, and she was spoiled and sassy and a lot of fun, while Katie was soft-spoken and sweet. Katie reminded me of a magnolia blossom. She had a round face, impeccable skin, and dark brown eyes.

The three of us had two jobs: to memorize the price of every ornament in the shop and to hand out baskets to customers who needed them. People came from as far away as New York to visit The Christmas Shop. It was a magical place and everyone said so.

My favorite place in the store was the leather shop because that's where Chad and Brian worked. Chad was a surfer and he looked the part—he had muscular arms and a radiant smile that set off his deep tan. "How's it goin'?" he'd ask in that offbeat way of his. I'd never met anyone from California, but I imagined this was how all the guys there looked and talked.

Chad had a girlfriend named Trish, and they lived together in a cottage on the beach called "The Tiny Bit." We liked Trish. She wore tube tops and sarongs from India and had long, straight hair that fell past her slender hips. When Trish walked, her hips swayed back and forth like one of those hula dolls you see on people's dashboards. We knew Chad was off-limits, so we stayed away.

Brian also had a girlfriend, Mercedes, who everyone called Mercy. She was blond and had long hair like Trish, but there was one difference: Mercy didn't like me. I suspected that she'd picked up on the chemistry between Brian and me.

Brian was good-looking, though not as handsome as Chad. He was average height, with a circular face and blond hair that he was always flipping out of the way. Brian's eyes were turquoise, like the stone he wore on a piece of leather around his neck. That stone fell right into his Adam's apple like it was meant to be there, and I was intrigued. Brian looked at me in a way no boy in high school or college ever had.

"Hey there," he'd say, glancing up from punching holes in a leather belt.

"Hey," I'd reply, blushing.

It wasn't long before Brian was taking my hand and pulling me into a nearby supply closet to kiss me. That closet was dark and primitive and it smelled of pine pitch and cowhide, and when I was there with Brian, I lost all reason. Kissing was all we ever did, but his kisses made my eyes close and my face flush and my body rush with warmth.

Sometimes when we were kissing I'd wonder, *Why is Brian going behind Mercy's back?* Mercy was twenty-six and stunning. I was just this eighteen-year-old girl who'd be leaving at the end of the summer. After work I'd get in my car and drive away from The Christmas Shop and ask myself, *Why am I cheating with someone who has a girlfriend?* I'd watched *Camelot* and had seen what happened when Guinevere fooled around with Lancelot. I knew this wouldn't turn out well.

What was wrong with me? I'd never done anything like this in my life. I wasn't even in love with Brian, and I certainly didn't have anything against Mercy. I just knew that when Brian kissed me I didn't feel any pain, so I pushed thoughts of Mercy—and being a good girl—aside. Brian made me feel alive. I just wanted more.

Our kissing sessions continued and I was afraid of getting caught, so I enlisted Katie and Cole to keep watch.

"Be careful," Katie warned me. "If Mercy finds out, she'll kill you."

She was probably right. I'd heard Mercy was the jealous type, and I knew why. My friend Glenda told me that before Brian, Mercy had been married to a guy named Steve Taylor.

"Everyone called them 'The Beautiful Couple,'" Glenda said. "Anyway, everything was good until their eyes started to wander. He'd be looking one way; she'd be looking another."

Glenda didn't say if either of them had had an affair, and I didn't ask, but the way she told it, all that looking had eventually ended their marriage. Mercy and Steve had divorced, Mercy had moved in with Brian, and now Steve was living at The Nags Header, an old, turn-of-the-century hotel and the hottest nightspot on the beach.

I'd only been at the beach a few weeks, but the words "Nags Header" and "Steve the Dream" seemed to be on everyone's lips. "Steve the Dream" was the name of Steve's DJ act. During the day, Steve surfed and waited tables at the Seafarer. At night, he hung up his surfboard and waiter's apron and spun records at the Tap Room in the basement of The Nags Header. He wore a silver lamé pantsuit strung with mini lights, and when he swayed to the music every girl in the Tap Room came under his spell. Or so I'd heard.

I wanted to know more, so I decided to ask Cole. She was practically a local, and I knew she went to the Tap Room all the time.

"Steve the Dream? Yeah, he's a pretty boy," she said. "He's also a pompous ass."

I chuckled. Cole had a way with words.

"He can't be that bad," I replied.

"Nah, he's harmless," she conceded. "It's just that every girl on the beach wants to get in his pants."

Later, I mentioned Steve to Glenda. It was raining and the shop was busy, so Edward had asked me to help her at the jewelry counter.

"You haven't seen 'Steve the Dream'?" she asked, incredulous. "Oh, girl, he's fine." She closed her eyes as if thinking naughty thoughts.

"That's what I hear," I said, smiling.

"You need to check him out," she said with conviction. Glenda was a single mom and older than the rest of us, and I trusted her judgment. I'd just have to go and see for myself what all the fuss was about.

"Katie and I are going to the Tap Room tonight. Wanna come?" Cole asked a few days later as we restocked ornaments. It was early June and the shop was swarming with sweaty, sunburned tourists.

"Sure," I answered eagerly.

After work, the three of us piled into Cole's red Spitfire, crossed the drawbridge, and headed up the beach to our destination. Night was just falling and the old hotel, with its shuttered windows and wraparound porch, looked majestic.

The Good Humor Band was playing on the main floor, but we headed for a door on the side. Nailed to a post beside the entrance was a hand-lettered sign that read, "TAP ROOM. Steve the Dream TONIGHT!" My stomach fluttered. After weeks of anticipation, I was finally going to see Steve. I tucked my hair behind my ear and looked down at my baby doll top. *Too girlish*, I thought, panicked. I'd spent an hour trying to find just the right outfit, and now it was all wrong. I lifted my head and took a deep breath. It was too late. This would just have to do.

Katie, Cole, and I showed our IDs to a girl who stamped our hands.

"I have to pee," Katie said, and slipped away to the bathroom.

"Want a beer?" Cole asked. I was eighteen and I'd never had a beer in my life. But I needed something to calm my nerves, so I said okay and followed Cole over to a small driftwood bar.

"Two Miller Lites," she said with confidence. She was younger than me, but I knew she had been drinking for years. The bartender set two plastic cups filled with foaming liquid gold on the bar.

"Two dollars," he said, and I reached into my pocket and pulled out my money.

After handing over the two dollars, I lifted the cup to my lips. The beer was foamy and bitter, but I liked it. I had just taken a sip, but it felt treasonous. I'd never seen my parents drink. The only alcohol in our house besides the rubbing kind was the scuppernong wine Mama kept under the kitchen sink for when my period cramps were bad. My close friends in high school had been Christians, like me. None of us drank. Now I was drinking beer in the Tap Room with my friends, and I felt liberated. Best of all, no one cared.

A few minutes later, Katie appeared with a beer in her hand and joined us. While the three of us stood there, I scanned the room. It was dark and cave-like, with a concrete dance floor, a few tables, and scattered chairs. A sheet hung over an open doorway that I guessed led to the beach. In the middle of the room was a tiny platform lit by a spotlight, which held a small table, a stack of records, and a turntable. *Ah. So that's where he'll be.*

People began to arrive, mostly girls in pairs. The prettiest ones wore midriff tops. They had perfectly coiffed hair and knowing eyes. Most had breasts much larger than mine. I was clearly not in their league. What was I doing here? I didn't know how to act at a bar. I wanted to run, but my eyes were on the stage. I'd come this far. I had to see this "Steve the Dream" person.

A few minutes later, a figure emerged from behind a curtain. His dark, wavy hair was combed back, Elvis style, and he owned the room.

Steve Taylor was the most gorgeous man I had ever seen. He wasn't at all like the blond surfers I knew; he was a six-foot-one Roman god. His deep brown eyes, chiseled jaw, and dazzling teeth were flawless.

I glanced around. The bar was now filled with scantily clad females. Like me, their hopeful faces were fixed on Steve. "Look at me!" their eyes said. Steve picked up his mic.

"Hey, everyone! Thank you for coming. How about a little David Bowie?"

"FAME!" Bowie's voice echoed across the room. I watched Steve, who closed his eyes and grooved to the booming beat. He moved like seaweed in water, fluid and untamed. After a few minutes, he opened his eyes, picked up an album, and glanced at the cover.

"FAME!" People started walking toward the stage to dance.

"Oh . . . my . . . God!" I reached over and yelled into Katie's ear. "He's perfect."

"Yeah, and he knows it," she said, chuckling.

Even I could see that, but I didn't care.

Night after night, we made our pilgrimage to the Tap Room. And night after night, I went hoping to catch Steve's eye. Sometimes I was sure he saw me as he looked into the crowd. Most nights I felt invisible. I stood by the bar, watching as he went through the motions of playing records. Sometimes boys would come up and ask me to dance, and I would, but only so I could move closer to the stage and Steve's line of sight. I'd close my eyes and imagine that Steve was watching me. Then the song would end, and I'd open my eyes to see him winking at a cute brunette across the room. It was hopeless.

The Fourth of July had come and gone. It was now mid-July, and Katie and Cole had asked me to come live with them in the double-wide trailer they shared at the end of the island. The timing couldn't have been better, and I was thrilled. Horace had a new girlfriend and was rarely home, and Tommy worked the night shift at the Holiday Inn. Our old house was often empty, and I didn't like being there alone. Besides, getting a little distance from Horace meant I didn't have to worry that he would report my comings and goings to Mama and Daddy. So I moved into the trailer, and the girls and I carpooled to work and made our nightly treks to the Tap Room.

I was surprised when Horace showed up at the Tap Room one night. *What is he doing here?* Surely he'd come to check up on me. I was annoyed.

Katie, Cole, and I were nursing beers by the bar. Horace moved toward us, sporting a winsome smile.

"Hello, girls," he said. "Hey, sis." He leaned over and kissed me on the check.

"Budweiser," he said to Sean. I watched as he paid for his beer, leaned back against the bar, and began scanning the room.

"I wanted to see what all the commotion's about," he said. "You all just do your thing and pretend I'm not here."

"Okay," I said, self-conscious but determined to have a good time.

Steve came out and spun his records. We danced to almost every song, then ordered a second round. I looked at my watch. It was already nine. Where had the time gone?

"I'm burning up!" Cole shouted over the music. "Let's take a walk."

I looked over at Katie.

"Sure," she said, so I followed the two of them out to the beach.

The night was breezy, almost tropical. The sand was lit by a hazy moon, but we could see our way to the water's edge. As we walked, I sensed we weren't alone. I turned and saw three guys following a hundred yards behind us. I could hear their drunken chatter, though I couldn't make out their faces.

What I didn't know was that there was a fourth figure following close behind.

"Hey, fellas! Why don't you leave those girls alone." It was Horace. He'd seen the guys follow after us and decided to tag along.

"Whazzit to ya?" a voice retorted. "One of 'em your sister or somethin'?"

"As a matter of fact, she is," he said.

They stopped in their tracks, then turned.

"Oh, hey man! We're sorry!" said the guy who'd shouted the snide remark. "We didn't mean to cause any trouble." They whispered among themselves, then promptly stumbled back to the Tap Room.

Maybe having a big brother checking in on me wasn't such a bad thing after all.

July grew unusually hot and humid, and the coolness of the Tap Room was a welcome escape. Katie and I had gone for a walk on the beach after work and decided to stop by for a quick beer before heading home. It was just getting dark when we arrived, so there were only a few locals hanging around. Tuesday was half-price draft night and we knew the bar would fill up quickly, so we ordered our beers and found a small table to the left of the stage.

I took a deep swallow. Beer had quickly become my new friend. It gave me a pleasant buzz and helped ease my anxiety about seeing Steve. He was standing in his usual spot on the platform, but something was different. Instead of his silver pantsuit, he was wearing a plaid shirt and jeans. His face looked different too. This was the first time I'd seen the person behind the act, and I didn't quite know what to think.

Then I realized: it wasn't "Steve the Dream" I was drawn to; it was the attractive twenty-six-year-old man standing in front of me. I'd suspected there was something behind all that showmanship and hype, and I was right. He seemed relaxed, not put-on like the cutout cardboard Elvis I'd seen night after night.

"Wow," I said to Katie, "look at that." Katie glanced up from her beer and over at Steve.

"Oh my, Laura Belle," she said, smiling. Laura Belle was the nickname I'd been given in high school, and somehow it had stuck. "What are you going to do now?"

"Get another beer," I replied. "Want one?"

"Sure." She reached into her pocket and handed me a crumpled-up dollar bill.

I walked over to the bar.

"The usual?" asked Sean. I was now a regular and I liked it.

"Yep," I said, "thanks." I paid Sean, picked up our beers, and was starting to turn around when I heard a voice say, "Hi."

I finished turning. It was Steve. It had finally happened.

"Hi," I replied, looking down, afraid my smile would give me away.

"I see you here a lot. What's your name?"

"Laura." I raised my eyes to meet his. He was even more beautiful than I'd realized, especially up close. My head suddenly felt light and my body weightless.

"Do you surf?" he asked. The question took me off guard. I was far from athletic, but I knew surfing was a big deal around here.

"No." I paused, not knowing what to say next.

"The guys and I usually go to Hatteras," he replied. He was referring to Cape Hatteras, the surfing haven known for its amazing swells. "You should come and watch us sometime."

"I'd like that," I said, pleased.

"It's quiet tonight," he said, studying the room. There was an awkward pause. "Good talking to you," he said, distracted. He turned and walked back to the stage, and I returned to my table.

"Oh my gosh," I said to Katie. "I can't believe that just happened."

"I can," she replied confidently. "I was watching him. He likes you."

"I don't know about that."

I looked over as Steve dropped the needle on another record.

Chapter Three

When I wasn't at the Tap Room, I was lying on the beach, trying to achieve the perfect tan. Katie, Cole, and I would wake up out of the previous night's stupor, pull on our bathing suits, and head over the causeway to a quiet stretch of beach behind the Ramada Inn. There, I'd lay out my things, slather myself in baby oil and iodine, then lie down on my towel and wait for the sun to work its magic. I figured if I could just achieve a golden glow, I'd be prettier and maybe Steve would notice. Maybe I'd stand out in the crowd. I no longer wore glasses, but I still had two silver braces on my lower teeth and they made me self-conscious.

One of my favorite things to do when I got off work was to drive my car down to Pea Island, a wildlife refuge about ten miles south of Nags Head. Pea Island was unlike any place I'd ever known, and I thought of it as my private hideaway. I'd park and follow the boardwalk to the sound to watch the sunset. Most days I'd take my journal along. Sometimes I would write. Often I would just look out over the water and think—about Steve, Lawrence, my friends, and the beauty I saw there.

Sitting in that primitive landscape, surrounded by marsh grasses and wax myrtles, I felt peaceful. My soul drank in that peace like a garden after a soaking rain. Often, in that stillness, I was able to feel God's presence. At other times, He seemed far away.

...

The fall after Lawrence died, I started high school and made three new friends—Pam, Sheri, and Robin. I was still a mess—a jumble of grief and insecurity—and they loved me anyway. That, plus their unmistakable joy made me ask one day, "What's it with you guys? You're always happy."

"We love Jesus!" Pam replied.

Then I want to love Jesus too, I thought. I'd gone to a Methodist church all my life, but it didn't really seem to have any impact on the way we lived. It was just something we did, like reading the newspaper. This was new. These girls had something different, something I wanted—joy, peace, a contentment that eluded me. They invited me to a community Bible study, where I felt accepted and loved, and I started to believe I had a purpose beyond my sadness. A few months later we all attended a Nicky Cruz crusade, and when the invitation was given to pray and receive Christ into our hearts, I walked down to the front.

From that moment until I moved to the beach, I was on fire for Jesus and was never even tempted to stray. I carried my Bible to school and even brought it to the dinner table.

"Laura, please leave that Bible in your room," Mama said, exasperated, as she bit into a hot dog one night. She and Daddy had raised me in church, but I knew they didn't know Jesus as their personal Savior and I desperately wanted them to.

My faith had filled a spiritual void. Then I'd moved to Manteo and out from under the watchful eye of my parents. My life had been small and sheltered. Now it felt expansive. I was living on my own, I'd made new friends, and I was testing my independence. For the first time, I felt free.

Did I really have to make a choice between faith and freedom? Surely I could juxtapose the two.

Untethered

The unfamiliar stirrings of liberty—and desire—took me by surprise. They didn't just appear overnight. They were much more cunning than that. They snuck in the back door of my soul and quietly took up residence. Before I knew it I was tasting Brian's kisses and my first beer and having lustful thoughts about Steve. Now there was only one frontier left, and that was sex.

In our house, the word *sex* was a four-letter word, even though my brothers and I were growing up in sexually explosive times. It was the 1960s and love was free. Perhaps that's the reason the subject was so taboo.

I never got a "sex talk" from Mama, at least not one that was actually about sex. My sex talk, instead, was about my period. Mama knocked on my bedroom door one day.

"Here you go," she said, before handing me a box of Tampax pads and a brochure called *Becoming a Woman*. "Read this and let me know if you have any questions." She gave me an awkward look, then left. I leafed through the brochure. It had illustrations of smiling girls doing fun things (while they were having their periods, of course), but it didn't talk about sex. It only told me that I would have a period and to use the pads in the accompanying box when the time came.

Only once did Mama ever say the word *sex* in my presence: I was ten and Horace was sixteen, and the three of us were in Horace's bedroom. Horace was standing in front of the mirror, brushing his hair. He was using a girl's hairbrush. That may have seemed odd to most people, but it wasn't to me; he had a whole collection of them in the glove box of his car. They were like trophies. I knew those hairbrushes had something to do with sex, but I didn't figure it out until many years later.

Mama pronounced to Horace, "If you want to have sex, come to us first and you can get married so you won't shame your father and me."

That's the stupidest thing I've ever heard, I thought. Everyone knew that you were supposed to marry for love. I'd seen a dozen Disney movies, and I knew it was true. Of course, I immediately considered how great sex must be if she was making such a big deal about it. I already had my suspicions, of course, because it was never discussed in our house. But now I was dead sure that it must be even better than the banana splits we got in those little plastic boats at the Dairy Queen.

It wasn't long after that I was sexually molested, on two different occasions, in both cases by adolescent boys—one a friend of Horace's who was at our house for a sleepover, the other an older cousin. Both times I knew something was wrong and told my parents and they took immediate action and I was grateful. Horace's friend was sent home in the middle of the night and never came to our house again. Mama and Daddy confronted my aunt and uncle about my cousin. The next thing I heard he was being sent off to boarding school, and I guessed it was because of what he had done to me.

I was approaching my preteen years and my ideas about sexuality were forming, and being touched that way only confused me. Why did I feel embarrassed and ashamed? Had I done something wrong? Mama and Daddy never said another word, and we carried on as though nothing had happened.

Those two incidents changed everything for me, though I didn't realize it at the time. Later, I would see they were part of the reason I'd filled my life with men. So many men.

Eight years had passed, and I'd pushed aside the memory of what happened with those boys. I was now living at the beach and I had made a decision: I was ready to have sex, and I wanted to have it with "Steve the Dream." Lawrence had always told me I could have whatever I wanted if I wanted it badly enough, and I believed him. I wanted Steve more than I'd ever wanted anything. It might take time, but I was convinced it would be worth it.

I knew God couldn't possibly approve of my decision. I told myself it would probably never happen—and if by chance it did, surely He'd understand. After all, hadn't He placed this desire in me? And placed Steve right in my path?

I was sitting by the sound at Pea Island one afternoon watching the sun slip down past the horizon when I came to that conclusion. From that moment on, it consumed my every waking thought.

While I waited, there were other boys. I'd usually meet them at the Tap Room, at work, or on the beach. Ross was one of them. He had brown hair and a bright smile. It was late July when Ross sailed his tiny boat into the Manteo harbor. He was hanging out by the dock when I saw him the first time. I walked by and he looked at me and asked, "Know where I can get a sandwich?" I did, and we walked there and had lunch together.

After lunch, we walked back and he showed me his boat and we sat on the dock and talked until dusk. He leaned over and pressed his face into my hair.

"You smell like suntan lotion," he said. "I'm going to call you Coconut."

For the next two weeks, Ross and I hung out together, though I never took him to the Tap Room or mentioned Steve. Once, in the middle of the night, I woke up to the sound of knocking on my bedroom window. It was Ross. He had climbed the side of the house and onto the roof.

"Are you crazy?" I asked, delighted.

"C'mon, Coconut," he whispered, "let's take a walk." I pulled him through the window, and we stood in my bedroom and kissed in the soft light of the moon.

"Turn around and don't peek!" I told him as I threw on cutoffs and a T-shirt.

After I had dressed, I took his hand and led him through my

room, down the stairs, and out the front door. When we got outside, he smiled at me and without saying a word grabbed my arm, and we began running down the middle of Sir Walter Raleigh Street toward the water. It was a still, warm night and I was with this boy and he was pulling me toward something and I was going willingly. *This is what adventure feels like*, I thought.

We slowed down as we approached the docks.

"It's a beautiful night," said Ross. "I just wanted to watch the stars with you."

We lay down on the pier, kissed, and gazed up at the sky until the sun came up. We didn't talk much, but we didn't have to. Just being there together was enough. Ross was easy and he didn't pressure me. I liked that, though I still thought about Steve. Steve was perfect, and he was the only one I would give myself to.

Summer was quickly coming to an end, and I wanted to savor every moment. One day as I drove up the beach to see Tommy, who was now the day manager at the Holiday Inn, something compelled me to pull into a small, sandy parking lot in front of a large blue-and-white tent. A hand-painted wooden sign with the words "The Circus Tent" hung over the entrance.

I'd seen flyers for this place and knew what I'd find inside: local bands playing Christian music and wholesome high school girls scooping up hand-dipped ice cream. Why in the world was I here?

I got out of my car, walked over to the corner of the tent where I wouldn't be noticed, and peeked inside. Loud, tinny music blasted from worn-out amps. There were rows of folding chairs lined up, church style, and a few plastic tables were scattered across the back. I looked around at the smiling, peaceful faces, which seemed familiar and foreign.

A vocalist on stage was singing something about holding on to Jesus. I recognized the lyrics—it was a song I'd heard at the JESUS

'73 concert I'd attended two years earlier. The words pricked my conscience. I'd once held on to Jesus, but somewhere along the way, I'd let go. With that thought, I got back in my car and drove away.

I'd been wrestling for weeks about whether to return to school. The truth was, I didn't want to. I was having way too much fun and wasn't ready for my time at the beach to end. I couldn't imagine going back to UNCG and my dull college existence after the summer I'd had. Edward invited us all to stay on at the shop, and we were grateful. Katie decided to return to Suffolk, and I was sad at the thought of her leaving. Cole was staying on indefinitely, though, and she told me I could keep my room at the trailer. At least I had a job and a place to live if I wanted it.

"Winter's not the same here," warned Glenda one day as we walked around the shop straightening displays. "Everyone leaves and it's pretty dead. The beach closes up—even the Tap Room—and there's not much to do."

I recognized that voice—a mama's voice. Glenda had lived in Manteo all her life and I knew she was telling the truth, though I didn't want to believe her, especially the part about the Tap Room. Mama and Daddy had left several messages on the answering machine back at our trailer. The semester would be starting in four weeks, and they were anxious to know what I was going to do.

On a Thursday morning in early August, I was leaving for work when I found a piece of notebook paper tucked into the windshield of the truck Horace and I shared. It was from Ross.

"I've decided to go back to Fort Mill and finish college. It's been fun, Coconut. I'll never forget you and that smile of yours. Love, Ross."

I was sorry but not surprised. Ross was one of those "summer romances" I'd been warned about, and now it was over.

...

That night, I went to the Tap Room. It was a Thursday, the slowest night of the week just before the tourists arrived. I'd had dinner with Horace, and Cole was busy, so Katie and I drove separately and met there.

Katie would soon be leaving the beach, and I already missed her. She'd been a good friend. We bought our beers and found a table. Steve came out, looking gorgeous, as always. I was feeling the buzz of the beer, and thoughts of Ross were already beginning to fade. I danced with the guys who asked me to.

Steve took a short break. I stood in the middle of the dance floor, watching him return a record to its cover. He looked straight at me and walked over.

"Hi," he said. His voice made me tremble.

"Hey," I said, smiling. "It's quiet tonight." I searched for more to say.

"Yeah, Thursdays always are." He paused for a minute and looked toward the stage. "I'd better get back. Want to go for a walk when I'm done?"

"Sure," I said. My pulse raced.

As he walked away, he glanced back and smiled that smile that he'd practiced on other girls so many times. I knew because I'd seen him do it.

I rushed to the table, excited to tell Katie. "He asked if I wanted to go for a walk later," I said, heady with emotion.

"It's about time," Katie declared, smiling.

I looked at her and thought about all the times we'd hung out in that very spot. "I'm gonna miss you, girl," I said, suddenly feeling nostalgic.

"Me too, Laura Belle," she said. "We'll stay in touch."

After more beer and dancing, the crowd thinned out, and I

knew it was almost closing time. Katie stood up to leave and gave me a hug.

"Be careful, Laura Belle," she warned.

The dance floor emptied, and I waited for Steve to finish up what he was doing. As he disappeared behind the curtain, I started to get nervous. What if he'd changed his mind? What if he came over and told me good night and that was the end of it? What would I do then?

"Hey." I looked up from my ruminating. It was Steve. "Ready to take that walk?"

"Sure," I said, relieved. I moved away from the bar, and Steve and I walked to the entrance that opened to the beach.

A full moon lit our way as we walked across the sand to the water. My heart was beating wildly in my chest. When we reached a nearby sand dune, Steve stopped and looked down at me and pulled me closer. I took in his face, the one I had longed to touch, and our mouths melted together.

His kiss was like fire; the heat of it flooded my body. We kissed a few moments longer, and then he took my hand and we walked to the water's edge and stood side by side, not saying a word. He reached down and kissed me on the forehead.

"Want to go upstairs?" he asked quietly.

"Sure," I said, with only a vague sense of what I was agreeing to.

Instantly, I felt both elation and fear. I was about to give up my virginity for Steve, and I was ready. Or was I? I wasn't sure. My close friends were all virgins, so I'd never talked with any of them about sex. What would it feel like? Would it hurt? Or be amazing? The words *lust* and *fornication* popped into my head. These were sins of the flesh and I knew it. What I was doing was wrong. But Steve was here—right now—and I was going to see this through no matter what. I pushed my thoughts aside and reached for his hand.

We made our way back to The Nags Header and climbed the wide plank stairs to the second floor, where the guest rooms of the grand hotel had formerly been. The narrow hall was lit only by a dim light bulb. Steve unlocked his door and I followed him inside.

The pine-paneled room was just large enough to hold the few pieces of furniture—a double bed, a bedside table, a dresser and mirror. At the foot of the bed, I noticed some dumbbells and hand weights. *So that's how he got those arms*, I thought. The one window in his room was covered by a sheer white curtain and faced the beach. It was open and the curtain billowed and I could hear the rhythmic whoosh of waves on the sand.

"You can put your things in the bathroom," he said matter-of-factly, pointing to a door.

Things? Was I supposed to bring things? A toothbrush? Change of clothes? I had a purse, but the only "things" it contained were my car keys, my driver's license, a hairbrush, and a few Kleenex.

Then it struck me: birth control. I didn't have any. Only "those kind of girls" planned for this kind of thing. Now I was one and I was unprepared. What if I got pregnant? *It won't happen. He'll use something.* I was sure of it. But what if?

Suddenly, there were a dozen what-ifs. I felt vulnerable and naive. Other girls knew about this stuff. Why hadn't somebody told me? Why hadn't I asked?

I walked into the bathroom, found a partially used tube of Colgate, squeezed out a dab on my finger, and ran it across my teeth. I looked in the mirror. The face looking back was only vaguely familiar. *What's happened to me? What am I doing?* I questioned for the dozenth time. The girl in the mirror answered with a smile that was half-happy, half-sad.

I hope he's patient with me, I thought as I opened the door and entered the bedroom.

Steve's eyes met mine and he gave me a knowing smile. Then

he reached behind me and turned off the overhead light. My eyes adjusted quickly, and I saw Steve pull off his shirt and pants and crawl into bed. I did the same. *Would he like my body?* I wondered. I was grateful the room was dark except for the glow of the moon. *What am I doing?* I thought again as Steve pulled me closer. Now he was on top of me, looking into my eyes. "Oh God," I whispered, but those words didn't have the same meaning they usually did. Or did they? I felt as though I was free-falling into an abyss from which I would never return. Maybe those words were simply a cry for help.

I could no longer contain the emotions welling up in me. I was euphoric and fearful and guilty and resolute, and his muscular body and our skin touching and his mouth searching were too much to resist. I couldn't believe this was happening, but when he slipped inside of me, I just let myself fall.

Ouch. I winced. My body tightened.

"Relax, just relax," he said as he brushed the hair from my eyes.

"I'm trying," I managed weakly. I was scared he'd be disappointed, but I didn't dare say a word.

I felt yet another rush of fear. Why did it hurt? Was something wrong? He was being gentle, so the problem had to be with me. I opened my eyes and saw his face hovering above me. I reached up and pulled him toward me as another wave crashed on the shore.

When it was over, we lay there and he kissed me on the eyes. I waited a moment, then gathered up my courage.

"You're my first," I whispered, hoping he would be pleased.

"I am?" He pulled away slightly and looked at me, surprised. "Why me?"

"I don't know," I lied. I couldn't tell him that I wanted him because everyone else did. That he was the most stunning man I'd ever seen and the one I'd chosen to give myself to. Most every girl I knew wanted to be with Steve, and tonight he'd chosen me. I'd finally gotten what I'd waited for, and I was happy. I put my head on his chest and fell asleep.

Early the next morning, we made love again. The previous night had been awkward, strange, and surreal. This time, it was easier. More natural.

After it was over, he closed his eyes and went to sleep. As I lay there watching his chest rise and fall beneath the rumpled sheet, I thought about Jesus. I knew He wasn't happy with what I'd done. My parents wouldn't be happy either, especially Mama, but I couldn't think about that now. Right now I didn't care about anything else. I was with Steve.

But the world—and my noon shift—hovered outside the door. He would wake up soon, and I would have to leave. Suddenly I felt blue.

A little while later, he woke up and we dressed without saying much. We made our way downstairs and out the front door to the large wraparound porch that faced the beach road. Together, we walked to the corner of the porch and sat down on the railing.

"I miss Virginia," he said wistfully. Then he began talking about his mother, who was widowed, his sister, and his hometown. He seemed relaxed and I took that as a good sign. I watched his face as he talked and thought about making love with him. I could sit here forever, but I couldn't stop myself from glancing down at my watch. It was getting late, and I had to work and needed to go home first and shower.

"I'd better go," I said reluctantly.

He reached over and kissed me. Then, unexpectedly, he picked me up in his arms and carried me down the stairs like a bride across the threshold.

"See you later," he said, setting me down next to my car.

Not knowing what that meant and afraid to ask, I got into my car and watched as he climbed back up the steps. *Look back. Please.*

He did.

...

An hour later, I entered The Christmas Shop and walked to the stock room to put my purse away. I opened the creaky door and practically ran into Cole.

"Ooh, girl," she said, grinning. "We all know what you were up to last night!"

That didn't take long, I thought, embarrassed and proud all at once. I'd known Katie would tell Cole about me and Steve when she got home from the Tap Room last night, and that it wouldn't take long for the news to spread.

"How was it?" she probed.

"Amazing," I said with a smile.

I immediately headed to the jewelry room. I knew Glenda would want a report.

"So, Laura Belle," she said, grinning from ear to ear. "Is it true?"

Our twinkle-light world was small and nothing was sacred, especially when it came to "Steve the Dream." I'd quickly come to see that Steve was a bit of a celebrity among locals. Now, because of what had happened between us, I was in the spotlight with him, if only in a small way.

"Yeah," I said to Glenda, "I still can't believe it."

I suddenly became antsy. What if Glenda started digging for details I wasn't willing to share?

"I'd better go," I said. "You know Edward's motto: Keep Moving!" She smiled.

As I turned left out of the jewelry room and wandered toward the art gallery, my thoughts returned to Steve. *What is he doing? Has he thought about me? About last night? When will I see him again? Will it be awkward? What will we say?*

"You look unusually cheerful today." The sound of Edward's voice brought my daydreaming to a halt.

"Yessir, I am," I replied, smiling. *Shit. It must be written all over my face.*

I strolled through the art gallery, making my way to the leather shop. I dreaded seeing Brian. I was afraid my newly awakened body would betray me, that somehow he would know. I took a deep breath and tried to act as though everything were normal.

"Hey," he said as I leaned over his table. He looked past his work lamp and into my eyes. I caught a glint of sadness and knew he'd heard about Steve.

"When's your break?" he asked matter-of-factly. "I was thinking about driving down to the point. We could stop and grab some lunch."

So it took my sleeping with Steve to rouse his attention, I deduced. *Maybe he does care about me after all.*

"Sure," I said, pleased. "My break is at two."

This was the first time Brian had asked me to lunch. It had always been too risky with Mercy—all she had to do was show up and discover we were out together, and all hell would break loose. It was a chance neither of us had been willing to take. Until now.

I anticipated our lunch conversation and didn't know what I was going to say. While I'd spent months thinking about being with Steve, I hadn't given a moment's thought to the consequences if it were to happen. How it might possibly affect my relationship with Brian, who was sneaking around with me while he was with Mercy who used to be with Steve. It was just like the soap operas I used to watch with Daddy, except now I was living in one of my own making.

How had everything gotten so complicated? I'd done whatever I wanted to do since arriving at the beach, and it had felt like freedom. Now it just felt like a big mess. I knew the Bible warned about this very thing. It was called sin. I'd run roughshod over God and Mercy (would she show me any mercy if she caught me with Brian?), and now I felt badly about it. But not that badly.

41

Wow. What's happened to me? I thought for a moment, but came up blank.

At two o'clock sharp, Brian entered the lobby and went out the front door. I waited a moment, then followed him. He walked just ahead of me and headed to his truck, and I caught up with him.

After all our rendezvousing in that dark supply closet, shouldn't this be a piece of cake? Instead, being out in the open together in the middle of the day felt treacherous and unsettling.

He unlocked the doors of his truck and we got in.

"Well, this feels strange," he announced, glancing my way.

"It sure does," I responded, my nerves frayed. I looked around. We'd made it out of the shop and into his car without any sign of Mercy, so we were good. Or were we? As he started the engine, it occurred to me that I was sitting in the seat where Mercy usually sat and I felt sorry for her, but it also seemed too late to change my mind.

Brian pulled out onto the main road that ran through the middle of town, and we headed north to a quiet spot near the Umstead Bridge. On the way, we passed the Elizabethan Restaurant and he turned into the parking lot and went inside to buy our lunch.

A few minutes later, he came out carrying two white paper bags. "Hold these?" he asked, handing me our lunch. "I hope ham and cheese is okay."

As he drove to the end of the island, we made awkward small talk, carefully avoiding any mention of the previous night.

We finally reached the bridge. Brian pulled his truck into the parking area, and we got out and walked over to a narrow pier and sat down. I looked at him, not knowing what to say.

"Why'd you do it?" he asked, breaking the silence. It was the moment I'd been waiting for.

"I don't know," I told him, and that was the truth. Up until last night, I'd thought it was only about wanting Steve. Now I wondered if there was something more. Something to do with Lawrence and the empty space left when he died.

"Besides, you're not available," I said, looking him in the eye. Even I was surprised by my tone.

"I know," he said. "Mercedes." Her name hung in the air like a heavy perfume. "We probably should stop fooling around now that you and Steve . . ." He hesitated.

"I don't know what's going to happen with me and Steve," I said. And I didn't. Steve and I hadn't talked about a "next time," much less a future. "Probably nothing," I added, resigned.

Brian reached over and kissed me gently on the cheek, and I knew it was his first effort at pulling away. I gave him a sad smile.

"We just weren't meant to be," I said. "Mercy is beautiful. You should give that your best shot."

We sat without saying a word. I glanced at the time.

"We'd better get back to work," I said. "Mercy might stop by."

As he took my hand and helped me to my feet, I realized we hadn't even touched our lunch.

On the way to see Horace that evening, I made a decision. I was going to take the semester off and stay at the beach. I didn't know how long I'd be there. All I knew was that I didn't want to go back to school. I'd been leaning this way for a while, but now, with Steve in the picture, everything had changed. How could I just pack up my things in two weeks and go home? I had to at least give this a chance. I felt a sense of relief.

"Steve the Dream?" Horace asked, incredulous. We were standing in the kitchen of the old house when I shared an edited version of my night at The Nags Header. There was no way I was going to tell him I'd slept with Steve. I couldn't risk a lecture.

"Be careful, sis. I know what guys like him want," he said with conviction. Steve had the reputation on the beach of being a player, but that was something I chose to ignore.

"How come you know so much?" I asked, annoyed.

"'Cause we're about the same age," he said. "Don't worry. I won't tell Mama and Daddy."

"Thanks," I said, relieved.

The next day, I told Edward I would take him up on his offer to work through the winter. Then I called Mama and Daddy to break the news.

"I just hope you've made the right decision," Mama said. I could tell she had her doubts.

"I have," I responded resolutely. I didn't feel like explaining myself.

That same afternoon, I made the difficult decision to stay away from the Tap Room. At least for a few days. I was embarrassed to face Steve and uncertain about our relationship. What were we, anyway? A one-night stand? A summer fling? Up until we'd made love, we'd barely spoken fifty words. I knew that night had been all about sex. Would we ever be anything more?

When I finally got up the nerve to go back the following week, Steve wasn't there.

I walked over to the bar. "Where's Steve?" I asked Sean.

"He took a couple of days off," he said.

I didn't ask anything more.

Katie left two weeks later, and I felt lonely without her around. Cole was a great bar buddy, but I'd always been able to confide in Katie. It was now mid-August, and more people than I'd expected were calling it a summer and going home. After Labor Day, everything would get quiet. Only Cole and Glenda–and Steve–would still be around.

Well, Brian would be around too. But things were different between us. He and Mercy had gone into counseling and things were better, and I was happy for them.

I thought of Glenda's warning about life at the beach in the winter. *Maybe I should have gone back to school*, I thought. But no. I'd been miserable there. Anything would be better than that.

I needed time to think, so after work I drove to the beach. I'd made several trips to the Tap Room since Sean told me about Steve being away. Each time, I'd been disappointed; those "couple of days" turned into seven, and then ten. Without Steve there, the Tap Room was just a place to go and drink beer. Still, it was something to do. It was late afternoon, however, and the bar wouldn't be open for several hours. A walk along the ocean would be just the thing to clear my head.

I turned off the highway at Dowdy's Amusement Park and cut over to the beach road. I decided to check and see if Steve's car was at The Nags Header. To my surprise, it was, so I pulled into the parking lot. *What am I doing?* I thought. I was incredibly nervous about seeing him again after a few weeks, but I had to. I was tired of wondering.

I walked up the front steps and into the large room where the bands always played. There was Steve, sitting at the bar drinking a Tab. *Always watching your figure*, I thought.

He looked up. "Hey." He gave me a vague smile. "It's been a while. What have you been up to?"

Had he missed me?

"I've been busy," I said. "One of my roommates just left to go home, and we've been hanging out."

"Ah," he said. "Want anything?"

"No, I'm good."

"Let's go outside," he said, getting up from his barstool.

The old screen door slammed behind us as I followed him out

on the back porch overlooking the beach. His room was just above us, and my thoughts drifted back to that Thursday night.

"I'm moving to New York," he announced out of the blue. My breath caught in my chest. "I went up last week to talk to some modeling agencies. Wilhelmina wants to sign me."

I was stunned. He was leaving? Now? Just when I'd decided to stay?

"That's great," I said, feigning excitement. This was terrible. I wasn't sure what to do next.

"Yeah, I'm pretty pumped," he said.

"I didn't know you were thinking about modeling," I said, trying to stay calm.

"Yeah, I have been for a while. I decided to give it a shot, and here I am." He looked at me and flashed that smile of his.

"I'm happy for you," I said. "That sounds amazing."

He smiled. "You're pretty," he said softly. "You should give it a try."

I was flattered. Did he mean it? "I don't know," I said coyly. My thoughts started racing . . . modeling . . . New York . . . being with Steve. "I'm not sure I'm model material."

"I bet you could do it. You just need photos. Ray Matthews took mine."

Ray was a popular Outer Banks photographer and a friend of Horace's. Maybe I'd give him a call.

"So you're leaving," I said, inviting a response.

"Yep. My DJ days are over, at least for now. The Tap Room closes after Labor Day. I leave for New York that Tuesday. Monday will be my last night."

So this was it. This wasn't going anywhere. I'd be at the beach and he'd be in New York having this big life and we'd never see each other again. My stomach sank.

"I'm meeting a friend," I lied. "I'd better go." I could barely hold it together. If I stayed a second longer, I knew I'd begin to cry.

"Okay," he said. "Good to see you." With that, he leaned over, kissed me on the cheek, and gave me one last smile.

"Good seeing you too," I said.

He turned and walked back inside. I stood for a moment and looked at the ocean, deeply regretting my decision to stay.

~๑·๑~

Chapter Four

The first time I saw the skyline of Manhattan—a full nine months after Steve and I said goodbye—I was captivated. I'd been traveling in a car for ten hours with someone I'd just met—an acquaintance of a friend from college—and already I was beginning to lose sight of why I'd come to New York in the first place. We'd driven through the night and the sun was just coming up when I turned my eyes from the yellow lines rushing under us and there it was: gold and shimmering and beckoning. My heart beat wildly and I fixed my eyes on those skyscrapers, afraid they might vanish and steal the fragile dreams I'd brought with me.

My fall season on the Outer Banks had left me disillusioned. Steve took off for New York the day after Labor Day, just as he said he would. The Tap Room closed and people started leaving the beach; soon, only a handful of my friends remained. I felt lost. Summer had been life-giving—the comfort of Katie's presence, the bliss of being with Steve. With all of that stripped away, who was I? I wasn't sure.

Four years had passed, and the pain of losing Lawrence began to surface once more. But this time it was worse. It was fermented pain, not just the everyday kind, and much more potent. I tried numbing it with beer and sex, but nothing helped. Instead of drinking for fun, I began drinking to forget—Steve, my brother, the things that caused me unspeakable heartache.

Scarcity led to scavenging. I slept with guys I barely knew to push away thoughts of Steve, but mostly so I wouldn't be alone. I'd meet them at The Atlantis or The Jolly Roger—the only bars open on the beach off-season. They were locals—waiters, carpenters, fishermen. They were attractive, always, with dark tans or alluring eyes or seductive smiles, and they'd buy me a beer or two, and before I knew it I'd be following them home. Then I'd wake up in a strange bed and look over and feel a wave of remorse and realize that things were going from bad to worse. And then, like an addict desperate for a fix, I'd do it all over again.

By November, the magic the Outer Banks had once held for me had disappeared. I'd drive up the beach road late at night and pass The Nags Header, now shuttered and silent, and struggle to make sense of it all. The beach was cold and desolate, and college seemed my only escape. Not knowing what else to do, I decided it was time to go home, so I enrolled for the spring semester and returned to UNCG after Christmas break.

Back at school, I quickly discovered I'd brought my unhappiness with me. I wore it like a thrift store sweater, shabby after years of wear but too comfortable to toss. I couldn't stay in Manteo, but I didn't want to be back in Greensboro either. My old roommate had moved in with a mutual friend, and everyone was now a semester ahead of me. It only took a few days for me to realize that I wasn't any happier now than I had been the previous year when I'd left for the beach.

To make matters worse, I felt like an outsider. While I was away, my friends had gone on with their lives. They'd made memories without me—gone to dances and concerts, had late-night chats. I was the girl who had dropped out of college to live on the Outer Banks, and they didn't know what to make of me. At least, that's how it felt. They were clueless about my newfound depravity, which I didn't dare let them in on. I told them about Steve, but only in vague terms. They were all saving themselves for marriage, and I was afraid they would judge me. How could they understand the lure of "Steve the Dream"? They couldn't possibly.

The only cure was to find a new distraction. Steve had told me I should try modeling, so I did. I went to an agency near campus called Marilyn's, and they started sending me out on jobs. It was fun going to department stores, dressing up in bridal gowns, and working in showrooms at the High Point furniture market, and getting paid to do it.

Marilyn wanted me to start building my portfolio. A friend on my hall had taken a few candids, but I needed professional photos. I called Ray Matthews, the Outer Banks photographer Steve had mentioned when we'd last met.

"Horace's little sister? I'd love to work with you," he said. The timing couldn't have been better. I was restless, and a photo shoot on the Outer Banks with Ray gave me an excuse to escape.

I'd already dropped one bomb on my parents when I told them I was sitting out the fall semester to stay at the beach. Now I was about to drop a second one: I wanted to go to New York to try my hand at modeling. Steve believed I had a good chance, and after modeling for a few months, I'd come to believe it too.

I started dieting—cutting out sweets and eating salads—and dropped most of the weight I'd gained over the summer. I bought fashion magazines and pored over the pages. I read stories about girls who came to New York from the South and made it big. If they could do it, why couldn't I?

But I wasn't interested in just seeing myself in the pages of a magazine. I wanted to see my face on the covers of *Glamour* and *Seventeen*. I knew it would be hard work. I also knew if I wanted it badly enough, it would happen. After all, wasn't that how I'd ended up with Steve?

Before long, I knew the names of the top New York models—Cheryl Tiegs, Lisa Taylor, Patti Hansen—and the top agencies: Ford, Zoli, and Steve's agent, Wilhelmina. Between classes at UNCG, I'd call directory information, get the agency phone numbers, and call to ask about their requirements. At five foot seven, I was tall enough. I needed photos, but I'd have those soon. What I didn't know yet was how I'd get to New York. Flying was too expensive. Maybe I could take a bus or train or find a ride? I started getting excited—the Big Apple, modeling, seeing Steve. Now I just had to tell Mama and Daddy.

Over spring break, I announced my plan.

"I want to go to New York for a few days, just to see what happens."

"You don't know anyone in New York. And how will you get there?" Mama asked. She was looking older by the minute. With a daughter like me, it was no wonder.

"I know Steve. And I can find a ride," I said confidently, though I had no idea that I could. I'd told Mama and Daddy about the handsome boy I'd met at the beach and how he'd encouraged me to model. But that was all I'd told them, and that was all they needed to know. I'd proved I could model. I'd done it locally and it had gone well; now I was ready for more.

I stood for a moment on the sidewalk and looked up at the sign above the door. "The Barbizon," it read, and just below it, "140," the address. This pink brick hotel was legendary. For years it had been home to some of the most famous actresses in the world: Grace Kelly, Joan Crawford, Lauren Bacall. They had come here with many of the same hopes I had. And each of them had made it big. Now it was my turn to watch my dreams and destiny collide.

I checked in at the front desk, took my key, and headed up the elevator to the third floor. The doors opened onto a dark, narrow hallway with worn carpet. I walked to room 313, turned the key, and walked in.

The pale green room was small and sparse. There was a twin bed, a dresser, and a desk with a lamp under a window that looked out on another building. The shared bathroom was out in the hall. I went to the window and took in the view of the brick building next door. The leftover light from the sun just made its way into my room. What did I expect for twenty dollars a night? But this was home for now. I was at The Barbizon, and I was going to make the best of it.

Each morning I'd rise early, dress, and go downstairs to have breakfast. The hotel restaurant featured a circular counter in the middle of the room with silver barstools covered in burgundy vinyl. A large chandelier hung from the ceiling, and a wall of windows looked out over Lexington Avenue. I'd sit at the counter and order a cup of coffee and half a cantaloupe with cottage cheese in the middle. After eating, I'd pay the bill, pick up my map, head out the door onto Lex (that's what New Yorkers called it), and walk down the street toward whatever agency I'd decided to visit that day, glancing into windows and staring into faces as I went.

I'd been told not to look people in the eye in New York—they'd know I was from out of town—but I did it anyway. I loved studying the faces of the people I passed. Maybe their vacant gazes or stern demeanors or crazy-eyed stares would give me some clue about what awaited me on the other side of fame. While I walked, I also thought about Steve and wondered what he was up to. Was he dating someone? Was he happy? I knew he was modeling for Wilhelmina, but other than that I didn't have a clue.

On the final day of my stay, I got up my nerve to visit Ford Models, the most prestigious agency not only in New York but also the world. Eileen Ford had a reputation for looking after the girls she signed, and I liked that. Some of them even lived with her at her home in Long Island so she could groom them for the business. She was also known to be steely and demanding.

I was nervous. When I reached the door with a plaque that read, "Ford Models," I took a deep breath and walked in. I entered the small reception area and approached the woman sitting behind the desk. "I'm here to show my portfolio," I said with all the courage I could muster.

"Great. Take a seat," she said curtly. I handed her my "portfolio," a modest folder of amateur photos. I didn't know how to react to her terse manner. I was used to southern hospitality, and this was different. I reminded myself of where I was and sat down.

Two other girls were waiting: a brunette with angular features and a leggy blond with long, straight hair. They were gorgeous and here for the same reason I was. Would Eileen Ford pick them over me? I sat down and fidgeted with my skirt. Every couple minutes I'd sneak a glance at the two girls. I knew they were checking me out too, though our eyes never met.

A few minutes later, a door opened and an attractive brunette stepped out. "Laura?"

"Right here," I said.

"Come this way." I stood up and walked toward her. "I'm Claire," she said, smiling.

What a relief, someone nice. I followed her down a short hall, and we came to an open door and walked in.

"Laura, meet Eileen Ford. Good luck," she said before walking away and closing the door behind her.

"It's so nice to meet you," I gushed to the woman sitting behind a desk overflowing with papers and photos. I couldn't believe I was standing in front of Eileen Ford, an icon who'd practically invented the modern modeling agency. She had fiery eyes, a toothy smile, and light brown hair in a flipped-out bob similar to the style my mother wore. I could tell in an instant she was all business. She looked at me intently, then lowered her head and began flipping through the photos I'd brought along.

"So, you want to be a model," she said, looking me in the eye.

I flinched. Hoping she hadn't noticed, I replied, "Yes, I do. More than anything."

"Really?" She seemed amused. "I need to see your legs. Stand up and pull your skirt just above your knees." I immediately stood up and did as she asked. Ugh. I had Daddy's muscular legs, and they certainly weren't my strong suit.

"Hmm," she said, sizing me up with a once-over. "Your legs are a little short for modeling, but I guess they'll do."

Then she reached down and slid an object out from under her desk. "Come here and step on this."

I walked over, looked down and saw a bathroom scale. A scale? I was mortified. This was the last thing I'd expected. I stepped onto it, wishing I'd skipped the apple crumble I'd treated myself to that morning.

"One twenty-four," she said with conviction. She paused. "Lose ten pounds and come back next week."

Good grief. I was five seven, and she wanted me to weigh 114?

"Okay," I replied eagerly, wanting to please. Then I thought about how hard it would be to lose ten more pounds. I'd been dieting since January, and I'd barely lost eight. Now I was supposed to lose ten in one week? *I can't do this.* I began to panic.

"Are you free this afternoon? There's a go-see I'd like to send you to," she said.

My ears perked up. I was just learning modeling terms and knew a "go-see" was like an audition, though some girls referred to them as "cattle calls."

"It's for *Elle* magazine," she said. "They're shooting a spread in France, and I think you'd be perfect. Claire will give you the address."

France? Oh, my God.

"Thank you," I said, beaming. I knew I'd have to make it through the go-see, but *Elle* magazine? I could barely contain my excitement. "It was nice meeting you."

"And it was nice to meet you," she said as she handed back my photos. "Lose that weight and I'll see you next week."

I grabbed lunch at a nearby deli—tuna salad and a few celery sticks—and pondered what had just happened. It all felt so surreal. I knew I had to go back to North Carolina and talk to my parents. Then I had to pack and drive to the Outer Banks to shoot with Ray. All that would take at least two weeks. If I got the job with *Elle*, I'd figure things out. I made the decision to call Eileen Ford when I got back to Raleigh and explain my situation. Surely she'd understand.

I arrived at the go-see a few hours later in the same outfit I'd worn that morning. I was nervous but confident of my chances. Eileen Ford thought I was pretty enough to send out even with the extra weight I needed to lose. That had to count for something.

I stepped off the elevator and walked into the lobby of *Elle*. It was filled with blond models. I panicked. Every face was perfect and every hair in place. Most of the girls were taller and thinner than me. Who knew there were so many gorgeous blonds in New York? And why did they all have to be in this room?

The confidence I'd felt moments before vanished. Meeting Eileen Ford had made me feel invincible. But it hadn't prepared me for this. *Look at these girls, they're so skinny. Why would Elle choose me when they could have their pick of any of these beauties?* I glanced at my hands. *Why didn't I get a manicure?* I wanted to throw up.

"Laura Whitfield?"

I glanced up. "Yes, here." I rose from my chair and felt every eye in the room fall on me. "Watch out," those eyes seemed to say, "if you get picked and we don't, we'll kill you."

The competition in that room was unlike anything I'd ever experienced. What had I gotten myself into? I'd never liked competing—it wasn't my nature. Growing up, I'd avoided sports and focused on things I could do well, like playing the piano and writing poems. I just wanted things to be easy and good. Clearly, I hadn't thought this through.

The go-see was much like my visit with Eileen Ford, except this time there were two people—a French photographer and an editor from *Elle*.

"Big smile," said the editor, looking over the glasses propped on her nose.

I smiled.

"Great. Now turn around."

I did.

"Again."

I followed her cue. She forced a smile. Then she and the photographer, who looked very French in his all-black attire, began flipping through my portfolio.

"Are these all the photos you have?" the editor asked.

"Yes, I just got to the city. I'm new."

"Hmm," she replied, unimpressed. "And Ford sent you?"

"Yes, Eileen Ford," I said, trying not to gloat.

She turned to the man, and they spoke together in French.

"Thank you, that's all," she said. "The shoot is in Paris in two weeks. We only need one blond. If you're chosen, we'll contact Ford and they'll be in touch."

The whole thing took all of ten minutes. I walked back through the lobby and pushed the elevator button, and when the doors closed behind me, I took a deep breath. I'd survived. My trip to New York had been a success. I had a good shot at becoming a Ford model, and I might even have a job in Paris. Things had gone better than I'd ever imagined. The next morning, I checked out of the Barbizon and hailed a Checker Cab to Penn Station to take the train home.

I arrived back in Raleigh the next day, heady from my successful trial run in New York. Mama and Daddy picked me up at the train station, and I talked nonstop on the way home. I could tell from their expressions they were pleased. I told them about my visit with Eileen Ford and about the ten pounds, though I left out the part about having to lose it in one week. They might think it was excessive and try and talk me out of going back, and I wasn't going to let that happen. I was determined to go to New York, so I laid out my plan.

"School is out in a few weeks. I can take the train up then. I even have a place to live." I explained to Mama and Daddy that while I was there I'd decided to look through the "Roommate Wanted" ads in the *New York Times* and found the right fit: "Female roommate needed. 2 BR on 79th & 3rd. $250/mo. Utilities included. Available June 1." There was a phone number, and then, "Call and ask for Valerie."

I did, and we'd immediately hit it off. Valerie was twenty, a year older than me. She'd won a Junior Miss contest back in Minneapolis and had decided to come to New York to model. I'd stopped by to meet her and see the apartment. It was perfect—a safe neighborhood on the bus line. There was even an A&P across the street.

"I told her I'd talk to you and let her know," I said, hopeful.

"You can take your five hundred dollars for fall tuition and go to New York, or you can use it for school. It's up to you. When it runs out, you're on your own." Mama's response was so measured, I was sure she had prepared it.

"Really? Thank you!" I said, elated. My thoughts raced. I needed to call Eileen Ford. And Valerie. Mama and Daddy would pay my return train fare. I could use $250 for the rent and the rest for food and expenses. I'd have to get a waitressing job until I got on my feet, but I didn't mind. Everything was set.

First thing Monday morning, I called Ford. I told them I was finishing up school and would contact them when I arrived in the city in a few weeks. I asked about the *Elle* shoot. They hadn't heard anything; they'd call me. I'd just have to be patient and wait. I went back to school, said goodbye to my friends, and took my finals before returning home. It was finally Memorial Day weekend—the weekend I'd scheduled my shoot with Ray Matthews—so on Saturday, I borrowed Mama's car and made a beeline to the beach. I was leaving for New York in a few days, and I wanted to go by The Christmas Shop and tell everyone my news.

It was dark by the time I arrived in Manteo. Cole had told me to meet her at The Nags Header, so I dropped my things at our old trailer and drove right over. The Good Humor Band was playing upstairs, and I was ready to dance.

As I passed The Christmas Shop, crossed the drawbridge, and headed up the beach road, the woes of the previous winter fell away. I rolled down my windows and turned up the radio. The air was hypnotic, heavy with the scent of the sea.

I wheeled into the parking lot of The Nags Header, which was packed with cars. It felt like old times. I thought about Steve, our last conversation. I stepped out of my car.

I hurried up the front steps, pushed open the screen door, and strode into the old ballroom. It was filled with people talking and laughing. Some were dancing. Almost everyone had a beer in their hand. I edged my way through the crowd, looking for Cole. Before I could find her, I saw Steve leaning against the old wooden bar, sipping a Tab.

I was astounded. How had we ended up at the beach at the same time? He caught my eye and broke into a big smile. "Well, well," he said.

Was it just my imagination or did he look thinner, more like a model?

"I didn't expect to see you here," I said, trying to contain my excitement. I walked over and he reached out and gave me a hug.

I'd spent nine months reliving the night we were first together. Now his arms were around me once more. He felt amazing. The first thing I noticed, besides how handsome he looked, was how relaxed I was. The week in New York had boosted my confidence. I thought about how far I'd come since I'd last seen Steve.

"Yeah," he said, "I'm just down for the long weekend. I have a shoot on Tuesday I need to get back for."

"How's it going?" I asked. "The modeling, I mean."

"Good. Wilhelmina is keeping me busy—lots of go-sees, work. I just did my first commercial. I'm happy." He paused. "You look great. Are you modeling?"

"I am," I said proudly, pleased that he'd asked. I hesitated before continuing, wondering how he might react to what I was about to say. "I'm actually moving to New York next week."

"That's amazing, congrats," he said, smiling.

I considered the ten pounds I needed to lose—*Shouldn't I order a Tab?* I thought, then immediately ordered a beer. Steve and I stood and sipped our drinks as I filled him in on the past nine months—modeling, my week in New York, Eileen Ford, *Elle*, my photo shoot with Ray, my decision to move. He told me about life in the city, his recent commercial, and about some of the other jobs he'd landed. The crowd was rowdy and the music so loud we had to raise our voices to be heard. We chatted like old friends. I could tell he was genuinely happy for me.

"If things don't work out with Ford, let me know. My agent would love you."

"I will, thanks," I said.

Just then a pretty brunette in a gauzy white shirt walked up as though I didn't exist and gave Steve a hug. She whispered something in his ear and he smiled, took her hand, and began following her into the crowd.

He glanced back at me. "See ya," he said before disappearing into the crush of bodies.

My heart sank. But what did I expect? He was still "Steve the Dream."

I found Cole in the crowd after that, and I told her about running into Steve. We chattered nonstop and drank too much, and I barely remembered driving back to the trailer when I woke up the next day.

I returned to Raleigh with my first photo shoot under my belt and packed my suitcase for New York. I was going by train, so I could only take what I could carry with me. I was excited and scared. There were moments when I felt like I could conquer the world and others when I was sure I was crazy. But my course was set and there was no turning back. One way or the other, I was going to succeed.

Mama and Daddy drove me to the station, and we said tearful goodbyes. I gave Daddy a big hug. Then I hugged Mama. Even though the two of us had been at odds for years, I would miss her. I climbed on the train, put my things away, and sat down. As the train pulled out of the station, I caught a glimpse of my parents, their faces reflecting a mix of hope and fear. I waved to them through the window. I was on my way.

~୬·ୖ~

Chapter Five

As I stood on the balcony of my apartment and watched people hustle up and down the busy crosstown street, it began to sink in: Steve and I were in the same city. I was living in my first apartment on the Upper East Side. I'd been on my first go-see, and I was just seven pounds from becoming a Ford model. Seven pounds. It had been more than two weeks since I'd met Eileen Ford, and I'd barely lost three. Could I even lose the rest?

I knew I needed to be more disciplined—I'd done it before—but I couldn't think about that now. All my energy was focused on one thing: money. Mama had given me $600—she'd graciously thrown in an extra $100—and I only had $300 left. I knew I'd been careful. I'd given Valerie $250 for rent, and I'd spent another $50 on groceries and a few things for my apartment. July rent was due in just three weeks, and I didn't know where it would come from. I was haunted by a nagging uneasiness, but I refused to let it take hold. Somehow, I'd figure it out. I always had.

I bought a *New York Times* and looked through the "Help Wanted" ads. I ran my finger down the column until I got to "Models Wanted." I scanned the various jobs—hand model, shoe model, runway and showroom models—and circled the ones that most interested me. The next day, I got up early and called the phone numbers listed for each one. This was why I needed an agent, to do this kind of thing for me. For now, I was on my own.

I started picking up a few jobs modeling collections in department stores. Soon, I made my phone calls a daily habit. As glad as I was to have the work, though, my heart wasn't in it. Like every aspiring cover girl, I wanted to see my face in print. Still, it was income.

"What time are you getting up?" Valerie asked me one night before going to bed.

"Nine o'clock," I told her. "There's a showroom job I want. They need blonds."

Valerie was blond too—her Norwegian heritage was visible in her whitish-blond mane.

"Cool," she answered, casually. "Sleep well."

The next morning, I stumbled into the living room at nine, anxious to make my calls. Valerie was sitting on the sofa talking on the phone; my *New York Times* "Help Wanted" section rested in her lap.

She finished her call, then looked up. "Hey, I just got a shoe job," she said, beaming. "And that showroom wants to see me this afternoon." I was stunned. I told myself we were in the same business and competing for the same jobs and this was normal. But this didn't feel right.

"Great," I lied. "Can I see that?" I pointed to the newspaper, hoping she'd pick up on the anger in my voice. I wanted to confront her, but I didn't dare. I was a nice southern girl, taught to avoid confrontation at any cost. It's better to shut your mouth and keep the peace, even if it means pushing your feelings aside. That's how we were raised. The truth is, after nineteen years of that training, I didn't know how to speak up for myself.

"Sure," she said innocently, handing over the paper.

Was she clueless about the trespass she'd just committed? I knew she was fiercely competitive, but I didn't believe she was malicious. She was just a local girl who'd made it big. She'd come to New

York with modeling experience and a Junior Miss title—I'd seen the interviews and photos of her in the *Minneapolis Star Tribune*. She was confident, talented, and clearly out to win—even at my expense.

From that day on, I saw Valerie as a threat and avoided her as much as possible. I quickly figured out her schedule. She got up at eight thirty to make her calls, so I started getting up at eight to leave messages on answering machines. Sometimes I'd get a callback. Most of the time I didn't hear a word.

Time was running out, and so was my money. I knew if I could lose the seven pounds and start modeling, everything would be okay. But that would take time, and more money, for makeup, clothes, photos. Money I didn't have.

The next morning, I picked up the *Times*, skipped the "Models Wanted" sections, and went straight to the "Help Wanted" ads. "Burger King. Now hiring. Cooks and counter staff needed. Applications accepted 10 a.m.–2 p.m., M-F, 1557 Broadway, NYC." I was strapped for cash and willing to do almost anything to earn it. Surely I could get a job at Burger King. Besides, what did I have to lose?

I got dressed, walked over to Broadway, and caught a bus going downtown. I got off at the corner of Forty-Fifth Street, right in the heart of Times Square—a seedy enclave of hookers and peep shows—and walked to the address listed in the paper. I pushed open the door and entered a small hallway.

A woman in a pin-striped suit sat at a small makeshift table cluttered with applications, a telephone, and an ashtray overflowing with cigarette butts.

"Can I help you?" she asked before taking a drag of her Virginia Slim.

"I'm answering the Burger King ad," I said matter-of-factly.

The woman took another puff and eyed me suspiciously. "Honey, you're too pretty to flip hamburgers. Just a minute."

She picked up the phone and dialed a number. I was confused.

"There's a young lady here I think you need to see. She's applying for Burger King." She paused to listen to the person on the other end of the line. Then she put her hand over the phone.

"What's your name?"

"Laura."

"Her name is Laura. I'll send her right up."

She hung up the phone, then looked at me.

"Take this elevator up to the tenth floor and ask for Mr. Guterman," she said, pointing to her right. "Tell the receptionist Dorothy sent you. And good luck."

"Thank you," I said, not knowing what to think but feeling as if God had spared me from some terrible fate.

I walked over to the elevator, got inside, pushed the button, and waited as the car rushed to the tenth floor. There was a "ping," then the doors opened onto a lobby with a single door and on it a sign that read, "Horn & Hardart." I knew this name from the famous Automats dotting the city, their walls lined with little refrigerated boxes of food. They were coin-operated; you put in quarters, turned a knob, and got to pull out whatever was inside. Burger King certainly wasn't the most glamorous place to work, but I knew I didn't want to be an Automat girl.

I opened the door and entered a reception area with a glassed-in office and a sign that read, "Fred Guterman, President." Wow, the woman downstairs had sent me to see the president of Horn & Hardart. I'd read about Mr. Guterman in the *New York Times*. He'd once given an aging vaudeville performer a chance to sing at his Automat on Broadway and Forty-Sixth. "She makes people happy," he'd told the reporter. "That's what counts."

"I'm Laura," I said to the woman behind the desk. "Dorothy . . ."

"Ah, yes," she interrupted. "Right this way." She smiled and led me to the glass office, where she knocked on the door.

"Come in," a man's voice said.

She opened the door into a dimly lit room with a large mahogany desk.

"You must be Laura," said the man, rising from his chair. So this was Fred Guterman. He looked to be about fifty and was striking in his three-piece suit.

"Have a seat. Dorothy tells me you want to work at Burger King." He seemed mildly amused.

"Yes," I told him. "I just got to the city and I need a job. I worked the counter at a hospital snack shop in high school," I finished feebly. It was the only experience I'd had working with food.

"You know our Automats, right?" he inquired.

Oh no, here it comes, I thought, and nodded.

"Well, we've been phasing those out and replacing them with Burger Kings. We've also bought a few restaurants around town. We own Kitty Hawk on Third Avenue. They need a waitress. Are you interested?"

"Yessir," I said eagerly. "Thank you." I felt an enormous weight lift. Now I'd be able to pay my rent.

"Here's the address," he said, handing me a slip of paper. "When you leave here, stop by Kitty Hawk and ask for Gary. I'll give him a call and tell him you're on the way." I looked down at the words "Kitty Hawk" on the paper. I couldn't believe it. Kitty Hawk was a town on the Outer Banks, my old stomping ground. It was near The Nags Header and where the Wright brothers had come to make the first powered airplane flight. Out of the thousands of restaurants in Manhattan, I'd landed a job at one called Kitty Hawk. I was sure it was a sign.

"Thank you again," I said as I reached over to shake his hand. "I'm very grateful."

Someone had just done me a great kindness for no apparent reason. Why? I hadn't done anything to deserve it. And perhaps that was the point. I'd spent my life trying to earn everyone's approval—first Mama's, then my friends', then Steve's—believing if I was perfect enough or interesting enough or pretty enough I'd be loved. Now I'd met Fred Guterman, a powerful man who'd given me a job when I really needed one—no strings attached.

I realized in that moment I was tired of trying to be good enough. Maybe I should just try being myself.

A couple of days after meeting Mr. Guterman, I began waiting tables at Kitty Hawk. I felt at home there: model airplanes hung from the ceiling, and old black-and-white photos of the Wright brothers were displayed on the walls. I'd never waitressed before, but I picked it up quickly. All you had to do was be nice to customers, keep your orders straight, get along with the wait staff, and be friendly with the chef. I knew I needed to focus more on my modeling, but right now all that mattered was making enough money to get by. I got a free meal on the days I worked, so I'd eat a spinach salad and skimp on food at home. By the time July rolled around, I'd saved enough to pay my rent.

My first month in New York had been difficult. The job with *Elle* hadn't materialized and I was disillusioned. I hadn't followed up with Ford because I hadn't lost the ten pounds. Other than making a few phone calls, I'd been hanging out in our apartment not doing much of anything. It was hard to admit it, but I felt depressed.

I knew from being around Mama that the best thing for depression was to get up and do something. So I'd make myself shower, dress, and walk—through our neighborhood, anywhere. The moment my foot hit the pavement I came alive—I felt that anything was possible. I'd walk onto Seventy-Ninth Street and turn right or left and just keep walking, sometimes for hours. I was fascinated with New York—the smells, the people, the latest fashions in store windows. On the way home, I'd pass the corner newsstand and catch the cover of *Glamour* or *Vogue* and remember why I'd risked everything to come here.

"So, you're a model," said Alex Behrman when Valerie introduced us one night at Elaine's, a popular celebrity hangout. He appeared to be about thirty and had black hair, sparkling eyes, and a playful grin.

"Working on it," I said, flashing my best smile. He asked me lots of questions, and I eagerly shared my story—how I'd ended up in the city, my meeting with Ford, my dream of being a cover girl.

"Maybe I can help you," he offered.

"Thank you," I said. "I'd appreciate that."

From that moment, Alex Behrman became my fiercest ally and one of my closest friends. As we chatted, I learned that he was from an affluent family. His father was the president of Wilkerson Steel, one of the largest steel manufacturers in the country. Alex was an executive at Hathaway Shirts and worked at Rockefeller Plaza. He lived in a posh apartment between Park and Madison and had a private limousine. Despite his apparent wealth, he was warm and friendly and I felt comfortable around him.

I gave him my number, and he called the next morning to say how much he'd enjoyed meeting me.

"Go to Caswell-Massey on Lexington and Forty-Eighth and buy yourself a good hairbrush," he instructed. "I'll pay for it. You need it for your business."

The next week, he sent me to a Madison Avenue hair salon for a designer cut. I'd never been treated this way, and I was thrilled.

One day we took his limo to Tiffany's, and his driver parked right outside the front door.

"I have a DPL plate," Alex explained. "It stands for 'diplomat'— it means I can park almost anywhere in the city."

I smiled, wondering how he'd swung something like that. I knew he wasn't a diplomat. He *was* eccentric, though. We went inside and pretended we were engaged, and I tried on diamonds just for fun. Then we went out for an extravagant lunch—right in the middle of the day. Alex treated me like a princess, and our adventures were a welcome escape from my otherwise uneventful life.

He was also a bit of an enigma, and that was part of my attraction to him. I wouldn't hear from him for days and then he'd call me out of the blue.

"Want to join me for dinner at Windows on the World?" he'd ask.

I always eagerly accepted his invitation.

It was 1976, America's bicentennial. Operation Sail was in full swing, and I felt lucky to be in New York. Tall ships had entered the Hudson River harbor for the festivities, and for weeks sailors from all around the world wandered the streets. They moved like animals, in packs, handsomely decked out in their dress whites. They'd wink and tip their hats and turn their heads as I walked by. Occasionally, a slender stranger would call out to me in French or Italian or some other language as his shipmates spurred him on. They'd laugh and I'd smile coyly. I enjoyed the fleeting attention, but I wasn't the only one. Every girl I knew seemed to be captivated by these exotic creatures in white.

Now that I had a job and wasn't as anxious about money, I could focus on other things. Like Billy the bartender. I enjoyed spending time with Alex and he was good to me, but I thought of him only as a friend.

Billy was thirty-two and attractive, with short, blondish hair and a muscular body. He was also a terrible flirt. "I'm half-Jewish, half-Persian," he'd say, "and you know what they say about Persians." Then he'd wink at me and stroke his moustache, the way he always did.

It wasn't long before I was smitten. He'd walk over, put a

quarter in the Kitty Hawk jukebox, and play "Don't Go Breaking My Heart," and I'd instantly start moving to the beat. We'd sing the duet together, and the regulars at the bar would chime in.

After that came stolen kisses and drinks after work, and soon we were sleeping together. Billy asked for one of my modeling photos and hung it over the bar to let everyone know we were a couple.

I had fun with Billy. On the weekends we weren't working, we'd hop into the little red convertible he'd won on *The Price Is Right* and drive to Connecticut or Long Island. He'd put the top down and tell me stories—about being a contestant on a game show and about his old girlfriend Barbara and her daughter Sunshine. He'd met Barbara as she was leaving an abusive marriage.

"I felt sorry for her and invited them to move in. Then I fell in love—with both of them. We became a family."

He didn't say why they'd parted ways two months earlier, but he looked sad when he talked about it.

"It's over," he told me.

I wanted to believe him, but it seemed like he was trying to convince himself.

In mid-July, I went to a party with my friend Sylvia, who'd been named for Sylvia Plath.

"You need to get out more," Sylvia teased. "Besides, there'll be some fascinating people there."

She had my attention.

The spacious loft was filled with models, actors, artistic types. I'd only been there long enough to grab a glass of wine when someone called out, "Anyone need a roommate?" The question had come from a curious-looking girl on a swing suspended from the ceiling. A swing in an apartment. *Only in New York*, I thought.

"I do!" I quickly replied, hoping to get first shot. Things had continued to deteriorate with Valerie, and I was anxious to move out.

"It's an L-shaped studio on East Sixty-Third," she said. "Third floor with an elevator and a doorman. Three fifty a month." That was a hundred more than I was paying now, but I was doing well at Kitty Hawk—I could probably make it work.

The girl hopped down and walked over to me. "Hi, I'm Cheryl," she said.

"I'm Laura. Happy to meet you."

Cheryl was tall and wiry. She had narrow eyes, heavy with eyeliner; bright red lips; and short auburn hair cut at an angle. She reminded me of the department store mannequins I saw along Fifth Avenue.

"Do you model?" I asked. "You look like you could do runway." Runway models were a unique breed: super thin, with legs that wouldn't quit.

"My boyfriend tells me that," she said, smiling. "No. I work at Macy's as a graphic designer, laying out ads and flyers. What about you?"

"That's impressive," I said. "I'm a model. I haven't signed with an agency. I've just been picking up a few jobs. I also wait tables." *That's pitiful*, I thought, so I added, "It takes time," a comment made less to reassure Cheryl than myself.

I learned that she was twenty-six and from Ohio, and that she'd lived in the city for two years. It would be nice to have an older roommate who wasn't a model. No competition.

"So, you have a boyfriend?" I asked, curious.

"Yeah, Brad. He's Canadian. He's forty-two and drives a Jag."

Forty-two? I couldn't imagine going out with someone that old, no matter what kind of car he drove.

"Well," said Cheryl, "are you still interested?"

"Sure . . . but I would like to see the apartment first."

We made plans for me to come by the next day.

•••

The place was ideal: small but modern, with sienna-and-teal walls and a courtyard view. There were bamboo shades on the windows and pots of succulents scattered all around. Cheryl had a platform bed; I'd be sleeping on a mattress on the floor. But I didn't mind. I liked Cheryl and I needed a change. We agreed that I would move in August 1.

I was still settling in when Mama and Daddy arrived for a visit. Billy wanted to impress my parents, so he'd gotten us second-row seats for *Godspell*. It was my first Broadway show, and I couldn't wait. I was also proud to show off my older boyfriend.

I wasn't sure what Mama and Daddy would think of Billy, but he was charming and they were polite and I thought it went well. At least until the actress playing Mary Magdalene came down the aisle during her number and sat in Daddy's lap. She threaded her red feather boa around his neck, looked him in the eyes, and belted out lustfully, "Turn back, O man," adding, "How's it goin', big boy?" before handing him a Hershey bar.

I watched Mama's face; she was dumbfounded, but we all survived.

Mama and Daddy stayed for a few days. It was sweltering—I could feel the hot pavement through my shoes. To escape the heat, the four of us went to the top of the Empire State Building. We also had drinks at Windows on the World. Before they left to go home a few days later, we stood in my apartment and Mama looked at me and smiled.

"I'm proud of you," she said.

"Thanks, Mama," I replied. It had been a long time coming, but I knew I'd finally earned her respect.

Mama and Daddy returned to North Carolina, and I waited tables and hung out with Billy. Things were good, or so I thought. Then, as we were walking back to my apartment on a balmy evening in late August, I noticed that Billy was quieter than usual.

We passed the block of shops on First Avenue that included Barbara's Bakery and Sunshine Flower Shop. Billy had pointed them out to me when we first started seeing each other.

"Isn't that funny?" he'd asked wistfully. "Their names both in the same block."

We walked along in silence. "You okay?" I asked.

"Not really."

"What's wrong?" My stomach knotted. We were happy. What could it possibly be?

"I'm still in love with Barbara. And I miss Sunshine. I want to see if I can make it work with them again."

"Okay," I said, not knowing what else to say.

He told me he had seen Barbara and asked her to move back in. I was shocked.

"I can't believe you didn't talk to me first," I said, hurt.

"I know." He looked away. "I'm sorry. I should have."

And that was that.

~୨·୧~

Chapter Six

I was more angry than heartbroken over Billy's disclosure. I'd invested weeks into our relationship. And for what? Those weeks had turned into months and here I was, still without an agent. When I first met Alex, he'd urged me to keep a small notebook of business contacts. Now I picked it up and flipped through the pages. There were the names of several agencies I hadn't been to—Zoli, My Fair Lady, and Steve's agency, Wilhelmina.

I'd avoided Wilhelmina for fear of running into Steve. What would I say to him? "I'm great," I'd lie. "Busy. Getting interest from the top agencies. Landing some great gigs?"

Besides, I'd just gotten a letter from Cole telling me that Steve was dating a top model—it was all the buzz at the beach. The news unnerved me. I'd come to New York in hopes of what? Being with Steve again? What was I thinking? I'd wasted so much time—depressed, moving, doing nothing, hanging out with Alex, dating Billy. I suddenly saw the vast chasm stretched out between where I was and where I wanted to be. I knew I only had myself to blame.

Ford had wanted me to lose weight. So had the other agencies I'd visited. Losing that weight was all that was standing between me and a modeling contract. It seemed so simple. And yet I couldn't even do that. What was wrong with me? Why couldn't I focus? The truth was, I was terrified of failing. I'd told everyone I was coming to New York not just to model but to become a cover girl.

I'd set the bar high. What if I fell short? How would I face them? I couldn't let that happen—it would be too humiliating. Somehow, I had to push through my fear and keep going. I had to succeed—at any cost.

I knew I should take my portfolio to Wilhelmina. I'd heard wonderful things about Wilhelmina Cooper—that she was warm and kind and, like Eileen Ford, was good to her models. She'd been a successful cover girl in the sixties, and now she'd opened her own agency. But there was the weight issue. Could I bear hearing that again? Maybe a smaller agency, like My Fair Lady, would be better. They'd just opened and were hiring models. I decided to give them a try.

The next day, I took my portfolio and went to My Fair Lady, located in a renovated apartment building on East Eighty-Fourth. I'd called to see if I needed an appointment, but the woman on the phone had told me I could just drop by.

My Fair Lady wasn't what I'd expected; it was just a spacious room with photos hanging on the walls. The photos—print ads and magazine covers—were all of one model, Melanie Cain. The owner, Buddy Jacobson, had partnered with Melanie, a former Ford model in her early twenties, to start My Fair Lady.

A pretty brunette approached me. "Hi, I'm Melanie."

Of course, I recognized her at once—she was about my age, maybe a bit older. Definitely the wholesome girl who'd been featured in Cover Girl makeup ads and *Seventeen*. She wasn't exactly a celebrity, but she was a successful model and I was impressed. It was hard to contain my excitement.

"Nice to meet you," I said, smiling. "I wondered if you could take a look at my book."

"Sure," she said. She offered me a chair, and I sat down as she flipped through my portfolio. "Great shot . . . nice."

So far so good, I thought.

"Let me get Buddy. I'll be right back." She got up and walked behind a black curtain at the back of the room.

A few minutes later, a man came out. He was average height, with a mane of ebony hair and a mustache. Something about him unsettled me.

"Hi, I'm Buddy Jacobson," he said, shaking my hand. "Melanie tells me you have a nice book. And that you're looking for an agent."

"Thank you," I said, hopeful. "Yes, I am."

"How long have you been in the city?" he asked.

"Four months." Had it really been that long?

"Been to other agencies?" he asked, looking at me directly. His eyes were black as coal and a bit foreboding. I'd never seen anything like them. He looked Italian and seemed to be in his mid-forties.

"Yes. Eileen Ford expressed interest." My body tensed. "I'm actually thinking a smaller agency might be better for me."

"Hmm." He hovered over one shot. Curious, I glanced to see which one. It was the same photo that had spurred Eileen Ford to send me to *Elle*.

"You have a great look. Fresh. Definitely Junior."

I'd been told this before. "Junior" was a category of models featured in ads geared mostly to teens—makeup, skin care, and fashion.

He opened a desk drawer, reached in a file, and pulled out some papers. "I want to sign you. This is our contract," he said, handing the papers to me. I tried to digest his words. "Take it with you, look it over, sign it, and bring it back. I can get you work. I hope you'll decide to come on board."

I looked down at the pages in my hand. A modeling contract. I couldn't believe it.

"Thank you so much. I'm thrilled," I said, smiling. I'd tried to play it cool, but now I couldn't contain my delight. This was the moment I'd been waiting for. My parents would be so relieved. "I'll bring it back soon. Thank you again. It was nice meeting you." I looked over at Melanie Cain. "And you too. See you soon."

Buddy handed me my portfolio. I smiled, turned, and steeled my emotions as I walked through the front door.

Once outside, I stood there for a moment, taking it all in. Then my thoughts turned to Alex, who'd been my greatest ally. He was the first person I wanted to tell.

When I called Alex to tell him my news, he suggested we meet for lunch the next day at a little café near his office. I was anxious to show him the contract and get his advice. I watched his face as he read the fine print, hoping to detect a flicker of excitement. Instead, he was serious and unmoved. He finally looked up and gave a faint smile.

"You can certainly sign this," he said, "but I think you can do better."

"Really?" I asked, hoping for an explanation.

"I believe you've got real potential. I think you should hold out for Ford or Wilhelmina. My Fair Lady might get you some work, but they won't get you the caliber of work the other agencies can."

I listened carefully to what he was saying. Then I listened to my gut. As much as I wanted to sign that contract and call myself a working model, I didn't want to compromise.

"You're right. I should wait."

"It's your decision, of course," he added. "You're smart. You'll figure it out."

After lunch, Alex and I hugged goodbye.

"I've been invited to the Yves Saint Laurent spring fashion show at the Basin tomorrow night," he said. "I'd like to take you as my guest."

"I'd love that!" Alex had kept his distance while I was dating Billy, and I'd missed doing things with him.

As I walked past department store windows and bus stop ads, my resolve deepened. I knew what I needed to do. When I arrived at my apartment, I picked up the phone and called Wilhelmina. Steve or no Steve, I had to look out for myself and give this thing my best shot. I made an appointment for Thursday, then called Mama and Daddy.

Just the day before, I'd called to tell them about the contract with My Fair Lady. Now I was calling to tell them I'd had a change of heart.

"Alex is right," I told Daddy. "I don't want to sign with the first agency that comes along." I wondered how that must have sounded to them. I'd been in New York now for four months, with nothing to show in the way of a contract. Was I foolish to walk away?

"I know you'll do the right thing," Daddy said with complete confidence.

There were a lot of things I doubted, including many of the choices I'd made about my life, but I never doubted Daddy's belief in me.

"I hope so," I said hesitantly. I hung up the phone and let the weight of my decision sink in. Part of me was terrified; the other part, relieved. Buddy Jacobson seemed a bit sleazy. Something about his eyes, the way he looked at me, made me uncomfortable. There was that. But wasn't it also risky to wait? Then I thought about how I'd held out for Steve. How I'd risked everything to come to New York. I considered that maybe something was wrong with me, but then I realized: *That's who I am. A risk-taker. It wouldn't be like me to do anything else.*

The person I'd spoken with at Wilhelmina had told me to come to their open call in a few days. What I really wanted was to meet Wilhelmina Cooper, or "Willy," as her models and close friends called her. If I could just get in to see her, I might have a chance. But first I had to get through the junior agent who'd review my book.

Please, God, I thought, lifting a prayer. Then I stopped. Why should He do anything for me? I'd pretty much pushed God aside when I moved to the beach. I'd ignored Him when I made the decision to move to New York, and certainly since I arrived. I believed He had a plan for my life, but now I was set on making my own. After all, didn't I know what was best for me?

That's when I remembered the letter. The one that had arrived back in June, while I was still living with Valerie. I'd known from the beautiful cursive handwriting that it was from Mama. I'd opened it eagerly and read along.

"The closer you got to New York, the more doubt I had about your going." *I had no idea she felt that way.* "I'm afraid your greatest desire is what the world has to offer. And that in trying for the bright lights, you may be blinded by the glare." *How dare she say those things. I'm not blind*, I told myself. But her words stung.

I looked down at the letter and sighed. I knew Mama had written these things because she loved me, and I longed for her love. If I was honest, I knew she was right. My faith was real—as much a part of me as my own heartbeat. Yet the choices I'd made—to give myself to Steve, to move to New York and pursue modeling—had distanced me from God.

I couldn't think about that now, however. It only made me feel guilty, and I needed to stay focused. So I pushed my guilt down to a place deep inside, far from Mama's words and God's watching eyes.

I was going to a designer fashion show. I imagined all the glamorous guests dressed in the latest styles. What would I wear? I didn't own anything glamorous. I was barely making my rent.

Cheryl had told me about a vintage thrift shop in the Village called the Unique Clothing Warehouse, so I took a bus downtown, hoping to find something spectacular to wear. It was just what its name implied—a large, open room full of inexpensive vintage clothes.

There, I stumbled across the perfect outfit: a 1940s satin slip with an organza top that was set off with delicate lace. It was only two dollars. I couldn't believe my luck. I bought the slip and brought it home. It wasn't couture, but I felt pretty when I tried it on.

We arrived at the Basin—a well-known marina located on the Hudson River at Seventy-Ninth Street—and walked into a party that was beyond my wildest dreams. Alex and I ordered a glass of wine each and walked around.

Cheryl Tiegs, one of the most famous fashion models in the world, came up and spoke to Alex. I was awestruck. I'd seen her face on TV and on numerous magazines, and here she was. Right in front of me.

A few minutes later, an entourage of young Black men approached us. The man in the middle wore glasses and an elegant navy suit with a white silk shirt unbuttoned to expose his chest. He looked important, though I had no idea who he was. To my surprise, he walked right up to me and offered his hand.

"Darling, I love your dress! Where did you get it?"

I couldn't believe he was talking to me, but I couldn't tell him about my two-dollar slip. What would I say?

"At a little place in the Village," I replied, trying my best to be cool.

"Well, it's fabulous!" He took both my hands in his, squeezed them, and walked away.

I turned to Alex. "Who was that?" I asked, clueless.

"Willi Smith. The fashion designer."

"Oh my gosh," I said, shocked. "I paid two dollars for this thing!"

Alex and I chuckled.

"Well, you look gorgeous," he said.

I blushed. It had been an amazing night. Willi Smith had complimented my outfit. And Alex had told me I was gorgeous. No one had ever said anything like that to me—not even Steve.

I woke up happy the next morning, feeling confident. It was Thursday, so I headed to Wilhelmina to show my portfolio. I walked into the small reception area decorated with Willy's *Vogue* covers. I approached the receptionist and gave her my name.

"Can I see your book?" she asked.

"Of course." I handed her my portfolio.

"Have a seat," she said, shaking me out of my dreamlike state. Then she stood up and carried it down the hall.

There was one other model waiting with me, a brunette. Soon others arrived, along with a string of Willy models—checking in with their bookers, on their way to go-sees and shoots. Each time the door opened I looked over, hoping to see Steve. Each time, I was disappointed.

Then I realized: *Someone's reviewing my book at this very moment.* I *really* wanted this. I still had the My Fair Lady contract—I'd decided to see Wilhelmina before giving Buddy Jacobson a call. Even so, my mind was made up. Something about Buddy made me feel uneasy. What's more, I didn't want to sign with My Fair Lady or another lesser-known agency. I would hold out for one of the big three.

"Laura?"

I looked up. It was the receptionist.

"Yes?" I stood and walked to her desk. My stomach was in knots.

She handed me my book. "So . . ."

Uh-oh, I thought.

"I showed your portfolio to several of the bookers, and they love your look. The only problem is, we just signed someone who looks like you. I mean, you two could be sisters. I'm sorry. Maybe try us again in a few months?" She smiled a conciliatory smile and I went numb.

"Thank you," I managed. "I appreciate it." What would I do now? I took a breath. "Do you know Steve Taylor?"

"Yes, of course," she said, smiling.

"He's a friend of mine from back home. North Carolina," I said. "Would it be possible to leave him a message?"

"Sure." She handed me a notepad with the word "Wilhelmina" in swirling script across the top, along with a pen.

I paused for a moment. What would I say? I began to write: "Steve, hi. I hope you're well. I stopped by today to show my portfolio. Sorry I missed you. Would love to chat sometime. Here's my number. Take care." I signed my name and added my phone number underneath. Then I handed it to the receptionist.

"Thank you," I said, nervous.

"You're welcome. I'll leave it in the men's booking room. They'll make sure he gets it."

"Great," I said, "and thank you again."

I turned and walked out the door. My cheeks burned. I'd really blown it. Why had I waited? Now someone else had a contract—someone who looked just like me. If I had come a few days earlier, maybe they would have picked me instead of her. My mind reached for something, anything but this. I thought about Steve. Even knowing that I might hear from him didn't help.

It was now early October. Several weeks had passed since my visit to Wilhelmina, and once again, I seemed to have lost my way. I'd called Buddy Jacobson to tell him I'd decided not to sign his contract.

"I have to tell you, I'm disappointed," he said.

I felt guilty, but only for a moment.

"Call me if you change your mind," he said before we hung up.

I knew I wouldn't. But with Wilhelmina out of the picture, I didn't have a backup plan. I hadn't been to see Zoli—but the truth was, I didn't want to. I wanted to be a Ford or Wilhelmina model.

Period. Now both of those options were off the table. At least, for the time being.

So I waited tables, slept, and hung out with Cheryl and her boyfriend, Brad. I was the third wheel, but Cheryl didn't seem to mind. And Brad always paid. On the weekend, the three of us would go to J.G. Melon's for Sunday brunch. We'd sit at the bustling bar, and I'd order coffee and shots of Kahlúa.

"You're the only person I know who can sit and drink coffee from a mug and leave the bar flat on her ass," said Brad. He was trim and self-assured and fairly attractive for someone in his forties. He treated me like a little sister, and I enjoyed the attention.

During the week, we'd go to Elaine's, hoping to spot a celebrity. Sometimes we'd have dinner at Patrick Sullivan's.

Patrick was a former Ford model—rumored to be one of Eileen's pets—who'd quit the business to open his own restaurant. Sullivan's was the hottest spot on the Upper East Side, full of models, actors, and sports personalities. When we came in, Patrick greeted us with his infectious smile and boyish charm. "Brad! Cheryl!" he'd exclaim, shaking Brad's hand and giving Cheryl a peck on the cheek. Then he'd turn to me.

"Well hello, beautiful!" he'd say in a seductive voice before reaching over and kissing my earlobe.

He did this with everybody. Still, this gesture always made my pulse race, and more so because his gorgeous fiancée, Jordan, was looking on. Jordan was a Ford model, about my height, with classic features and a very large diamond on her left hand. I'd never seen a diamond that big except when Alex and I had gone to Tiffany's. She bent her hand down as though it would break from the weight.

After Patrick kissed me, he would pull back and look me straight in the eye.

"Right this way!" he'd say, and before you knew it we were seated at one of the best tables in the house.

Sometimes Patrick would break away and come over to our table to chat with us. One night, we were talking about modeling and I told him about my encounter with Eileen Ford and how I was trying to lose weight.

"You should try the Atkins diet," he said confidently. "You get to eat as much protein as you like."

It wasn't long before Patrick was making house calls, showing up at my apartment with boiled eggs and jumbo shrimp from the restaurant. I knew he didn't expect anything in return, but I'd put the food in the fridge and then we'd kiss and make our way to my makeshift bed. We'd make love, and then he'd get dressed and go back to work.

Once I asked him as I stood stark naked in the middle of my apartment, "What about your fiancée?"

"Oh, Jordan," he said, flashing his model smile. "Don't worry about her. This is our secret."

Then I'd go back to Sullivan's and see her with that very large ring. If he loved her that much, why was he sleeping with me? But I wasn't one to judge. I was sleeping with other people too. There was Rob, the handsome blond attorney who lived in the Village, who'd set off a poetry-writing frenzy in me for the one week we dated. And Leif–like the Viking–the Finnair steward I met at Kitty Hawk. He'd stop by when he had a layover and whisper to me in Finnish, and then he'd fly off to a new city and into the bed of another waiting girl like me.

Then I met Jacob Levine, who had taken over his family's furniture business. He was in his thirties, Jewish, and divorced. I thought things might work out with Jacob. Then one night we went out to dinner, and when the waitress came over to take our order, he told her what he wanted and then said, "That's all."

"What about me? I asked as she walked away. I was sure there must be some mistake.

"You're trying to lose weight," he said matter-of-factly. "I didn't want you to be tempted."

"Tempted? I still have to eat," I said, exasperated. I wanted to be loved, not controlled. I sat there, simmering.

"You're quiet," he finally said. "What's wrong?"

"It's not your job to manage me. I can take care of myself."

"I was just trying to help," he muttered.

We finished dinner and walked home in silence. It was our last date.

After Jacob, there were others—a whole string of others. They were all types—Italian, Jewish, short, blond, tall, athletic. I'd sleep with them and wake up hating myself. I'd tell myself, *No more*. Then I'd do it all over again. It was familiar pattern, but I'd reached a new low. Unlike the beach, in New York there were hundreds of men to choose from. And unlike the fishbowl I'd lived in there, nobody here had to know. I wanted to stop, but I didn't know how.

I wrestled with a darkness that I just couldn't shake. Why was I doing it? Was it to purge something from my body or mind? To fill the gaping hole left by Lawrence? Wasn't it also the novelty? The thrill of being with a new person? I didn't want familiarity. I liked the unknown; it gave me a rush. I believed if someone really got to know me, they might not like me, and they'd be gone. I was a risk-taker, but I couldn't risk that. Loss. Abandonment. I'd had enough of those for a lifetime.

Like every other girl my age, I knew I wanted to fall in love, get married, and live happily ever after. And I had a vision of who that person would be—someone like Lawrence, or Steve. None of these men measured up. They were poor substitutes. Mere diversions.

One day in late October, the phone rang. I picked it up.

"Hey," a voice said. "Laura?"

"Yes?" *Oh my gosh.* It was him. He'd finally called.

"It's Steve Taylor. Hi."

"Hi! How are you?" I replied, trying to act surprised while nervously pacing the floor.

"I'm great. Things are going well."

It was so good to hear his voice. I wondered if he could detect my elation over the phone.

"Hey, thanks for leaving a message. How'd it go with Willy?"

I told him about my visit and about the model they'd just signed.

"Yeah, that happens," he said. "But things in this business change overnight. I'd try back.

Listen, I just did a shoot with this amazing photographer named Bruce Weber. I thought it'd be fun to take some photos together. You know, with Bruce."

Bruce Weber? Whose photos I'd seen on the cover of *GQ*? "I'd love that," I gushed.

"He'll want to meet you first, see your book. I have his contact information. You can call him and set something up."

We hadn't seen each other for months. I was astounded that he would even suggest such a thing.

"Thanks! I'm excited!" I said.

"He's a great guy. You'll like him."

He gave me Bruce's number. Then he told me he had to run, and we hung up. In that moment I was the happiest I'd been in a long time. I knew Steve was dating someone—at least I thought he was—but now I knew he hadn't forgotten me. And that was enough.

I picked up the phone and called Bruce Weber.

"Steve Taylor?" He paused. "Yes, I remember Steve."

I told him Steve had suggested I call to see if he'd be interested in shooting the two of us.

"Sure," he said. "I enjoyed working with Steve. I would like to see your book first," he added. Then he gave me his address and told me to stop by the next day.

...

Bruce Weber lived on East Fifty-Eighth between Madison and Park. I went to the third floor and knocked on the door. A few moments later, I was greeted by a beautiful golden retriever and a woman with reddish hair and a kind smile.

"Hi, I'm Nan," she said as she motioned me inside.

"I'm Laura. I'm here to see Bruce."

"Right this way." She led me into a dark room with drawn curtains that barely let the afternoon sunlight filter through. There was a sofa with throw pillows, a few worn, overstuffed chairs, and an ottoman piled with newspapers.

"Have a seat," she said. "I'll get Bruce."

A moment later, a man entered the room and I stood to greet him. He was in his late thirties and had a full beard and a colorful bandana tied around his head. His smile immediately put me at ease.

"You must be Laura." He shook my hand. "Well, what have you got?"

I handed him my portfolio and walked back to the sofa.

He sat down, opened my book, and started to look through my photos. Nan walked in holding a tray with two glasses of lemonade. She handed them to us without saying a word.

"I take it you met Nan," said Bruce, looking up at her. His eyes narrowed into a smile, and I could see that he adored her.

He flipped through my portfolio, then stopped and looked at me. He stared at me for a moment without speaking. The silence was uncomfortable. What was he thinking?

"I'm going to call you 'The American Beauty,'" he announced, pleased with himself.

I blushed.

"Thank you," was all I could manage. Bruce Weber had just

called me 'The American Beauty.' I didn't know what to say. He flipped through a few more photos, then closed my book.

"I'd love to shoot you and Steve," he said. "I've got a big job coming up next Wednesday with Ralph Lauren. Give me a few weeks, then call me. We'll see what we can arrange."

"Great," I replied cheerfully. "Thank you for your time."

"My pleasure." He handed me my book.

I took it, then stood up to leave.

"I'll get Nan to show you out."

"That's kind," I said, "but I can let myself out."

He nodded and smiled and stroked his beard, and I thought I saw his eyes twinkle.

"Thanks again," I said before turning and exiting the dark room.

As I walked out onto Fifty-Eighth Street, the afternoon light flooded my eyes. I stood there for a moment, basking in the warmth. Bruce Weber. American Beauty. Shooting with Steve. It had been a very good day.

Chapter Seven

Two weeks passed and November arrived. My encounter with Bruce Weber began to fade into obscurity, like all the other near misses I'd experienced in New York. What was it with me? I called and left several messages on his answering machine—just as he'd instructed—but he never called back. Then I called Wilhelmina and left a message for Steve. Maybe he'd have an idea of how to move things forward with Bruce. Again, nothing. It felt like rejection, though I tried to tell myself otherwise. I knew they were both busy. Why was it always too little, too late? I'd been so hopeful. Now I was crushed.

This just buoyed my growing disdain for men. I was fed up with the opposite sex—the whole lot of them. Dating and sleeping with a string of men had proven distracting and demeaning. I'd had enough. So I resolved to steer clear of beds that weren't my own. At least for the time being.

That's when I met Jay Hersch, the new assistant manager at Kitty Hawk. Jay wasn't the type of guy I usually went for. He was in his mid-thirties and had the physique of someone who'd indulged in one too many donuts. But he was sweet and funny and polite, and I could tell he liked me. It all started with a few minor flirtations—a joke, a wink. Then he started asking me to serve lunch to him and Gary, my manager. It soon became clear why.

"I'm going to marry you," he said one day, completely out of the blue. Gary had stepped away from the table, and I had just put down a platter of fries. I was partly intrigued, partly amused. *That's bold*, I thought. We'd only known each other a few weeks.

"I don't think so," was all I could muster. I knew I'd never marry Jay. He was cute—in a way. But he wasn't model material. He was also Jewish. I certainly didn't have anything against Jewish people. Alex was Jewish. So was my ex-boyfriend, Billy. Dating a Jewish guy was one thing. But marrying someone who wasn't a Christian? That's where my parents would draw the line.

A few days later, Jay invited me to a wedding. "It's a traditional Jewish wedding," he told me, "complete with a chuppah, band, and all-night smorgasbord. You'll love it."

The couple were friends of his and Gary's. I was curious, more than anything, and thought it might be fun. So I agreed to go.

We drove out to Long Island to a ritzy country club buzzing with activity. All night long, Jay introduced me as his girlfriend. That was news to me. I'd agreed to come to the wedding, but we definitely weren't dating.

A week later, Jay insisted on taking me to the Grand Café for my twentieth birthday—an art deco revival restaurant on East Sixty-Third between Madison and Park. I was excited, even though I wondered what kind of message I was sending him. I wasn't sure I was interested in him, though I did like spending time with him.

A write-up in the *New York Times* said the Grand Café's "hazy pink color was like seeing the world through rose-colored spectacles," and they were right. As I walked with Jay down the sweeping marble staircase that led into the dining room, I felt like a movie star.

He stayed over that night. And lots of other nights after that. I felt comfortable around him and trusted him; he made me feel safe.

Thanksgiving arrived five days later. The city was dressed up for the holidays—from the colorful floats in the Macy's Thanksgiving

Day Parade to the glittering window displays along Madison Avenue—yet none of it captivated me. In fact, it only made me more depressed. I was longing to go home; Thanksgiving was a time to be with family. I didn't have a penny to spare, though, and I was too embarrassed to ask my parents for help. So I stayed.

Cheryl invited me to watch the parade from the windows on the sixth floor of Macy's, where she worked as a graphic designer. It should have been a magical day—I'd been watching the parade on TV since I was a little girl, but I was so homesick that I had to work hard to fight back the tears.

Cheryl went home that afternoon to spend the holiday with her family in Ohio, so Jay, Gary, and Gary's fiancée, Suzanne, invited me to join them for dinner at one of Fred Guterman's new restaurants on East Seventy-Ninth, a place called Chic's.

Unlike Kitty Hawk, Chic's was light and airy, with pale yellow walls and black-and-white tile floors. When we arrived, there was a sign on the door that read, "Closed. Private Party." I was eating Thanksgiving dinner with my boss and his fiancée and my other boss (whom I was dating), and I was miserable.

It was one of those moments when you realize you've hit a new low—when the weight of your life choices topples you into some deep, unscalable pit. That's how I felt that day. Like a loser. My modeling was going nowhere. I barely made enough money waiting tables to pay my rent. And I was dating a nice person whom I wasn't all that attracted to, a guy whom I knew my parents wouldn't approve of. My life was closing in on me, and I didn't know how to escape.

"Come on, baby, marry me," Jay said to me in the back of the taxi as he took me home that night.

"I haven't even seen your apartment," I replied, annoyed, "and you want me to marry you?" It seemed irrational, even crazy.

We'd been going out for over a month, and we'd always stayed over at my place. What was that about? It was beginning to get old.

"Okay, okay," he conceded. "Next weekend. I promise."

He was true to his word. That Friday night, he took me to his apartment on East Eighty-Second. It was tastefully decorated and had exposed brick walls and lots of light. Being there made me feel like we were a real couple. I imagined us living there together, and the thought made me smile.

"Nice," I said. We went out for Italian, then came back and fell asleep in each other's arms.

While he showered the next morning, I poked around. What could it hurt? After all, he kept talking marriage and there was so much I didn't know about him.

The first thing I could see was that he was meticulous. His suits were carefully hung in the closet and his clothes neatly tucked away in the drawers. His order brought comfort to my chaotic mind. Maybe it wouldn't be such a bad thing to marry him. I'd only been in the city six months, and already I was weary. The incessant focus on my body was taking a toll on my self-esteem. It was always about how I looked, never about who I was inside. I was scraping to make ends meet and discouraged about ever finding an agent. I put on a brave face, but the truth was, I wanted to give up. Maybe it was best to call it quits and settle down. Jay was a nice guy, and I'd figure out how to deal with my parents. After all, wasn't my happiness what mattered most of all?

On the way home that Sunday afternoon, I stopped at a newsstand and bought an issue of *Modern Bride*.

One day in early December, Jay announced, "My rent is too high. I need to find a cheaper place. I was thinking somewhere closer to you."

His remark caught me off guard, but I was delighted that he wanted to be more involved in my life.

"Okay," I said, smiling. "I can help."

I took it upon myself to scour the *New York Times* rental section. Jay wasn't helpless. But it was a welcome distraction from waitressing, and it gave me something to do. Within twenty-four hours, I'd found a one-bedroom apartment over my favorite Greek deli—just a block from my place. I went to Bloomingdales, bought sheets, and used the sewing machine I'd brought to the city to fashion curtains for the windows. I was proud of my handiwork. The place sparkled.

"Wow. This looks great, baby," he remarked as he looked around.

I was happy that he was pleased.

Having Jay closer meant we could spend more time together. As we were walking along the East River one day on the way to our favorite bar, I had an epiphany: I loved being with Jay because when I was with him I didn't have to act like a model or even think about modeling. I could forget about my failures and just be me. The more I thought about it, the more marrying Jay seemed like a good idea. It was safe, a haven from the discomfort I felt in my own skin. I had serious doubts that I could ever make it as a model, much less a cover girl. Maybe I could make it as someone's wife.

Two days before Christmas, I flew to Raleigh to spend the holidays with my family. While I was there, Jay called me almost every day.

"Who's that?" Mama asked one day after I hung up the phone.

"Just Jay. The guy I'm dating."

"Oh," was all she said.

I told her we worked together and that he was nice, and that seemed to satisfy her. I omitted the part about his not being a Christian, of course, and I didn't dare tell her about his marriage proposals. I wasn't sure I'd ever get up the nerve to marry Jay, but if I did, I'd deal with Mama then. One thing at a time.

I came back to Manhattan in early January and was greeted by

17-degree temperatures and a foot of snow. How did people survive in this place? I didn't have snow boots or a warm winter coat. I'd lost my summer tan, my skin was breaking out, and I had zero tolerance for the cold. I told myself January wasn't the time to tromp around the city trying to pursue modeling, and especially to find an agent. Taking on a few extra shifts at work and seeing Jay was all I could handle.

Life finally settled into a tolerable rhythm—until one fateful Sunday in February. Valentine's Day was the following week, so I was anticipating something special from Jay, perhaps a more formal proposal. The staff at the restaurant had just finished up one of our famous Kitty Hawk brunches. I was adding up my tips at the back table with Steph, a veteran New York waitress who seemed perpetually annoyed with me—partly for my southernness (which my male customers loved) and partly because I'd been bringing in more tips than her.

In Steph's mind, that day must have been as good a day as any to get even.

"Jay's married, you know."

"What?" I asked, thinking I'd misunderstood.

"He's married," she repeated. "Everyone knows it." She paused for effect before adding, "Everyone except you."

My heart raced and my face went hot. I frantically reached back through my memories to find some explanation. I was unable to utter a word.

"He can't be," I finally said. The words fell out like concrete. "I was at his apartment . . ."

I'd never said a word to Steph about my personal life. This was definitely more than I wanted her to know.

"Jay swore us all to secrecy," she continued. "Gary played along."

My stomach wrenched. "I have to go," I said weakly.

I gathered my tips and tossed them into my purse. I grabbed

my coat, then walked through the restaurant and out the front door onto Third Avenue. The day was unusually sunny, and the light on the snow was blinding. It was almost thirty blocks to my apartment, but I started walking, fast, hoping the pattern of one foot after the other would purge my mind of the words Steph had just spoken.

When I got to my apartment, I immediately called Jay. I tried him at home, but there was no answer. Then I tried him at work, where he'd just arrived for the closing shift.

"Is it true?" I blurted out when I got him on the phone. I spoke with a fierceness he'd never heard.

"*What*, baby? Is *what* true?"

"Are you married?"

"Yes, I am," he admitted, "but I love you. Carol and I aren't happy. I'm going to ask her for a divorce."

I rarely got angry, but now I was livid and the words came easily. "I can't believe you. You're an asshole. You're married, and you were asking me to marry you? What were you thinking?" I shook my head in disbelief. "What about the weekend we stayed at your apartment? How did you pull that off?"

"Carol's a sales rep. She was on a trip," he stammered.

"What about her things? Did you hide them? I didn't see a trace of anyone else."

I was dazed by the words I was uttering. It was only starting to come together. Not only was he a liar, but I was also beginning to believe he was sick too.

"I can explain . . ." he started.

"Never mind," I said. "I don't want to know."

"Can we at least talk?" he pleaded. Before I could respond he added, "I'm coming over."

"Don't," I said firmly. "I won't let you in." I slammed down the phone.

He'd be here in forty minutes. I knew I had time to get to his place, and I had a key. I headed downstairs, nodded at Danny, the doorman, and hurried up Sixty-Third to First Avenue. As I walked I felt a renewed conviction to rid my life of this man and everything associated with him.

I unlocked the outside door, walked up a flight of stairs, and let myself into Jay's apartment. I stripped the bed, took the curtains down from the windows, and removed the personal items I'd used to decorate his place. With my arms full, I pulled the door shut behind me and headed back down the stairs. When I got to the street, I looked around to see if anyone was looking and dumped everything in a pile by the curb. Then I went back and got a lamp and the few pots and pans I'd left behind. I took what was mine and added Jay's things to the waiting pile. Within fifteen minutes, I was done. I took one last look at the mound of discarded memories. Good riddance.

I walked back to my apartment, pulled the door shut behind me, and secured the lock. Only then did I realize I was shaking. I had no idea what he might try next.

Twenty minutes later, there was a knock at the door.

"Baby, it's me," Jay said through the door. "Let me in!"

"No! Go away! I don't want to talk to you. Ever again." Then I added, "I emptied out your apartment. Your things are on the street."

My words only spurred him on. The knocking and pleading continued.

"You're crazy!" I yelled, as my whole body trembled. "Go away. Stop bothering me!" I sat down in a chair and waited until the knocking finally stopped.

When I was sure Jay was gone, I called Gary.

"I'm quitting," I said indignantly. "I'd appreciate your mailing my paycheck."

He didn't ask why, but I knew he knew. He'd duped me. They

all had. I knew I'd been naive, but what they'd done was despicable. Since Steph's fateful announcement, I'd racked my brain to uncover some minute detail I'd missed. The only thing I could think of was Jay's hesitation in inviting me to his apartment. But hadn't I looked around? I hadn't found one shred of evidence to suggest he was married.

Early the next morning, I called Fred Guterman. He dropped by Kitty Hawk from time to time and always seemed glad to see me. Now I needed a favor. I told him I'd just quit my job, that I needed a change.

"Do you have any openings?" I inquired.

To my relief, he didn't question why. "I need a hostess at Chic's. I hired an all-male wait staff, and business is slow. Having a pretty girl up front might help bring in customers. Interested?"

"Yes, thank you!" I was thrilled. I liked Chic's—it was classy, it had a backgammon lounge, and it was close to my apartment. While hosting would mean no tips and less money, it would allow me to sever all ties with Jay. I could begin a new chapter.

Ending my relationship with Jay and getting a new job restored my confidence. And working at Chic's was fun. I quickly made friends with my male coworkers—Randy, Chris, Dusty Rhodes, the list went on. Most of them were actors or models trying to break into their respective businesses, like me. Being with them was easy. There were no sexual or romantic overtones—we were simply there to cheer each other on.

Now that I was hostessing, I needed new clothes. I'd only bought a few things since moving to New York, so I headed over to Saks Fifth Avenue on my day off to see what I could find. Mama and Daddy had given me money for Christmas; I'd set it aside for emergencies. This didn't qualify as an emergency, but I decided to treat myself. After what I'd been through, a new skirt and blouse might be just the thing.

I made my purchase and headed to find the escalator. On the way, I passed the coat department and stopped to browse. It was late February and everything was deeply discounted. As I looked through the racks, I noticed a separate room—The Fur Salon. I'd never even thought about furs; only wealthy women wore them. Still, it might be fun to try one on.

I ran my hand down a gorgeous full-length mink. It was luxurious. I pulled it off the rack and slipped it on. Then I walked to the mirror to get a better look.

"Beautiful," said a voice behind me. I turned and saw a man standing there. He gave me an artful smile.

I smiled back. "Thank you," I said, a bit embarrassed.

He was a few years older, I surmised, than my father. He was thin and graying at the temples—more dignified than handsome—and he was nicely dressed. Surely he knew I couldn't afford a fur.

I looked at him sheepishly. "I thought it would be fun—"

"It suits you," he said before I could finish. "William. William Reinhold." He held out his hand.

"Laura Whitfield," I said, offering mine.

"Are you a model?" he asked. I was flattered but slightly irritated, because now I felt compelled to offer a satisfactory response. "Yes, I am." Then, out of habit, I added, "I don't have an agent, but I'm working on it."

"I know Wilhelmina," he said without hesitation. "Maybe I could help."

I was astonished. I'd randomly walked into the fur department at Saks and met someone who knew Wilhelmina Cooper? *Thank you, God.* It was a miracle. I rarely sought God's guidance these days. So for this to happen? He must have been watching out for me.

"Let me take you to dinner. We can talk more."

I'd just met this man and knew nothing about him. Still, I couldn't pass up the opportunity. "I'd like that," I said.

Untethered

He reached in his coat pocket, retrieved his wallet, pulled out a business card, and handed it to me. "My card."

I looked at the engraved lettering. *William Reinhold, Esq. 912 Fifth Avenue, New York, New York 10021.* So he was wealthy. He must be. I didn't know anyone who lived on Fifth Avenue, not even Alex.

We chatted for a few minutes, and I gave him my phone number. Was I crazy? He seemed like a nice person, and the card seemed like the real deal. We agreed to meet the next night at Lutéce. I was nervous, but if he could get me in to see Willy, it would be worth it. I'd just have to take the chance.

"I'll see you at seven," he said, giving a subtle bow. He wasn't much on looks, but he certainly didn't lack for manners.

"Seven it is," I agreed.

I showed up at Lutéce the following night wearing the most elegant dress I owned. It was the premier French restaurant in the city, and I knew he was trying to impress me. It worked. It was nice being with an older man who had money and connections. I wasn't attracted to him physically. It would be like being with my father; the idea made me sick. But I didn't have to worry about that. Wasn't he just a businessman, like Mr. Guterman, who wanted to help me out?

William listened attentively as I told him about Eileen Ford, *Elle* magazine, My Fair Lady, and my lack of success with Wilhelmina.

"About Wilhelmina," he said as we finished up dessert. "I could give her a call. Set up an appointment for you to see her."

"Really? That would be amazing." My entire body vibrated.

"I can't guarantee you'll get a contract. She'll either sign you or she won't. That's up to her."

"Yes, of course," I said, trying to be cool, though I could barely contain my excitement.

"I have good instincts about you." He smiled. "But before I call

98

her, there is one thing. I'd like to spend more time with you, get to know you better. It's just that I'm asking a favor from a friend. You understand."

I did understand. He was going to pressure me to sleep with him. Could I do that? He was old, too old, I reasoned. But he was my only hope of meeting Wilhelmina. I stopped for a moment and took a breath. *Maybe I'm wrong. Maybe I'm jumping to conclusions. Shouldn't I just take it one step at a time and see?*

A few days later, my hunch about William Reinhold proved right. It began with that first dinner. Then other dinners, followed by snifters of Grand Marnier at his place and unpleasant late-night trysts. He'd pull me to him, and I'd close my eyes against his advances and think about Steve or the beach—anything to escape. I hated myself, but I justified my behavior. William was my ticket to Wilhelmina, possibly my last ticket.

Then one night I stayed over and woke up sweating—like an animal trapped in a net. He asked what was wrong, and I told him I felt sick and needed to go home. I dressed quickly and walked down to Fifth Avenue and hailed a taxi. I fell into my bed at three in the morning and stayed there most of the next day.

I'd come to see sex as a way of getting the attention I wanted. I wasn't proud of that fact, but it was true. However, I'd never seen it as currency for selling my soul. Until now. I'd refused plenty of men. I'd even walked out of a photo shoot because the photographer had started coming on to me. Other girls slept around to get ahead, but I'd never dreamed that would be me. I'd always strived to make my own way. Now I was compromising myself for a shot at a modeling contract. I felt sleazy. And cheap.

I never breathed a word about William to anyone, not even Cheryl. I was too embarrassed. I knew I couldn't keep sleeping with him—it felt incestuous. I finally got up the nerve to confront him.

"Have you had enough time?" I asked over the phone one day, hoping he wouldn't detect the edge in my voice.

"Enough time for what?"

"To know I'm okay. That it's all right to call Wilhelmina."

"Ahh, that," he said smugly.

I resented the way he'd used me, though the truth was, we'd used each other. We had an unspoken agreement. I'd given him what he wanted. Now I expected him to come through.

"I'll call her this afternoon," he replied.

He phoned back a few minutes later. "You're all set," he said. "Two o'clock tomorrow. I wish you the best."

That was the last time we ever spoke.

It was now March, and it had been six months since I'd first walked through Wilhelmina's doors. This time, things were different.

"I have an appointment," I told the receptionist. "With Wilhelmina." Just speaking her name felt surreal.

"I'll let her know," she said, smiling.

I went to sit down. I wasn't there long.

"Willy will see you now," someone said. I snapped back to reality, stood up, and walked over to where a young woman was waiting.

We made our way down the hall and entered an office with two swivel chairs covered in a bright, geometric fabric, a cube table with an arrangement of fresh flowers, a large picture window, and in front of it, a large desk.

"I'm Willy," said the woman sitting behind the desk. She smiled warmly and motioned for me to sit down.

"I'm Laura," I said.

Wilhelmina Cooper was the most beautiful woman I had ever met. A Dutch immigrant who'd graced more than three hundred magazine covers during her decade-long modeling career, she was thin and had a long, slender neck and dark, inquisitive eyes. Her smile was gracious and inviting, and she immediately made me feel at ease.

"William Reinhold called me, as you know, and asked if I'd be willing to look at your book. He had nice things to say about you."

"Yes. He's a nice man," I offered, pushing down the unpleasant images bubbling to the surface. "I so appreciate your time."

"Of course," she said. "Tell me a little about yourself."

I shared my story—how I'd come to New York and had a few promising, though unrealized, opportunities, but held out because I wanted more than anything to work for her.

"Let's see what you've got," she said, pointing to my portfolio. I laid it on her desk and watched as she flipped through the pages. I tried to read her expression, but I wasn't sure what she was thinking. I waited for her to speak.

She closed my book and looked at me. "I want to sign you."

"You do?" I was incredulous.

"Yes, you have potential. In fact, if you play your cards right, I believe you could make six figures a year." I let her words sink in. Six figures? A hundred thousand dollars or more? But play my cards right? What did that mean? Starving myself? Sleeping my way to the top?

She handed me a piece of paper with lots of fine print. "Here's your contract. Sign it and bring it back and you can get started. We're excited to have you." She flashed me a warm smile.

"Thank you," I uttered, barely able to speak. I'd paid a price with William to get in the door—but ultimately, I knew, I'd gotten this contract because Willy saw my potential.

I was a Wilhelmina model. My dream had finally come true.

Just like that, everything changed. I was still hostessing at Chic's, but there were test shoots and go-sees most days, so I started working nights. I went on commercial auditions for Noxzema. And Breck

Shampoo. Once I was waiting in the lobby of *Glamour* magazine and Christie Brinkley, one of the new supermodels, walked in wearing a stunning red suit. She was gorgeous.

No doubt about it, the competition was tough. Day after day, I went on go-sees to sell my looks, and day after day, I was rejected—wrong eye or hair color, too short, too heavy. Sometimes I made the cut and landed a job. But that was rare. I began to understand why girls burned out in this business. As a model, you were treated like a commodity. Models were fish wrap, as we liked to say—your photo might appear in the *New York Times* one day and be used to wrap fish the next.

I was still the same person—striving for perfection and constantly worried I'd fall short. But now I was being propped up—by Willy and her husband, Bruce, by my bookers, and by Peter, the nice man who headed the men's division. I was venturing into new territory, and they were all there to keep me from straying off the path. Willy was kind to me, and patient. She answered my questions and gave me advice. Just knowing I could drop by her office made all the difference.

Yet not a day went by that her words didn't haunt me: *Play your cards right. Six figures.* Did she really think I was that pretty? That I could make that much money? I wanted to believe it, but it seemed so far out of reach. I'd worked hard to get here. What if I screwed up? Or worse yet, failed? Then what?

While I put on my makeup each morning, I'd put on another face—the one I presented to the world. It was confident, self-assured. I hoped it would be convincing. *You're doing great,* I'd tell myself after botching an audition or losing out on another modeling job. In reality, I was fear-stricken. Afraid of the slightest misstep. I felt fragile. Vulnerable. If I could just keep up the façade, I thought, maybe I could fake my way through. That terrified girl underneath—would be a tightly held secret only I knew.

...

I opened my eyes one Sunday morning in early April, and the first thing to pop into my mind was church. *That's odd.* I never thought about church, except when I passed St. Patrick's or one of the other large cathedrals. In fact, I hadn't been to church in over a year.

I got up and dressed, hopped into a taxi, and gave the driver the address of a Methodist church I'd found in the Yellow Pages. A few minutes later, he pulled up in front of a very unassuming building.

Hmm, I thought. *That's odd.*

"Miss?" he said, opening the partition behind him. "This isn't a church. It's a funeral home."

"That's strange," I told him. "I was sure I'd written down the right address."

"There's a church around the corner. I'm not sure what kind."

I glanced at my watch. It was ten till eleven. Most services started at eleven. I didn't have time to be choosy.

"Yes, thank you," I said, still trying to make sense of what had just happened.

A few minutes later, he deposited me in front of a beautiful old brick building with an ornate stone carving over the front entrance. I still wasn't sure why I was there, but I felt compelled to find out.

As I stepped through the door, I was greeted by a firm hand-shake and the strains of a Bach prelude. I felt a sense of relief, like coming home.

I made my way down the aisle and slipped into a pew. I knew somehow that God had orchestrated the events of that morning. The urgency I felt, the mixed-up address—for some reason, He wanted me here. I sat and listened. Expectant.

I came back the next Sunday, and the next. For the first time in years, I felt safe. Maybe there was hope for me after all.

A week later, Alex called out of the blue. We'd been out of touch, and it was great to hear his voice.

"How's it going?" he inquired.

I excitedly told him my news.

"Fantastic!" he said. I could tell he was genuinely happy for me. "Listen, there's someone I want you to meet. She's the head of Revlon."

"Really?" I said, delighted. "I'd love that. Thank you." I didn't ask how he knew her, but it didn't matter. It seemed that Alex knew everyone in New York.

"I'll call her and see if we can arrange something for later this week. It will be great to see you."

I'd forgotten how much I liked Alex. He was a good person. Solid. There were no hidden agendas or games with him.

I hung up the phone and sat down for a moment to take it all in. Revlon? This was huge. It just might be the big break I'd been hoping for. Alex's call lifted my spirits.

He phoned back to tell me he'd be by on Wednesday. It was now Monday. I soared through the next couple of days, upbeat and confident as I went on my go-sees.

On Wednesday, Alex picked me up and took me to Barbara Miller's apartment in Midtown. We got on the elevator and he pressed "PH." Of course the head of Revlon would live in the penthouse. We knocked on the door and were greeted by a maid who showed us to an opulent living room with gilded furnishings and plush Persian rugs.

After introductions, Mrs. Miller looked through my portfolio. Revlon owned Fabergé and Babe perfume, the hot new scent for teens. It smelled like raspberries, and girls everywhere were wearing it. I'd seen the commercials and print ads in my favorite magazines. They featured Margaux Hemingway, the famous novelist's granddaughter. She was fresh and outdoorsy. Most importantly, she had the Hemingway name. Everyone knew about Margaux's contract with Babe—it was the first million-dollar contract ever awarded for an ad campaign.

A million dollars. I couldn't imagine.

"Alex tells me you're with Wilhelmina."

"Yes, that's right," I said.

She closed my book and looked at us both. "You're prettier than Margaux. I'd like you to have her contract when it comes up in September."

Did I hear her correctly?

"It will be a lot of work, but we'll make it worth your while."

What? I sat there, dumbfounded. I quickly did the math. It was now May. September was only four months away. Becoming a Wilhelmina model had been a dream come true. But this was almost too much to absorb. My smile spread into a grin.

"Thank you, that's so kind," I managed.

"We'll have to go through the agency, of course. Logistics. We'll stay in touch." She reached into a small gold case on the table beside her and handed me a business card.

"Thank you again," I said as I shook her hand.

She showed us to the door.

"I knew she'd love you," Alex said as it closed behind us.

We got into the elevator. As he pushed the button, I glanced at him. He was beaming.

"Well, look at you," he said. "The new face of Babe."

I smiled too, taking in what had just happened. As the elevator rushed to the first floor, it felt as if I were in a dream. If I could just hold on for four months, my face would be everywhere. In newspapers, magazines. On billboards and TV.

"It's just a verbal exchange, mind you," Alex cautioned. "But Barbara is good for her word."

The elevator opened, and we walked out into the marble-tiled lobby.

"Do you have plans this afternoon?" he asked.

"Uh, no." I chuckled. "My head is reeling. I'm pretty worthless."

"Then let's celebrate," he said. "How about a little champagne?"

How can a life be so completely perfect one moment and so completely in shambles the next? But a few days later, that's just what happened. It began with a knock on the door.

"It's Brad," said the familiar voice from the hallway outside our apartment. "I forgot something. Let me in?"

I opened the door and saw Cheryl's boyfriend standing there in his signature khakis and rumpled Ralph Lauren shirt.

"Sorry to bother you," he said, sweeping past me. He made his way to the bed and picked up a paperback book.

It wasn't odd for him to be there; Brad usually stayed over a few nights a week. But seeing him there without Cheryl was awkward. We'd never been there alone.

I shifted nervously on my feet. The room began to shrink around us, and the air grew eerily still. He asked how the modeling was going, and we made small talk about this and that. Then I saw him glance at the empty wine bottles and ashtray of spent joints by Cheryl's bed.

"She's become a pothead," he said, annoyed. "And she drinks too much."

His remark didn't surprise me. Lately he'd seemed disenchanted with her—a comment here, a jab there.

Without another word, he locked eyes on me. He ambled over, kissed me, and pulled me down onto the platform bed. Cheryl's bed.

Early on, I'd found Brad charming. Over time, I'd come to see him as arrogant. Cheryl, on the other hand, was crazy about him. They'd been dating for two years, and she was sure he was going to propose. What was he doing? What was *I* doing?

"This is insane, we shouldn't," I urged, but I was defenseless against his touch.

He kissed me gently, then harder. Then he unbuttoned my shirt and pulled off my pants, and before I knew it we were both naked and I was scared.

The sex was frantic and tenuous. The moment it was over, I regretted it. Deeply. As I rose to get dressed, I detected a key in the door. I heard Cheryl's voice.

"Laura?"

Oh, my God. No. In that moment, time stopped, and all I could hear was the sound of my heart pounding in my chest—then footsteps. She rounded the corner. Her face froze in disbelief.

In that instant, one thought consumed me: *I've been caught.* For someone so adept at hiding, it was the worst of all possible fates. I'd become a pro at hiding. From my parents. And many of my friends. I hid because I'd changed, and not for the better. I was the good Christian girl who'd moved to the beach, started drinking, and lost her virginity. Over the past year, there'd been dozens of one-night stands, but no real consequences. Until now.

"I want you out. By Sunday night," she blurted, her eyes welling with tears. She turned, walked out of our apartment, and slammed the door.

Brad and I stood with our eyes riveted on the space she'd just occupied. Then we looked at each other. I searched his face. *What am I going to do? Where will I go?*

"It's okay," he said, as if reading my thoughts. "We'll get away. To Long Island. I'll take you to Sag Harbor."

I'd always wanted to see the popular weekend destination. Now I didn't care—about Sag Harbor, about anything. "Okay," I managed.

"I'll pick you up in an hour," he said. He dressed, then walked to the door, where he turned around. "Don't worry, we'll figure things out." Then he was gone.

It all felt surreal—as if I were a passenger peering out the window of a speeding train. I stood in the middle of the living room, immobile. It was Friday. The trip to Sag Harbor would buy me a few days. Then I'd need a place to stay. Who could I call?

I thought of Alex. He was my closest friend. But I didn't dare call him. What would I say—*I slept with Brad, and Cheryl's kicked me out on the street?* Alex was classy. He'd done so much for me. Now I'd behaved like trailer trash. I couldn't bear for him to know.

Then I thought of my friend Greg, who bartended at Chic's. He was a southern boy and we'd hung out a few times. He might understand.

"Greg?" I said when I heard his baritone voice on the line. "It's me, Laura. Could I come stay with you for a few days?"

"Of course," he said. "Are you okay?" His kindness brought welcome relief.

"No, but I will be. And thank you. I'm heading to Sag Harbor for the weekend. I'll call you Sunday night when I get back." I hung up the phone and sighed. At least now I had somewhere to go when I returned.

As I packed, I replayed over and over what had happened, my thoughts like a needle stuck in the groove of a record. *What will I tell my parents? Where will I go?* I walked into the bathroom and stood at the sink with my head down. I was so disgusted by what I'd done, I couldn't even look at myself. Then I remembered something I'd seen on a detective show on TV. A police officer had shot and killed someone, and he was filled with remorse. His sergeant told him to look himself in the mirror—literally face what he'd done—so he could move on. I lifted my head. My eyes met my reflection.

The girl looking back at me was only vaguely familiar, as though she might be someone I'd passed on the street on a Tuesday after-noon. But that was all. Her eyes stared off into the distance—blank, void of any spark. As I observed her, I knew one thing: If she were to stay in this city much longer, she'd become completely unrecognizable. She'd risk losing her mind and ending up at Bellevue, the famous New York psychiatric hospital. Whoever this stranger was, I had to step in and save her from that fate. If what she'd experienced up until now was difficult, a breakdown would be worse. She needed to leave now, get out. She needed to go home.

On Sunday night, I returned to the apartment I shared with Cheryl on East Sixty-Third. I stood and looked at the gold letters on the door: 6C. My heart sank. This was the last place on earth I wanted to be. I knocked to see if Cheryl was there. No answer.

I entered cautiously. It was dark and hauntingly quiet. I was grateful to be alone. I walked over and switched on a lamp by the sofa. That's when I saw it: a large arrangement of flowers in a glass vase sitting on the coffee table with a note attached. I picked up the note and read the typewritten message: "Cheryl, dear. Please forgive me. I love you. Brad."

When did that happen? I felt dizzy. It was clear I'd been used. We'd just spent the last forty-eight hours together, and now I'd come home to this?

I knew Brad didn't care about me. The weekend had just been about getting away from Cheryl—and yes, sex. Still, I'd thought they were over. He'd never said so—I'd assumed it. It had helped me make sense of what had happened between us.

Now I was furious. I called Greg and asked if he could come right away and pick me up.

"See you in fifteen," he said.

I quickly crammed the few things I owned into a suitcase. Ready to go, I stood there alone in the middle of our L-shaped studio, and a wave of memories flooded in. I'd had some good times here, especially in the beginning. Now my life was like a bad soap opera. It was time to move on. I walked to the door, opened it, and pulled it shut behind me. Then I locked the dead bolt and slid the key under the door.

A few minutes later, Greg and I were headed down First Avenue to his apartment in the Village.

Greg was bright and attractive and had a shock of red hair. He lived in a small brick tenement on East Fourteenth Street, a three-story walk-up with a rooftop view. He told me he had majored in English at Duke and was writing a novel about a homeless man living in The Battery.

As he cooked dinner, we drank cabernet and passed a joint. I leaned against the counter and sipped my wine and listened as he told me about the research he'd done for his book—dressing up as a homeless person and living in Battery Park for three days.

"Wow, that was brave," I said, impressed.

"Brave—or stupid," he said. "I almost got myself killed." Then he explained how a beggar had mugged him but he'd managed to get away.

I soon felt a buzz from the alcohol and pot. That, plus his soft southern drawl, lured me into a temporary state of well-being. For a moment, I forgot why I was there.

After dinner, Greg led me to his matchbox bedroom. "You okay with this?" he asked thoughtfully.

"Yes," I said, and I was. His apartment was tiny—I'd already thought about the fact that we might share a bed.

I undressed in a daze. The incident with Brad had left me completely shattered. I was just an assortment of body parts, not unlike Lawrence's remains—an arm here, a leg there, some semblance of a heart. I wasn't sure I wanted to have sex with Greg—or with anyone, for that matter, ever again. I was too raw. What I wanted was for someone to tenderly gather me up, take me in his arms, and tell me everything was going to be all right.

But not just anyone. Someone I trusted. And I trusted Greg.

Greg lit a candle, and we crawled into bed and held each other in the flickering light. Slowly, my defenses weakened. When we finally made love, he was gentle and sweet. The contrast to Brad was striking.

Sometime in the night we woke up, covered in sweat. He grabbed my hand and I followed him, bare-skinned and giggling, up to the roof. He pushed open the door, and we ran out onto the black tar surface, still warm from the day's heat. We stood looking out at the hazy Manhattan skyline, not saying a word. It was late, but I imagined someone else might be up and looking at us standing there, naked, scanning the sky. It didn't matter. The night air felt good against my skin.

So this is what it feels like to come out of hiding. To be free.

Over coffee the next morning, I thought about Wilhelmina and the contract with Revlon. Then I thought about the girl I'd seen in the mirror—the one staring blankly back at me.

"I'm done," I said to Greg. "I'm not sure how I'll get there, but I've got to go home."

"I'll take you," he said without hesitation. "I need to make a trip to Durham anyway—see some friends, pick up a few things."

"Really? Thank you," I said, relieved. Greg had been a good friend. I was grateful.

He had to ask for the time off at work. I needed to tie up loose ends. It was Monday. If we left on Wednesday and drove through the night, we'd arrive Thursday morning. We now had a plan.

I called Mama and Daddy and, in my best upbeat voice, told them I wanted to take a break from modeling. I explained that I was coming home and I had a ride. They were happy to hear from me. As far as I could tell, they didn't suspect a thing.

I spent the next few days saying goodbye to friends. I called Chic's, and finally, Wilhelmina. I informed Willy that I was going home for a week, and she was gracious, as always.

"I'll black out those dates," she said. "Just let us know when you return."

I hung up the phone. *When you return.* I might be lying to Willy, but I couldn't deceive myself. Something deep inside told me I'd never be back.

Dusk was falling when Greg and I packed up his faded brown Valiant that Wednesday and drove out of Manhattan. As we sped down the Jersey Turnpike toward North Carolina, I glanced at the same shimmering skyline that had beckoned me just twelve months before. I'd arrived with a suitcase of fragile dreams, and one by one I'd thrown them away. Now I was leaving empty-handed. I fixed my gaze on those same skyscrapers—the lights pulsing and throbbing, more piercingly beautiful than I'd remembered. As alluring as it was, I knew there was no turning back.

~༢·༡~

Chapter Eight

As I opened my parents' refrigerator door and felt the wave of cool air, my eye caught something pink peeking out beneath a piece of aluminum foil. A baked ham. I took a paring knife, cut off a chunk, and stuffed it into my mouth. Then I spotted a hoop cheese—the squishy, orange kind that almost melts when you bite it. I unwrapped the cellophane and tore off a piece. It wasn't until I reached for a Pyrex dish of banana pudding that a wave of guilt swept over me. I shut the door quickly, slipped back to my room, and plopped down on my bed.

I thought I was alone, but the guilt followed me. It began to whisper: *Look at you!* I'd begun this destructive eating pattern before leaving New York, and the pounds had started piling on: five, then seven, above my ideal weight. *You're fat!* it shouted. *More food? Are you kidding? That's the last thing you need!*

Back to the kitchen. Ham. Cheese. Guilt. Repeat.

Mama's cooking was hard to resist, especially now that I was back in Raleigh, a twenty-year-old college dropout with nothing to do. She was the best cook I knew, and everyone else thought so too. Mama had been raised on a farm in Eastern North Carolina; her specialty was comfort food—homemade biscuits, fried chicken, sweet, sticky pies—and I needed comfort. So I ate. From boredom and depression, and to forget.

I thought back to New York and the many times I'd called the

Greek deli near my apartment and ordered an apple crisp for delivery. And about the afternoon I blew off a go-see and, instead, sat in front of the TV and ate strawberry jam sandwiches until I felt sick. I knew I was punishing myself, but I didn't know how to stop. And a part of me didn't want to.

Now I was home and nothing had changed. Eating made me feel better, but only momentarily. Then I'd get on the scale and watch the needle totter above the number I'd hit the day before. Ten, twelve, fifteen, above my modeling weight. *Now you've done it. You're a fuckup. It's what you deserve.* I'd step off the scale and skulk to my bed and pull the covers over my head and sleep to shut out the images of Brad, Cheryl, and my last, fleeting glimpse of Manhattan. I'd only been home for two weeks, but the details were already fading like an old photograph. Even my potential million-dollar contract with Fabergé seemed surreal. Other than telling my parents, I hadn't said a word to anyone about it. It would be too humiliating for anyone to know I'd blown such a huge thing.

When I could bring myself to look in the mirror, I saw the one thing I'd done right since surviving that afternoon with Brad: I'd successfully hidden the old me under layers of fat. The face looking back wasn't that of the pretty, thin girl who'd modeled for Wilhelmina. It was softer, rounder, less striking. *You'll never model again,* the reflection said. Part of me was relieved.

Now I had a new problem: an ill-fitting wardrobe. So I drove to a nearby fabric shop, bought a few yards of rose-colored fabric, and made myself a dress. Not just any dress but one to cover my plump physique. I worked all day and finished it by that evening. I pulled it over my head and zipped it up. There. Now I could go out in public and no one would notice. At least, that's what I hoped.

I wasn't sure what I was going to do with myself now that I was home, but I knew I couldn't continue sitting around day after day eating and feeling sorry for myself. I needed a reason to get out of bed in the morning, so I decided to look for a job.

I'd dropped out of college and didn't have many skills. I was smart, and an excellent typist. But I couldn't imagine sitting at a typewriter all day in a corporate office. The very thought made me cringe.

"Why don't you try a temp agency?" Mama offered as we cleaned up after breakfast one day.

The word *temp* resonated with my restless heart. "That's a thought."

"Just until you figure out what you want to do," she said.

What I really wanted to do was finish college. All my life I'd dreamed of going to the University of North Carolina at Chapel Hill, Lawrence's alma mater. When I met with my high school counselor to discuss my college plans, he told me I was a shoo-in for UNC and I'd ace the SAT. Then my anxiety got the best of me. With my disappointingly low scores, I got a rejection from Chapel Hill and ended up at UNCG, miserable. Since then I'd made a lot of haphazard choices—moving to the beach on an impulse and then to New York, where I'd grown tired of New Yorkers treating me like a dumb blond, telling me I'd end up barefoot and pregnant and never get my degree. Hardly a week had gone by that someone hadn't mentioned it—either Danny the doorman or some mouthy, intoxicated customer.

They were wrong. College was in my DNA. My parents were college educated, and so were my brothers. Only now wasn't the time. I'd just gotten home from New York, and I was spent. Dropping in and out of college had been stressful. When I did go back, I wanted it to be for good.

Temp work, it turned out, was not for me. After one particularly unpleasant job, I decided I was done. That afternoon, I curled up on the corduroy sofa in Mama and Daddy's den and looked through the *News & Observer* "Help Wanted" ads.

Temp work. Forget it. Waitressing. I'd had enough of that for a lifetime. *Maybe this*, I thought as my eyes fell on an ad for a local nightclub called The Pier. They were looking for someone to work the door—check IDs, collect covers. Perfect. I'd get to meet the musicians and enjoy the amazing shows they were known for. Most important, I'd have an excuse to get out of the house. My parents were great for letting me move in with them. They'd never once asked why I'd left New York, and I was grateful. Still, being around them every day was draining after living on my own for so long.

I picked up the phone and called the number listed in the ad. I introduced myself and asked about the position.

"Sure, it's still open," said the manager, a man named Travis. "Why don't you stop by tomorrow morning at ten?"

The Pier was one of five nightclubs in The Village Subway, a cool underground entertainment complex located in Raleigh's Cameron Village shopping center and fashioned after the Atlanta Underground. It wasn't as hip as the Underground, or as chic as the discos I'd frequented in New York, but it was the best my hometown had to offer. I drove to Cameron Village and walked down into the cavernous underground space originally built to serve as a bomb shelter during the Cold War. *Bands and beer are a much better use of this space*, I thought as I followed the signs to The Pier.

The beach-themed nightclub was just as I'd imagined it—dimly lit and cave-like and smelling of stale beer. It reminded me of the Tap Room. And Steve. As my eyes adjusted to the dark, I looked around. Wooden tables stacked with chairs were scattered everywhere. There was a bar in the corner and a stage in the front with rope dividers to keep the crowds at bay.

Light flooded the room as a curtain to my right parted and a man with scraggly hair walked over and introduced himself.

"I'm Travis. You must be Laura."

"I am," I said, shaking his hand. I handed him the scanty résumé I'd brought along.

He looked it over. "Uh-huh. Okay," was all he said. When he finished, he set my résumé on a nearby table and gave me a pointed look. "Only one concern, you being a model and all." He paused. "Can you be tough?"

"What do you mean?" I asked, mildly irritated.

"People will make up all kinds of shit to avoid paying their cover." He paused and looked at me intently. "You'll need to be firm. No freebies, understand?"

"Of course not," I offered, not really knowing how hard people would push me and if I'd be able to comply.

"We have a big show tomorrow night, and I need all the help I can get. Come at five to fill out your paperwork and you can start."

"I'll be here. Thank you."

I had a job. I was elated. No more dreary stockrooms or typing stints. Beginning tomorrow, I'd get paid to have some fun.

I left The Pier energized and hungry. My high school friend Pam was waiting tables at Pizza Hut, so I decided to stop by, grab some lunch, and say hello.

"Hey, girl!" said Pam as I pushed my way through the lunchtime crowd. She gave me one of her bright, toothy grins. "It's great to see ya!" She was holding a tray of soft drinks but managed to give me a hug, then pointed to a two-top by the window. "Have a seat; I'll be right there."

I walked across the food-strewn carpet and slid into the red banquette. I pulled a menu from behind the napkin holder and opened it. I loved pizza, but it had been a while since I'd had one. Pepperoni, mushrooms. My mouth watered.

"Hey!" She slipped into the seat across the table.

I looked up and smiled. I'd always loved her enthusiasm.

"I just have a minute. How *are* you?" she asked. Pam had shiny, shoulder-length blond hair and a captivating smile.

"I'm good," I said. "I just landed a job at The Pier." Everybody in Raleigh knew about The Pier. I was excited to share my news.

"That's cool! And I'm working at Pizza Hut," she said, playfully rolling her eyes. "I need to save money. I want to buy a car. And go to grad school."

Grad school? I could hardly get my head around an undergraduate degree. And savings? I didn't have a penny. I wasn't surprised. Pam had always been a high achiever. I knew she'd accomplish whatever she set her mind to.

"When'd you get home?" she asked.

"A few weeks ago," I told her. "Modeling was brutal. I got burned out."

"Ahh," was all she said. My thoughts raced. Could she tell I'd gained weight? Was she wondering why I *really* left New York? My face went hot as I became aware of the large "F" flashing in the middle of my forehead. FAILURE. Surely she could see it. *Stop it*, I told myself. Pam was a good friend. She wouldn't probe.

"I'm just glad you're back. We'll definitely have to get together."

My instincts were right. If she was curious, she was keeping it to herself.

"Yeah, I'd like that," I said, relieved. I gave her my order, then watched as she ripped a sheet from her pad and scribbled something down.

She handed me the paper. "Here's my number. Call me." Then she slid out of the booth and stood up. "I'd better get back to work. Did you see Troy McConnell? He's sitting over there." She pointed to the middle of the room. "You should say hello."

Troy was two years older than Pam and me; he'd been a senior when we were sophomores at Paige High School, and the three of us had sung together in the mixed ensemble. I remembered his blond hair and blue eyes. And his beautiful tenor voice. But I didn't want to speak to Troy. Not now. I was too fat. I just wanted to eat my lunch in peace, unnoticed.

"Go on," she prodded, sensing my hesitation. "What have you got to lose?" She smiled, then dashed away.

Maybe she was right. Troy was just an acquaintance from high school; I didn't really care what he thought. I should at least go over and say hi.

I stood up and looked to where Pam had pointed. There he was, sitting with a girl. Was she his girlfriend? If I went over to speak to him, would she think I was flirting? This was awkward. All I wanted to do was say hi. I paused. Oh, what the heck. I walked over.

"Troy?" I said tentatively, wondering if he'd remember me. I glanced at the young woman with him. She was plain and wore very little makeup. She looked nice, but he'd always preferred pretty girls. Probably not his girlfriend, I surmised.

"Laura? Laura Whitfield!" His face broke into a curious smile. He stood to greet me, then sat down just as quickly. He looked at the girl as if for a moment he'd forgotten she was there.

"Laura, this is Sharon. Sharon, Laura. We were at Paige together." I nodded and smiled.

"Well, well. I heard you were modeling in New York."

"I was. I'm taking a break," I lied. I was fifteen pounds heavier than when he'd last seen me. I felt self-conscious.

"How about you? What are you up to?" I asked quickly, hoping to avert further inquiry.

"Bagging groceries at Food Lion," he said. "For the summer. I teach during the school year. Social studies. In Granville County."

"Wow," I said. "A school teacher. That's great." Mama had been a teacher for many years, and I admired anyone in the profession.

I glanced at Sharon, who seemed bored. I shifted on my feet. "I should probably get back to my lunch."

"Okay," he said. "Listen, I'd like to call you. Can I have your number?" He pulled a pen from his shirt pocket, then tore off a corner of his place mat and handed them to me.

I was flustered. Call me? Why? Sharon must be just a friend, I concluded.

"Sure, of course." I wrote down my parents' phone number and handed it to him.

"Thanks," he said as he took the scrap of paper. I was struck once more by his boyish good looks. He reminded me of Robert Redford, who I'd seen in person once at the Clinique counter at Bloomingdale's. Troy's face was rounder, less angular, but he was cute nonetheless.

"Great to see you"—I looked at Sharon—"and nice to meet you."

I walked back to my table smiling. Maybe being back in Raleigh wasn't so bad after all.

The next night, I started working at The Pier. Travis had been right about needing my help. A popular local band called Arrogance was performing, and even before the doors opened people were lined up down the hallway, waiting to get in.

I was anxious, though I wasn't quite sure why. My job was simple; all I had to do was greet customers, collect their three-dollar covers, and stamp their hands. Then it came to me: I'd spent the past few weeks eating excessively and hiding in my room, and now I felt exposed. The Pier, with its hot musicians, pulsating music, free-flowing beer, and bumper crop of new guys, would surely be too much for me to bear. What if I met another "Steve the Dream" and fell under his spell? Look where that had gotten me. I certainly couldn't risk that again.

"Let's do this!" said Travis as he unlocked and opened the door.

I took a deep breath. *Here I go.*

The first guy who entered looked barely old enough to drive.

"ID, please," I said in my firmest voice. He handed it over, and I examined the photo on his driver's license. This was my first customer, and I didn't want to screw up. Was that really him? I studied his face, then glanced back at the image. It had to be him. Why would someone with a fake ID be the first one in line?

"Three dollars," I said. I took the crumpled bills he handed me, then stamped his hand.

"Enjoy!" I added, trying to sound friendly and professional to cover my scrutiny. Behind him were four girls, a couple, and then a cute guy who winked at me as he approached the counter.

"Hello, gorgeous!" he said in a sultry voice.

"Thank you," I said, blushing. "ID?"

This was exactly the thing I'd worried about: some renegade bad boy looking for a good time. A guy like this, with dancing eyes, a dazzling smile, and a confident come-on, would be hard, if not impossible, to resist. *Lucky I'm living at home*, I thought, knowing I could only get into so much trouble under my parents' roof.

But after another smile, the guy moved past me and entered the club, and I refocused on my job, determined to make a good impression.

For the next few hours, time flew by. It was almost eleven thirty when the last person left and Travis locked the door. It had been a good first night. The band packed up as I helped the waitresses stack chairs on the tables and clear off the floor.

"Good job," Travis said with a nod. He wasn't the effusive type, so I took the nod as a positive sign.

"Thanks," I said, "it was fun."

I walked out of The Pier and climbed the stairs to the front entrance leading to the empty parking lot. At that moment, I felt the most alive I'd felt since leaving the city. It was good to be busy. As I mounted the last step, pushed open the glass door, and walked into the night, the warm air enveloped me. It was heavy with humidity and the faint smell of crepe myrtle. *Rain,* I thought. There was almost nothing I loved more than a good, soaking summer rain. I unlocked Mama's car, climbed in, and headed for home.

I slept in the next morning, exhausted from staying up later than usual. When I woke up, I walked into the kitchen to grab a glass of milk—just as the phone rang.

Mama answered it.

"Hello?" she said, then paused. "Yes, just a moment." She put her hand over the receiver.

"It's Troy McConnell."

Boy, he didn't waste any time. In all the excitement about starting my job, I'd completely forgotten about Troy. She handed me the phone.

I took it and cupped it to my ear. "Hello?"

"Laura, it's Troy. Troy McConnell," he said in a formal but upbeat way. "How's it goin'?"

"Great," I said, happy to hear his voice.

"How's The Pier?"

"Good, thanks," I said, pleased that he'd remembered. "Last night was my first night, but I liked it. It was fun."

"Glad to hear it." He paused. "Listen, I wondered—if you're free—would you like to go to Umstead Park on Sunday? I'll pack a picnic. It's supposed to be a nice day."

I listened to his lilting voice and smiled. A good ol' southern boy. I'd missed being around people who talked like me.

"I'd love to," I said. "What time?"

Then it occurred to me: he was asking me out on a date. The whole idea of dating felt strange. New York hadn't been about dating. It had mostly been about meeting and sleeping with strangers. I thought back to the last person I'd dated: Jay, my married boss from Kitty Hawk. Jay the Asshole.

"Great! I'll pick you up at noon. In my new car," he added, sparking my curiosity.

"Wow, what'd you get?"

"Crown Victoria," he said proudly.

"Nice!" I said.

Troy was a smart, hardworking schoolteacher who'd taken on a second job and saved enough to buy himself a new car. He seemed mature and responsible.

"Thanks," he said. He paused as if searching for something to say. "Well, I guess I'll see you on Sunday!"

"Okay, see you then!"

I hung up the phone and stood in the middle of the kitchen, smiling. Umstead Park. A picnic with Troy. What would I wear?

On Sunday, I was ready just before noon. I pulled on my new outfit—a flowered top, white pants, and a pair of strappy sandals—and stood at my bedroom window to watch Troy drive up in his new Crown Victoria. *Hmm, a family car.* I wasn't thinking about marriage or family or anything of the sort, but that's what came to mind.

Troy stepped out of the car and made his way to the sidewalk that led to our front door. He was wearing khakis, Top-Siders, and a blue polo shirt, the unofficial uniform of every male Carolina grad. My pulse raced. I hadn't been with anyone since New York, and I was nervous.

Troy and I talked nonstop in the car as we drove to William B. Umstead State Park, located on the outskirts of Raleigh. I told him about the beach and New York. He told me all about college—how he had gotten into Carolina and his mom had wanted him to become a doctor, but he loved sociology and had decided to major in that instead.

As we ate lunch, he asked me if I'd dated anyone special. I told him about Steve and how he'd encouraged me to model and how I'd ended up in New York. I briefly mentioned Billy, then Jay, though I didn't tell him about the part where I found out he was married. Troy said he'd had a serious girlfriend named Rachel and they'd broken up just before graduation.

"She was beautiful," he said matter-of-factly. "We were talking about getting married. Then we started arguing. It just didn't work out."

We cleaned up our lunch of Kentucky Fried Chicken and Coca-Colas in bottles.

"I'll be right back," said Troy.

He picked up our picnic basket and disappeared down the path. A few minutes later, he returned with a guitar case.

"Surprise," he said, grinning. He set it down on our blanket, opened the case, and pulled out a Martin guitar.

"I didn't know you played," I said, breaking into a smile.

"Yeah, I taught myself. I like to mess around with chords. I know a few songs."

"And a Martin. Impressive." I knew a bit about guitars from friends who were musicians. Many of them considered Martin to be the best.

"Yep. I got a good deal on this baby," he bragged.

"Play something!"

He picked up his guitar, tuned the strings, put on a capo, and started to play.

Ah, *"Part of Your Life." Kris Kristofferson and Rita Coolidge.* I knew it well.

I chimed in, and our harmonies melded as though we'd been singing together all our lives.

After our first date at Umstead Park, Troy and I fell into a rhythm— going out for dinner or ice cream or to his apartment to listen to music, make out, and, sometimes, make love. Three weeks later, we were engaged.

It was mid-June, and Troy invited me on another picnic, this time to Pullen Park. We strolled along the lake, stopped to ride the carousel, and then found a grassy spot under a large oak tree and spread out a quilt. I set down our basket, opened it, and began pulling out our food.

"I think we should get married," Troy said.

I was speechless. He'd told me he loved me on our fourth date, and even that had seemed too soon. Now he was talking about marriage? I was nervous but excited.

"Will you marry me?" he blurted out.

"Yes. Yes, I will!"

As I reached over to kiss him, I felt a wave of relief. *Somebody wants me*—the promiscuous, backslidden Christian who'd failed at every turn. Now I'd have another chance to make something work without screwing it up.

"I'm sorry, I don't have a ring for you," he faltered. "We'll get one, of course. But I didn't want to wait."

"It's okay," I said, delighted by his enthusiasm.

And just like that, we were engaged.

That evening, Mama and I were in the kitchen making banana bread.

"You've prayed about this, right?" she asked when I told her the news.

Her question caught me off guard. Prayed? Hell no, I hadn't prayed. I should have, of course. This was the biggest decision I'd ever make, and I should at least have consulted God. It occurred to me that I'd just said yes without giving it a second thought. With her single question, my carelessness had been exposed.

My faith had been so important to me. In theory, it still was; in practice, not so much. The truth was, I'd been doing things my own way for so long that I'd simply gotten out of the habit of asking

Jesus about much of anything. The way I saw it, Troy was cute. We enjoyed each other's company. He was from a nice family and he had a good job. What was there to pray about? And suppose I had? I certainly couldn't risk God telling me no.

Mama stopped, wiped her hands on her apron, and looked me square in the face. I knew that look. I squirmed.

"Of course I prayed," I said, lying through my teeth.

I knew what was behind her question: she was afraid, as Daddy was, that I was marrying too young. But I wasn't. I might be twenty, but I'd already lived a lifetime–the beach, New York. How many people my age had done the things I'd done? Not many, I reasoned.

But there was another thing: I wasn't sure Mama even *liked* Troy. I thought back to that night just after we'd first started dating. Mama had invited him for dinner, and they'd gotten into an argument over something trivial. Mama rarely argued with anyone; she simply spoke and that was the final word. But not with Troy. They started to joust and his face went red and Mama's volume escalated and Daddy and I sat there nervously, shifting in our seats. I looked over at Daddy, hoping he might intervene. Instead, I found him focused on his peas, pushing them around with his fork. It was going to be up to me.

"Would you both stop?" I interjected in the middle of a sentence.

It worked. Troy looked up, disgruntled. Mama fumed. No one said a word for what seemed like minutes.

When Troy finally spoke, his voice was flat. "Thank you for dinner. I'd better get home."

"You're welcome," Mama replied coolly. I recognized that tone, and I knew there was no easy forgiveness in it. So there was that.

But what if no one else proposed? I wasn't exactly a catch–modeling failure, college dropout–though I'd recently signed up to take an Evening College class at Chapel Hill. What if I spent the rest of my life alone? I simply couldn't take that chance. Troy would make a good husband—at least, I thought so. I imagined our life together—him teaching, me getting my college degree and, when the time came, staying home to raise our two blond, blue-eyed children. What more could I ask for?

Besides, I'd been with lots of guys. I knew what I wanted. I was ready to be with one person, settle down. Wasn't I?

Then came that night at The Pier. It was a Wednesday in mid-July—a little over a month since Troy had proposed—and an old acquaintance, Kevin Chandler, was performing.

Kevin was a local singer-songwriter; he was tall and lanky, with long brown hair and a warm smile. My friend Teresa had introduced us when we were juniors in high school. Kevin was several years older, and he'd been attending college at North Carolina State when we first met. He'd asked for my phone number, and when he called I'd invited him over for a Coke. He'd brought his guitar and we'd sat on the front porch and he'd sung to me and I'd been smitten. He'd stopped by the next week, and the week after that. The last time, as he was leaving, he'd given me a kiss. I'd been hopeful that something might come of us, but then he'd stopped calling. I knew he liked Teresa and she liked him and our friendship came first, so I'd let it go.

Four years had passed since then, and I was excited to see him again. Would he even remember me? Would it be awkward? What would I say?

"Well, hello," he said as he walked into The Pier and gave me a hug.

My heart jumped.

"How have you been?" he asked in that open manner of his.

"Great," I said. "I've been in New York, modeling. Now I'm back home. Working here." I knew I should say something about being engaged, but for some reason I didn't.

His eyes rested on my face. Then his mouth spread into a smile, like butter melting on toast. "Listen, I need to set up. Maybe we can talk after the show."

"I'd like that," I said. I watched as he turned and walked toward the stage. *What are you doing?* I asked myself at once. *You're getting married in four months.* I drew in a breath and looked away. *What's the big deal? You're old friends. He just wants to talk.* And just like that, I gave myself a pass.

At seven thirty, Travis opened the door and customers started trickling in. It was midweek, and things were slow. I stood behind the counter, watching Kevin from a distance. He hadn't changed at all. I thought about the times he'd come to my house, our one kiss.

"Hey," a familiar voice said, jolting me out of my reverie. It was Troy. "I wanted to surprise you," he said, pleased with himself.

"Great," I said, trying to muster some enthusiasm. Yet all I felt was disappointment.

He handed me his money, and I placed it in the drawer and stamped his hand. "I'm gonna grab a beer. Can you come over and talk?" he asked.

"Maybe in a few minutes. When the musician finishes his set."

The musician. I didn't dare say *Kevin* for fear I might betray myself by the way I spoke his name. Then again, wasn't Kevin just someone I'd known briefly in high school? Still, Troy might not understand. I'd told him very little about the beach or New York—about Steve and all the other guys after him. I'd meant to. But in the few months we'd been dating, he'd changed. Now when I mentioned the past, I'd catch an eye roll, a sideways glance, or, increasingly, a snide remark. If he knew I'd been with dozens of men, he'd toss me out like a pair of worn-out jeans. It was too risky to tell him the truth. So I said nothing.

Ten minutes later, Kevin took a short break. I wasn't busy, so I locked the cash register, slipped from behind the counter, and walked over and sat down beside Troy, who was sipping draft beer from a mug.

"Want to do something after work?" Troy asked, wiping a hint of foam from his upper lip.

My eyes searched the stage and locked on Kevin, who glanced in our direction.

I stiffened. "Not really."

I felt Troy's eyes on me. I turned from Kevin and looked down at the table, unable to meet his gaze. "I feel like being alone."

"Thanks a lot," he said.

I met his eyes. I could see he was annoyed.

"You know him?" he asked, nodding toward Kevin.

"Yeah, I met him in high school. Teresa Fogleman introduced us."

"I see." His voice was edgy. He downed his beer and set the empty mug on the table.

"I think I'll go. I can tell when I'm not wanted."

He was clearly angry, but I didn't even try to console him. "Troy . . ." My voice trailed off, and I exhaled as I watched him walk away.

As he disappeared through the entrance, I felt relieved. The nerve of him, just showing up without telling me. But he was my fiancé. We were getting married. Or were we? I imagined him calling, breaking off our engagement. After the way I'd acted, it's what I deserved. But he wouldn't, I told myself. He couldn't. Our wedding invitations had arrived just two days earlier. Wasn't it too late to call things off? What would we tell people? And what would they think?

Suddenly, I felt sick. I looked at my watch. It was only an hour until closing. Kevin had one more set and then he'd be done. I went back to my station and tried to stay busy to pass the time.

"Thanks for coming," I heard Kevin say to the audience. "I'll be back in August. I hope to see you then." The house lights came up and piped-in rock 'n' roll began to play; I walked over to help the waitresses clear tables and put up chairs.

One by one, the customers left until it was just the bartender, a waitress named Jess, Kevin, and me.

I moved to the stage and waited as Kevin put his guitar in its case.

"Are you done?" he asked.

I nodded.

He picked up his guitar and I walked beside him to the door, passing Jess on the way. She gave me a look. *Bad girl*, her eyes said.

"See ya," I said slyly. I knew she was right.

Kevin and I walked in silence through the empty subway. We climbed the stairs, pushed open the door, entered the parking lot, and made our way to his car. My stomach fluttered with nerves.

He unlocked the doors, opened the trunk, and arranged his equipment inside. Then he shut the trunk, walked closer, and took me in his arms. We stood there for a moment, holding each other, and my body started to relax. I turned my head and pressed my cheek against his chest, feeling the rise and fall of his breath.

After a moment, I pulled back and looked up at him. I'd forgotten how tall he was. I drew my mouth toward his face, hoping for a kiss.

"That guy . . . is he your boyfriend?" he asked.

I stood there, unable to answer.

"Why did he leave?" he pressed.

"I told him I needed some space. That I wanted to talk to you."

"This isn't a good idea."

"It's okay, really," I said, fighting back tears. "I explained that we were old friends."

"You should go to him," he said gently. He leaned down and kissed me on the cheek. "It was great seeing you," he said, then climbed into his car.

What a mess, I thought as I watched Kevin pull out of his parking spot and drive away.

I followed the white-lined spaces to my car. As I turned on the engine and began the drive home, my mind raced. I had no idea what I would say to Troy, but I couldn't think about that now. It was almost midnight and I was bone-tired. I'd figure it out tomorrow.

I went home, where I fell into bed and a restless sleep.

Troy called early the next day. I told him I was sorry for hurting him and that I wouldn't do it again. I explained that nothing had happened with Kevin. That I'd gotten cold feet about the wedding and needed some space. Within a day or two, everything was back to normal.

But then my thoughts would drift to Kevin, and I would feel embarrassed; I'd thrown myself at him and almost thrown everything else away. Why would I do that? Troy was a great guy; I knew I was lucky. Still, something wasn't right. Was this a sign? I felt unsettled, but I was in too deep to question why. So I pushed it down, hoping it would go away.

The next sign came a month later, in late August. The phone rang, and when I answered, I recognized the voice. It was Katie, my old buddy from the beach.

"Stewart!" I was thrilled to hear from her.

"Laura Belle," she said, subdued. "I have some news. About Brian."

I knew instantly that something was wrong.

"He's at Norfolk General. In intensive care." She spoke in fragments. "Mercy is with him; they're still together. Someone found him in a ditch on Collington Road. He was on his motorcycle. They think he took one of the curves too fast. He's unconscious."

I stood there, frozen. I thought of Brian's turquoise eyes, of our stolen kisses in the leather storeroom at The Christmas Shop. This couldn't be. All I wanted to do at that moment was get in my car and drive to Norfolk and sit by his bed and hold his hand. But that was crazy. Mercy was with him. And I was engaged. I couldn't go. I stopped and gathered my thoughts.

"Is he going to be okay?" I asked, not really wanting to hear the answer.

"They're waiting to see. The next twenty-four hours are critical. Say a prayer."

"I will," I mumbled. "Keep me posted. And thanks for letting me know."

I hung up the phone and sat down on the edge of Mama and Daddy's bed as memories of Brian poured in—the way he looked at me, the hunger that passed between us. My body stirred, and that's when I realized: I'd never felt that way with Troy. We'd made love, of course. Things were good. But was "good" enough? Shouldn't I feel passionate—deeply passionate—about the person I was going to marry?

I was a traveler embarking on an arduous journey. I had a map in my head and signs pointing me in the right direction, and I was ignoring them. At my own peril, I was speeding down the highway, whisking past signs warning me to STOP and SLOW DOWN. Now they had my attention.

You should call off the wedding, I heard something deep inside me say. Then, even more insistent, a voice said, *You can't*. Despite what had happened with Kevin and Brian, I knew I had to go ahead with my wedding plans. Everything would be fine, I told myself. We would be happy. I stood up, walked to my bedroom, and dressed for work.

~୨·ୡ~

Chapter Nine

Troy and I were married on Thanksgiving Day–November 24, 1977–just three days after my twenty-first birthday and six months and two days after our first date. The ceremony was held at Longview Methodist Church, the church my family attended and where I had gone to kindergarten. The sanctuary was nearly full; most of my relatives were there, along with our closest friends. I wore a white Victorian blouse with cutout lace, an ankle-length skirt, and ballet slippers. Mama pinned up my hair and added a few sprigs of baby's breath. I carried a bouquet of peach silk roses, something I could keep to remember that day forever.

Our reception was in the church basement–the same place I'd eaten lunch and taken naps as a five-year-old. It wasn't my first choice; its drab cinder block walls and linoleum floors lacked charm. But it was free and we were keeping the wedding simple, so I gave in. We had wedding cake and apple cider and all the usual suspects you'd find at a southern wedding–cheese straws, ham biscuits, and sausage balls. The church ladies who'd watched me grow up refilled platters and made sure everyone had enough to eat.

Afterward, my aunts and uncles and cousins all came to Mama and Daddy's for Thanksgiving lunch.

"Have a seat!" said my aunt Karen, patting an empty chair.

"Thanks, but we need to get going," I told her. "We have a long drive ahead of us."

I loved my relatives and appreciated the trouble they had gone to to be there. But I had no interest in hanging around making small talk or enduring red-lipstick kisses from my bevy of aunts. What if they started asking questions? I'd only seen two of them since I'd returned home, and I knew they were curious about New York. I couldn't endure an inquisition, especially on my wedding day. Part of why I was marrying Troy was to put all that behind me. I'd tucked New York into a box labeled "Do Not Disturb," and I didn't intend to open it. Besides, we were driving to the mountains for our honeymoon—to a place about five hours away called Banner Elk—and I was ready to hit the road.

Troy and I slipped through the kitchen and back to my old bedroom to change clothes. It felt strange being there with him; except for Daddy and my brothers, I'd never been alone in my bedroom with a guy. *But we're married,* I told myself. *It's okay.* We dressed quickly and exchanged sheepish looks in anticipation of the night to come.

I'd chosen a brown tweed suit for my going-away outfit. Troy pinned a white carnation corsage on the velvet lapel. We headed to the living room to say goodbye to my cousins, and then to the dining room, where my aunts and uncles were gathered.

Mama and Daddy excused themselves and followed us into the kitchen. Mama straightened my corsage, then gave me a hug.

"Have fun," said Daddy. "We love you." He flashed a tender smile.

"We love you too," I said. I kissed him on the cheek, and then Troy took my hand and pulled me out the door to our new life.

It was two o'clock and we'd been driving for about an hour when I began to feel achy and warm. I felt my forehead. It was hot to the touch, and my throat was swollen and sore.

I looked at Troy. "I can't believe it. I think I'm getting sick."

"You're just tired," he said dismissively.

At that moment, sitting in the car beside my new husband, I felt all alone. I regretted that we hadn't lingered a while longer in the refuge of my family.

That's when it hit me: now Troy was my family. *We* were a family. It seemed so unreal.

As we crossed the Watauga County line and made our way up the steep hill to Banner Elk, the snow began coming down in torrents. By the time we got to the Holiday Inn, the roads were blanketed in white. We checked in, unloaded the car, and walked to our room. I went to the bathroom, pulled on a nightgown, and crawled into bed. By now I could hardly swallow. Here we were on our honeymoon, and all I wanted to do was disappear under the covers and sleep forever.

It's a sign, I thought, desperate to make sense of what was happening. *Another sign*, because it certainly hadn't been the first.

After returning from our honeymoon, Troy and I moved from Raleigh to Durham, thirty miles away. We rented a second-floor apartment in a rambling brick house on North Gregson Street near Duke's East Campus. There were two rooms down the hall—one occupied by an undergrad named Lisa, the other by a law student named Ted. Our apartment consisted of one bedroom, a bathroom, a living room, a breakfast nook, and a kitchen. The living room was spacious. Light flooded through the windows from sunrise until the streetlamps came on at night. We filled the place with furniture passed on from our parents—a rocking chair here, a bedside table there—until it felt like home.

Troy taught junior high in a rural county thirty minutes away. I sold greeting cards at a Hallmark store at the mall. Two nights a week, I drove to Chapel Hill to attend a continuing ed class—an easy way to get my foot in the door at UNC. Most nights we ate casseroles made from family recipes. On special occasions, we drank cheap wine from the stone goblets Horace had given us as a wedding present. Life was simple, and we soon settled into a routine.

Then it began: the awakening that would bring about our demise.

It was a dreary Sunday in February–a steady rain was falling and a few dead leaves clung to the trees–when we invited Lisa and her boyfriend, Kirk, to come over for dinner. Lisa lived down the hall, and we ran into each other and chatted from time to time. They were midwesterners, unassuming and soft-spoken, and I was fond of them.

"Nice!" said Lisa, when she noticed the Mateus rosé, cheddar cheese, and saltines I had set out. It wasn't much, but with their diet consisting mostly of canned soup and peanut butter and jelly, I knew it was a treat.

"So, tell us about New York!" she said, taking a sip of wine. "You mentioned you were a model."

"Yes, I was." I glanced at Troy. I was learning to watch his face for cues of what and how much to say.

"Do you have photos? I want to see them!" she said.

Troy's face became rigid. I wasn't sure what it was, but I knew at that moment I'd done something wrong.

"Yes, my portfolio." I walked over to the library table and pulled out the large brown leather case hidden beneath a stack of books. "Here." I handed it over.

She flipped through the pages as Kirk moved closer. "Wow, these are amazing."

"Thanks," I said, smiling. As I watched her eyes move from one photo to the next, something inside of me stirred. I hadn't looked at my portfolio in months. The last time I had, it had reopened an old wound, one I was desperate to heal. But this time was different. Now I felt a swell of pride. I'd lived in New York. I'd been a Wilhelmina model. No matter how badly it had ended, those things were true. Surely that counted for something.

Over dinner, Kirk and Lisa talked about their upcoming graduation. With engineering degrees from Duke, their futures looked bright. I thought again about what it would be like to launch into the world with a degree in my field, though I wasn't yet quite sure what that would be. Like Daddy—and Lawrence and Horace after him—I'd probably major in English. I loved literature and I enjoyed writing. I'd published in our literary magazine in high school and done well in my English classes at UNCG. On several occasions, I'd entertained thoughts of following in Daddy's footsteps and becoming a writer.

I was excited about the evening classes I'd been taking—but being a writer? That all seemed a distant dream. For now, my life was here, in this attic apartment, predictable and small.

Lisa and Kirk finally excused themselves—they had an exam the next morning and needed to study. I watched at the door as they returned to Lisa's room. We began clearing the table, and I noticed that Troy was unusually quiet.

"What's the matter?" I asked, dreading his reply.

"Why did you have to bring up modeling?" His words fell like a hammer on my heart. *So that's it. He's jealous.* I looked at him in disbelief.

"That's all over," he announced.

I stood there, unable to speak. What had he just said? I'd started modeling long before we started dating. Steve, the beach, New York, Wilhelmina; that life, those memories, were mine. Who did he think he was, trying to take that away? Yes, he was my husband, but I knew one thing: I wouldn't let him.

"I didn't bring it up; Lisa did."

"That's not the point," he fumed. "New York is behind you. Your life is here now. With me."

With those words, my chest tightened and my breath became shallow.

"That's true," I agreed. "But modeling is part of who I was. Who I am now. Why is that a problem? I don't understand."

He didn't answer; he just turned and walked away. I felt as though I'd been kicked in the solar plexus, that place where many believe the soul resides. Others believe it's the center for self-esteem and personal power, of which I had none. At least, not at that moment.

After that, I was careful not to talk about modeling in Troy's presence. I went to work, put out greeting cards and joked with my boss, Jill. Then I drove back to our apartment and waited for Troy to get home from school. When he did, we ate dinner, watched TV, and went to bed.

We made love once a week. Sometimes, when we'd finished, I'd lie there and think about Steve. I knew he'd hit the big time because I'd started seeing him everywhere—on toothpaste commercials, in ads for JC Penney and Sears. I didn't dare tell Troy I knew him, much less that he'd been my first. I was afraid he'd ply me with questions I didn't want to answer. It was best to keep that to myself.

The months passed by, and summer arrived with its roiling wave of humidity. I'd signed up for summer school classes—tennis and film critique—and they soon became the highlight of my week. I wasn't very good at tennis—I'd never been athletic—but watching movies and discussing them was fun.

When I wasn't in school, I moved wistfully through my days. I'd now successfully escaped my past—at least, I thought I had.

One Sunday afternoon in mid-August we were in Raleigh, visiting Troy's parents. I was sitting at the kitchen table, copying a recipe, while Troy thumbed through the paper.

"I'm gonna help Dad wash the car," he announced. He folded the paper, set it down, and walked through the kitchen and out the front door.

I put down my pen and picked up the *News & Observer* and held it to my nose. I loved the smell of newsprint. Because of Daddy, it was in my blood. I riffled through the pages, thinking I might catch a glimpse of Steve, and that's when I saw it: "LOVE TRI-ANGLE: BUDDY JACOBSON ARRESTED FOR MURDER OF MELANIE CAIN'S LOVER." I gasped. *Buddy Jacobson*. The same Buddy Jacobson who owned My Fair Lady? The one who'd offered me a modeling contract?

I scanned the story, desperate for details. Phrases like "jealous rage," "bloodstained apartment," and "charred body" leapt from the page. Then this: "Police are investigating the possibility that Jacobson used his modeling agency as a front for an escort service."

Escort service? Dazed, I put down the paper and stared past the bowl of fruit sitting on the counter. I easily imagined the progression from modeling to sex to murder.

My eyes focused on my mother-in-law, Helen. She was up to her elbows in soapy dishwater, singing a hymn from my childhood: "Just as I am, and waiting not, to rid my soul of one dark blot."

I thought about the dark blot that was Buddy Jacobson's soul.

"Wow," I said to no one in particular.

"What is it?" Helen turned to me with that worried look of hers, the one that drove Troy crazy. I liked that she worried about us; I found it endearing. But worry, in his mind, was fear, and fear meant weakness, a trait he couldn't tolerate in others and wouldn't acknowledge in himself.

"Something I read. A modeling agency. New York." My words emerged as Morse code. "A contract . . ."

As I sat in the safe haven of my in-laws' kitchen, I felt utterly alone. I didn't dare share the salacious details. What would she think of me? I certainly couldn't share any of this with Troy. It might set him off.

"Oh." She smiled sweetly then turned back to her dishes.

"Oh"? That's it? "Oh"?

But what did I expect? The McConnell clan rarely even asked about my life before Troy. It was as if none of that mattered. But it did. Those events had shaped me. They were real.

I'd come to believe that I couldn't talk to anyone in this family about the things that were important to me—Lawrence, modeling, my dreams for the future. I remembered a conversation I'd once had with Helen about taking classes so I could finish college.

"Oh honey, you don't need a college degree."

I was only twenty-one, but there was one thing I knew about myself: if you told me I couldn't or shouldn't do something, then by God I'd go and do it, simply to show you I could.

"You're just gonna stay home and have babies." She smiled.

The phrase "barefoot and pregnant" popped into my head. This was the twentieth century. Did anyone in their right mind still think that way?

I wanted children one day, of course. But I also wanted more.

"To Thee whose blood can cleanse each spot, O Lamb of God, I come!"

I was lucky to have eluded My Fair Lady and a sordid life of sexual encounters for hire. I was grateful for Alex's wise counsel, and that, ultimately, I'd followed my gut. Though I'd done nothing to deserve it, I knew God had been looking out for me.

"Just as I am, though tossed about, with many a conflict, many a doubt," my mother-in-law warbled.

Tossed about. I thought of the tiny boats I'd seen tossed about during a particularly menacing storm on the Outer Banks. Though safe in the shallows, they'd had to take care not to be cast up on the shore. I was grateful to have escaped New York and my brushes with danger. How many other compromising situations had I put myself in? Hadn't I done the right thing by marrying Troy? Wasn't I safe?

In some ways, I was. In other ways, I wasn't so sure. I was like one of those boats, except mine had a slow leak. Moment by moment, I sensed it filling with water. I wondered, sitting there listening to Helen, how it would all end.

I loved Troy and, in many ways, found our life together comforting. I was a good wife. It was something that came naturally to me. Unlike modeling, I didn't have to try too hard. Sometimes he'd pull out his guitar and sing "The Boxer," and I'd join in and harmonize, and we'd look at each other and smile and I'd think, *What could be more perfect?*

Moments later, however, that feeling would pass as I remembered it wasn't perfect at all.

Most days, I just went through the motions. Something was missing, though I couldn't quite put my finger on what. As I ruminated, my thoughts always drifted to the beach or New York, and I'd feel a twinge of sadness.

When I looked in the mirror now, I saw just one thing: a wife. I couldn't deny that I'd always longed to be part of someone. After Lawrence, or "A.L.," as I'd come to refer to life since his death, I'd gone on a relentless quest to find someone who would fill the hole left by his absence. Wasn't that at the heart of my fling with Steve? And why I'd slept with so many guys in New York?

Then I'd found the one person who'd loved me enough to want to be with me forever.

But by then, that hole was so vacuous, Troy and our marriage had filled it completely. Now there was nothing of me left. Or was there? Wasn't I still my own person? Didn't I have hopes and aspirations apart from him? Surely I could be married and still be me. I had to find a way.

I started by taking a new job at a women's clothing store called Ups 'N Downs. It was early September, just a few weeks after I had read the news about Buddy Jacobson. Vicki, the assistant manager there, frequently dropped in to buy cards at Hallmark, and when she mentioned one day that they had an opening for a salesperson, I applied. The manager, Joanne, was a New Yorker, and we instantly hit it off. Even Troy was supportive, though I guessed it was because I'd be making more money than I had selling cards.

I loved working at Ups 'N Downs. The clothes were sassy and stylish, and I got a generous discount. Vicki and I dressed windows, put up displays, and helped customers while we grooved to the latest hits. It didn't take long for me to realize that I was good at my job. I could pull together the perfect outfit and make a customer feel beautiful, no matter what her body type. A few clients even started asking for me by name.

Six months later, though, when Joanne was promoted to regional manager and Vicki, now in Joanne's old position, offered me a job as her assistant manager, I hesitated. I liked the idea of a career in retail—having a title, working in fashion. But then I remembered the skimpy pay and the long hours I'd be spending on my feet.

College. The word came like a whisper. I was already working on getting the credits I needed to go full-time. After giving the assistant manager position some thought and talking it over with Troy, I told Vicki no. Still, I was grateful she had asked.

It was March of 1979 and the country had just come out of a recession—the worst since the Great Depression. We were struggling to save for a house, and I needed full-time employment. We lived just a few blocks from Duke—and I thought it might be fun to work in an academic environment—so I put in an application and was hired as the departmental secretary of the music department.

I was ecstatic. What could be more enchanting than working in a place where music wafted out of classrooms, drifted through stairwells, and lingered in the halls?

I'd always loved music—and in many ways, it had shaped my

existence. When I was six, Mama and Daddy bought seasons tickets to Friends of the College, a concert series at NC State. I'd sit between them in Reynolds Coliseum and listen as artists like Van Cliburn and André Watts worked their magic. I'd swing my feet to the music until the lilting melodies lulled me to sleep and Mama and Daddy would wake me for the trip home.

As a young girl, I'd watched Lawrence sit at our piano and play "Moonlight Sonata," stroking the keys with his long, tapered fingers. I also played: Broadway hits, Bach's Inventions, and the hymns I'd heard at church.

Now music would fill my days.

I knew I was lucky to have this job. My boss, Frank Tirro, was a renowned jazz musician with a warm manner and ready smile. My desk was wedged into a compact reception area just outside Dr. Tirro's office; there was a sofa, coffee table, filing cabinet, record player, and locker to store my things in. An oriental rug and a few philodendrons made it feel homey. Dr. Tirro's assistant, Marion Turner, worked in the adjoining office. She had salt-and-pepper hair and was always kind. Just being in her presence was comforting.

I enjoyed the work—typing letters, greeting visitors, and interacting with students. It was a welcome relief from the fault-finding at home. I'd come to realize that the barbs and innuendos were directly proportional to Troy's insecurity on a given day. Work was different. People were thoughtful and saw me for who I was. Two in particular, Dr. Paul Bryan and Dr. Allan Bone, treated me like a daughter.

Dr. Bone and his wife, Dorothy, invited Troy and me to come to Vermont that June and visit them at their summer house in the Green Mountains. Though as a couple Troy and I were not especially adventurous, we went and had fun. On the way home, we stayed overnight at Wheatleigh, an Italian-style villa built in 1893 as a wedding present from a father to his daughter, who was marrying a Spanish count. While Troy showered the next morning, I slipped out and roamed the grounds. As I walked through the formal gardens, I wondered what it would be like to live in such opulence with a man I truly loved.

Before we left, Troy took a photo of me sitting on the steps by a marble fountain. When the photos came back from the processor, I hardly recognized the girl I saw there. She wasn't the same girl who'd returned from New York and used food as a way of numbing. This girl was slender, and pretty. Her long hair was tied back from her face, and her chest and arms were tanned. She was wearing a long white skirt and a navy top. When I looked closely, though, I noticed that her eyes were vacant and her smile sad.

That fall, Troy and I joined the Duke Chapel Choir. We'd heard members were paid a thirty-dollar-a-month stipend and we needed the money, we both loved singing, and the European-style Gothic cathedral in the middle of Duke's campus was awe-inspiring. Who wouldn't want to sing there? We signed on.

Week after week, we listened to sermons about Jesus feeding the five thousand or Moses crossing the Red Sea. Most of it fell on deaf ears when it came to me. It wasn't that I'd stopped believing; I hadn't. It was just that I'd become accustomed to making my own choices, without praying, without considering God at all. Gradually, I'd sealed off my heart.

I'd known from day one that Troy was a Christian. We all were, the whole bunch of us who'd grown up in ranch houses in East Raleigh. We went to school during the week and to church on Sunday. Like me, he'd prayed the prayer of salvation. On our wedding day, we'd taken sacred vows before God and a sanctuary of witnesses without giving much thought to how we'd live out our faith together. The truth was, we'd barely even discussed it. Though it wasn't the thing that had brought us together, I wondered, in moments of clarity, if it was the one thing that might keep us from falling apart.

Sometimes, when I was alone, I'd think about the girl I'd been back in high school, the one whose heart had beat so wildly the night she'd heard that altar call, she couldn't stay in her seat—she'd walked to the front and prayed to receive Jesus, and known without a doubt that He had come into her heart to live forever. That moment had changed her. She'd lost all hope when she'd lost her brother. Taking that step of faith had made her come back alive.

Where had that girl gone? What had she gone looking for, and where had she thought she would find it? She hadn't found it at the beach. Steve had left for New York and taken every bit of hope with him. She hadn't found it in New York, though, Lord knew, she'd tried. Every relationship, every bed, every giving of herself had surely been her groping to find her way. Getting married hadn't been the answer. She was still lost, on a one-way train to nowhere, staring out the window as the landscape of her life passed by.

Troy was still teaching and working part-time at a men's clothing store, and he was eager to try something new. When he met our next-door neighbor, Roger, who'd recently started a new company in downtown Durham, they instantly hit it off; after a formal interview, Roger offered Troy a job.

"I'll be an account manager," he explained. "They know I don't have any business experience, and they say they'll train me."

I was excited at the news. He was a gifted teacher, but he'd grown restless. He was tired of his commute and the meager pay. And after so many years of his mother's comments about how he should have been a doctor, he needed something to prop up his fragile ego. I believed this job could be it.

He started his job in June, and two months later we bought a house—a two-bedroom 1940s bungalow with gleaming hardwoods and a fireplace. Our parents urged us to wait. The country was still in a recession, they said, and investing in real estate was risky. But all we could see were the positives. We both had good jobs. We didn't have any debt. We lived frugally—except for our morning treks to Dunkin' Donuts, a splurge for a young couple struggling to make ends meet. So, ignoring their warnings, we forged ahead.

We painted the kitchen a buttery yellow. I sewed blue-and-white gingham curtains to hang in the windows and displayed blue willow plates on the walls. When we'd finished, it looked like a spread in a Country Curtains catalog.

With the new house and new job, I'd hoped things between us would improve, but they only brought new pressures and made things worse. The economy was stalled. Prices for gas and food were at an all-time high, and layoffs were rampant.

"I was the last one hired; I'll be the first to go," Troy kept saying. It was the same almost every night. Our dinners would start out in silence. Then I'd ask about his day. Then he'd unleash.

"I'm the low guy on the totem pole. I don't have experience. Or a business degree."

"They just hired you," I'd say, trying to reassure him. "They're not going to fire you."

"That's what you think," he'd say with contempt.

"I'm sorry." Those words were automatic, and my response to almost everything. But I *was* sorry. For him. For us. I'd thought this job would boost his confidence. Instead, it had the opposite effect. He'd lost his spirit, and with it the swagger that had drawn me to him in the first place. In just a few months, my cocksure schoolteacher had turned into a worrier. He'd become the thing he'd always resented about his mother. And he didn't even see it. Try as I might, I just didn't think things were that bleak. Roger liked Troy. He'd hired him because he'd seen potential. Surely he wouldn't let him go.

"Everything will be okay," I'd say, believing it.

"Yeah, right."

"I'm sorry," I'd say again, this time under my breath.

I prided myself on being the consummate cheerleader. Even though I'd never made the squad in high school, I was a natural—eager to find the right words, quick to reassure him that there was hope. But it didn't do any good. His response was always the same: a put-down here, a stab there.

During the year and a half that Troy and I had been married, I'd become adept at apologizing: "I'm sorry" for this, or "It's my fault" for that. Looking back, none of it was really my fault at all. But that's not how it felt. It felt as if I were to blame for everything. I must be. Why else would he be so unhappy?

There were moments when I'd begin to emerge out of my self-doubt and loathing. Then I'd shrink back. I'd find myself captive once more, and barely able to breathe.

One such moment came in the early fall. My supervisor, Mrs. Turner, knew that I'd modeled and told me that her son, John, was breaking into fashion photography.

"He was wondering if you'd model for him?" she inquired one day.

"I'd love to!" I said.

John and I talked over the phone and arranged a date and time.

"I thought it might be fun to shoot at the Horace Williams Airport," he said. "Do some shots of you standing by a plane." The airport was small and located right in the middle of town.

"Sounds great," I said, immediately knowing what I would wear: a two-piece periwinkle-blue silk outfit with fuchsia trim on the neck and sleeves. It had been a present from Cheryl, and it was the most stylish thing I owned. It had hung in my closet since I'd returned from New York. Now I'd finally have an excuse to wear it.

It seemed as if the world was opening up to me. There were so many possibilities, and I was eager to try each one.

I came home from work excited to tell Troy. I hadn't brought up modeling for months. Surely he wouldn't mind.

"It's Mrs. Turner's son," I said as his face became set. "He's trying to build his portfolio," I added, hoping to elicit a positive response. "I think it will be fun."

"Fine," was all he said.

But I knew from his tone that it wasn't fine at all. My chest tightened. I'd done it again. Whenever I explored something new, it upset him. I hated that about myself. So why did I keep doing it? Why couldn't I figure out how to keep him happy and keep the peace? After all, I was his wife. Wasn't that my job?

On the day of the shoot, I got into my green '68 VW Beetle and drove away from Troy's lingering disapproval. I stood on the wing of a plane and John shot several rolls of film and I had a blast. I watched with envy as he changed out his lens and raced to capture the fading light. His passion was palpable.

My modeling days might be over . . . but maybe I could learn photography? I knew what it was like to be on the other side of the camera, and I had a sharp eye. I bet I'd be good.

I got home just before dark, went to our bedroom, and changed into a T-shirt and pair of jeans. Then I went to the kitchen and started supper.

"How was it?" Troy asked as he took a bite of chili.

I was pleased that he had asked, though I was surprised by his interest in my latest creative pursuit.

"Great!" I said, smiling. Still excited about the photo shoot, I let down my guard. "I was thinking I might like to study photography."

"Why?" The word fell from his lips with a thud.

"I think I'd be good at it," I said, suddenly nervous. "I'd have to go to school. But it would be cheaper than college."

"But it's expensive. Photography school. All that equipment."

I didn't disagree. I didn't dare. I just shrank into myself and remained silent.

Three months later, just before Christmas, one of my favorite music professors, Dr. Bryan, asked me if I'd like to be the rehearsal accompanist for a production of *H.M.S. Pinafore*.

"It's for a group called the Durham Savoyards, and I'm directing," he explained. "They're a bunch of talented people from the community who do this for fun."

I readily said yes. I'd been an accompanist for my high school ensemble, but I hadn't played much over the past few years and I'd missed it.

The score was one of the most challenging things I'd ever tackled. I practiced daily, pushing through the difficult passages until I could play them with confidence. The weekly rehearsals were lively and filled with laughter, and Dr. Bryan and the performers were grateful to have me there.

Several weeks before opening night, I was sitting at our piano working on an especially tricky section when Troy walked in.

"I don't understand *why* you're doing this," he said, his voice filled with disdain. There it was. That word. *Why* was his response to most everything: *Why did you have to bring up modeling? Why do you want to study photography? Why, why, why?*

"You're spending all this time, and they're only paying you seventy-five dollars."

My eyes fell. I lifted my hands off the keys and placed them in my lap. When I finally looked up, I knew from his expression that he was pleased with the blow he'd struck.

Now I was angry. *I'm not doing it for the money,* I wanted to say. *I'm doing it because it makes me happy.* Instead I simply placed my fingers back on the keys and continued to play.

Chapter Ten

It was now March and I'd been working at Duke for a year. It was the first day after Duke's spring break and I'd come in early, glad to be back at work after a week off. I unlocked the door and turned on the light. As my eyes adjusted, I noticed a beautiful seashell sitting on my desk right by my nameplate: a small, spiky conch with brown and white stripes. It was so exquisite, I knew it must be a gift. *Hmm. Who in the world left that there?* It must have been one of the students, I reasoned. But how did they get in?

I walked around my desk and put my jacket and purse away. Then I sat down at my desk and picked up the shell. I smiled, wondering again about the giver of this delicate gift from the sea. Then I returned it to its place and went to work.

A few minutes later, Dr. Tirro arrived, and not long after, Mrs. Turner.

"Welcome back," she said in her warm way. "Have a nice break?"

"Yes," I said. "It was quiet."

"Sounds lovely." She paused. "Do you mind updating the faculty directory? It's been a while."

"Happy to." I turned around in my chair and took the cover off my typewriter. Through the door, I could see students scurrying down the hall to their classes. The bell rang, one last door shut, and all was quiet.

I fed a piece of paper through my typewriter. I loved typing; it was therapeutic for me, like gardening or cooking was for other people. I enjoyed watching my fingers run across the keys. I was fast and I was proud of that fact.

"Like the shell?"

Startled, I looked up to see an attractive young man standing at my desk. He looked vaguely familiar, though I didn't know his name.

"Luke Buchanan," he said, as if reading my mind. "I work in tech support."

"Of course," I said. I couldn't remember exactly when or how often, but I knew I'd seen him around. He was about six feet tall. He had wiry hair and close-set brown eyes that turned up at the corners when he smiled. He was wearing khakis and a white shirt with the sleeves rolled up just below his elbows, and his arms and face were tanned.

I sat up taller in my chair. "Yes." I glanced at the shell. "It's beautiful. Thank you."

Our eyes met. I blushed.

"I went to Sanibel Island over break. With my mom," he explained. "I saw the shell and thought of you."

I saw the shell and thought of you.

There are times when a look—or an object—can cause an imperceptible shift in the universe. If, in that fleeting second, you knew what it would set in motion, you might do everything in your power to stop it. But that's the thing about moments. They come and they pass and life goes on. And yet it doesn't. Because afterward, nothing is ever the same.

He was thinking about me. In Florida. I paused. *But he doesn't know me. And I'm married.*

"Well, I gotta run," he said, breaking the silence. "I'll see you around."

"Okay," I said as he moved to the door. "Thanks again."

He smiled and disappeared down the hall.

Luke started stopping by more regularly to say hello, and whenever he appeared, I felt something I hadn't felt since Steve.

What are you doing? I'd ask myself. *You're married. This is wrong.* But then he'd show up unexpectedly and I'd look into his eyes and see the tiniest spark and something inside of me would ignite. It wasn't long before I was thinking about him all the time.

"Want to grab some lunch?" he asked one morning. "I thought we could walk over to The Dope Shop and get a sandwich." It was early spring; flowers were in bloom and East Campus was a vibrant green. How could I say no?

That lunch was followed by another, and another, and another. Then letters—long ones, handwritten on lined notebook paper, folded into envelopes, and left on my chair at work with "Laura" penned on the front. I came to work each morning hopeful to find another one. At the sight of one, my breath would catch in my chest and I'd sit down quickly and read each word before anyone arrived.

Each letter was the same—line after line describing the passion he knew we'd share when we were finally together. Given and read in secret, each one was a puff of wind on a smoldering ember.

Then, one day in early April, about a month after we'd met, I opened my locker and found a perfect long-stemmed yellow rose in a beautiful crystal vase. I smiled, then quickly shut my locker for fear someone might see.

"Thank you for the rose," I whispered later that morning when he appeared at my desk.

"I wanted to surprise you," he said, flashing that smile.

"You did," I reassured him. "You always do."

So many things about Luke reminded me of Lawrence. His intelligence. His quick wit. The fact that he didn't need external props, that he was comfortable in his own skin. Perhaps that was what drew me most of all. He'd brought me that shell, and now this rose, knowing each would capture my heart.

"A perfect rose deserves a perfect vase. I searched everywhere for just the right one. It's Scandinavian. Boda."

I was taken back by his sophistication. How did he know about these things? He'd grown up in Spain and Malaysia, for Pete's sake. And he was only twenty-four.

He looked around to make sure no one was listening. "Spend the weekend with me," he said suddenly. "Tell him you're visiting a friend."

I searched his face for some reassurance that it would all be okay. But all I saw was desire.

"Okay," I said, with as much confidence as I could muster. "I'll see what I can do."

On the drive home that afternoon, I devised a scheme. We didn't have any plans for the weekend. I'd tell Troy I was going to see Katie, my friend from the beach. She'd gotten married and lived in Suffolk, Virginia, about three hours from Durham. I'd say that I'd be leaving from work on Friday and coming back Sunday night.

When I got home, Troy was sitting in his favorite chair, reading the paper.

All at once I felt guilty. And sad. I took a deep breath. "I'm thinking about driving to Suffolk this weekend to see Katie Stewart." There. I'd lied. I kept going. "I called her. She said it was okay." I'd made the decision not to ask permission. What if he said no?

"Fine," he said nonchalantly. He looked up from his paper.

It took everything in me not to look away. It was at that moment that I began to break free.

Friday afternoon, I drove to Luke's apartment—a 1930s red brick structure tucked away on a tree-lined street—and parked my car behind the building, away from view. I grabbed my overnight bag from the trunk, walked up to the second-floor landing, and knocked on the door.

A few seconds later, the door opened. There was Luke, his face mirroring my emotions. This wasn't an easy choice, for either of us. And yet it felt like the only one we could make.

I set down my things and fell, trembling, into his arms. The tears came, first in gasps, then in waves, and he held me until I caught my breath. Without saying a word, he took my hand and led me through the kitchen and spacious living room and into his bedroom. The golden light of the late afternoon peeked through the bamboo shades and fell across a large platform bed draped in white. Other than the bed, a few plants on the windowsill, and a framed souvenir print of a performance of Bach's *Requiem Mass*, the room was bare.

He lowered me onto the bed and kissed me deeply. I closed my eyes against the onslaught and we melded together, and soon we were lost and there was no turning back.

We made love again and again, as if we were lovers who'd parted in the past and only now found each other again. His body knew mine fully from that first moment. How could that be?

Afterward, we lay there, sweaty, entangled, and silent. What had just happened? And what were we going to do?

That's when I remembered the lyrics of an old Scottish ballad Karla Bonoff had recently recorded: "The water is wide, I can't cross o'er."

As close as we were, there was an impenetrable gulf between us.

Still, there was something about this man that drew me in a way I'd never been drawn to anyone before. I lifted my face to the air and breathed in an elixir of possibility and hope.

For the next few months, my life consisted of three things: lying, sneaking around, and living in fear of being discovered. For years,

I'd successfully hidden my wanton behavior from my parents. Now I was telling myself that this was the only thing I could do, when all the while I knew better. I'd read *The Scarlet Letter* in eleventh grade. Yet here I was, walking around with a red "A" emblazoned on my chest. I'd technically had one affair already, with Jay, my crazy married New York boyfriend. But I'd given myself a pass because I'd been in the dark, and when I discovered the truth, I'd ended it immediately. So, was I really at fault? I told myself I wasn't.

But this was different. There was no pass. Troy was my husband, and I'd made promises to him that were supposed to be forever. Then Luke had come along and penetrated my heart, body, and soul, and those vows just hadn't stood up. They hadn't been weight-bearing. Now I was watching them fall in slow motion, crashing around my feet like an imploding building.

I thought back to a demolition I'd witnessed in Midtown Manhattan. There was an explosion, then from top to bottom that skyscraper came tumbling down, concrete and metal and residue and smoke. Within moments, it was only a heap of what once was. It was no longer a place people could enter to find shelter from the cold; it was only a wasteland, a mess waiting to be cleaned up.

That was now the state of my marriage, and I was to blame. I carried the rubble on my shoulders as I moved through every waking minute, thinking about Luke and the mess I'd made, wondering what to do next.

I started to feel like a stranger in my home. But that wasn't the worst of it. I'd become so emotionally removed from the person with whom I shared my meals and my bed that he seemed like a stranger too. I constantly wondered if he could feel the breach between us. I sometimes searched his face for clues, but even then, I couldn't trust myself to read them correctly. Were they real? Or just a product of my guilt? I wasn't sure.

I was grateful for the refuge of work, a place to escape to and steal a few moments with Luke. I held it together Monday through Thursday. But Friday was another story, as it meant two days and three nights at home. Every Friday, as five o'clock rolled around, my mood would go from a vibrant cerulean to a stormy gray. I'd gather my things, and Luke would meet me outside the music building and walk me to my car. We'd stand in front of Rosebud, my VW Beetle, and hope no one would see us as we said our goodbyes. He'd kiss me tenderly and tell me everything was going to be all right. Mostly I believed him, though sometimes I'd see the disquiet in his eyes. The truth was, neither of us knew how it would turn out. We just knew we loved each other, and hoped that it would.

I'd get into my car and cry all the way home, ripped away from Luke and driving toward my faux life with Troy. I didn't want to hurt Troy, but that's exactly what I was doing. I'd once loved Troy. In some ways, I still did. Yes, he'd been critical. Yes, he'd chipped away at my heart. But I didn't believe for a minute that he was a bad person. We were just a bad fit.

It was increasingly clear that we never should have married. I'd come home from New York with my self-esteem in tatters. Before I'd had time to recover, I'd jumped into our relationship. I'd believed it would save me from my past and heal my tarnished soul. But with time, I'd gotten stronger. The management offer at Ups 'N Downs, modeling for John Turner, playing piano for the Savoyards, my job at Duke—all those things had shown me I didn't need Troy to validate me. I was worthy in and of myself.

Then I'd met Luke, a person who recognized my potential and supported me in whatever I wanted to do. As I began to emerge, he was there, cheering me on—not so I could fall helplessly into his arms but so I could fly.

It was now the middle of May, and life at home had become unbearable. At night I'd lie awake, worrying. During the day, I was so in knots I couldn't eat. I was down to 107 pounds—the smallest I'd ever been, and 7 pounds below the weight Eileen Ford wanted me to reach. That's when it occurred to me that I should return to New York and try again.

"I'm thinking of calling Wilhelmina—to see if they'd take me back," I announced to Luke one afternoon. It was a Saturday, and I'd managed to get away for a few hours. We'd made love and were lying together, staring into the canopy of trees just outside his bedroom window.

I'd just started summer school at Carolina and had applied to go full-time in the fall. I was one step away from getting my degree. But now that I'd lost all the weight—something I never thought I'd do—it had suddenly dawned on me that I might be able to model again. As much as I wanted to finish college, I knew I wasn't getting any younger.

If Wilhelmina did sign me, it would mean moving back to New York, away from Luke and any possibility of a future together.

"I think you should go," he said. "I'll take you."

"You will?" I asked, relieved and subdued all at once. I wasn't surprised. I knew he would do anything for me.

I'd read in the paper that Wilhelmina had died of lung cancer just a few months earlier. I'd been saddened by the news; she'd been like a surrogate mother to me. In the short time I'd known her, I'd grown to love her. There had been rumors around the agency that she and Bruce had a troubled marriage. She'd never said a word, but there had been the cigarettes, lots of them, and that faraway look I'd sometimes see in her eyes.

It had been three years since I'd been in New York. Without Wilhelmina to turn to, I'd have to find another way.

I left work a little early that Monday. I went home, called the agency, and spoke with Sarah, the person in charge of new talent. I told her my story—that I'd worked with Willy, that I'd returned home for a few years and was ready to come back.

"Send me some photos," she said. "We'll take a look and get back to you."

"Thank you, I will."

I hung up the phone. What would I tell Troy? How could I possibly get away? But this was my one chance. I'd figure it out. I had to.

That night, I went through my portfolio and pulled out the best photos to bring to work with me the next day. I spent the first part of my lunch hour typing up a letter to Sarah, using the music department address so Troy wouldn't be tipped off. Then Luke walked with me to the East Campus post office to put the package in the mail. I paid the postage, then turned around to face him.

"Well, I did it," I said, searching his eyes for reassurance.

He reached over and squeezed my hand. "I love you," was all he said. It was enough.

It was a Friday afternoon in late June when I found myself in the reception area of Wilhelmina, waiting for Sarah. It had taken several weeks after I'd gotten her letter to line everything up. I had a break between summer school sessions—an ideal time to make the trip—so I called Sarah and set up an appointment. Next, I told Troy that I wanted to go to the beach for a few days. Horace was there, so he didn't suspect anything. Then Luke and I put our plan into place: We'd take off around noon on Thursday. I'd drive to his apartment and leave my car, and then we'd make the ten-hour trip to New York and arrive before midnight. I'd have Friday morning to rest before my appointment at two. It would be grueling. Still, if everything worked out, it would be worth it.

Being back at the agency felt surreal. I looked around. The wallpaper was different, but the photos of Willy were the same. I thought about Steve. Was he still here? Would I run into him? The beach, our relationship, it all seemed so far in the past. There'd been Troy. Now Luke.

"Laura?" I looked up to see a pretty brunette holding open the same door I'd walked through dozens of times.

"Sarah?" I stood up and walked toward her.

"Hi! Do you have your photos?"

"Right here," I said, handing her my portfolio. Until now, she'd only seen samples from my book.

"I just want to take them back so everyone can have a look. I'll come get you when we're done." She turned and walked away, and the door closed behind her.

I went back to my seat and waited. Luke had decided not to come with me to the agency. We'd discussed the fact that I'd appear more professional without my boyfriend in tow. Twenty minutes passed, then thirty. What in the world were they doing? Surely it was a good sign.

All at once, Sarah appeared at the door. "Come with me."

I stood up and my heart jumped to my throat. As I followed her down the hall to a small office, my mind swirled—a new contract, a fresh start.

I found a chair as Sarah walked to her desk, sat down, and looked at me.

"I passed your book around. Everyone loved it. You have a great look. And you photograph well. We talked about it at length. The truth is, the economy's bad. We're hiring younger models. Eileen Ford signed Brooke Shields two years ago. She's fourteen now. They'll get a good ten, fifteen years out of her." She paused. "How old are you?"

"Twenty-three." I felt my whole body tighten.

"Yeah . . . I'm afraid you're too old." Her eyes met mine. "I hope you understand."

"Of course," I lied. *I'm twenty-three and too old? How can that be?*

I took the elevator down to the lobby, then walked out to Thirty-Fifth Street and looked up. The sky was pale blue and the air was heavy with fumes. As I walked back to the hotel, I thought of the events that had brought me here. Waiting to hear from Wilhelmina. The lies I'd told Troy to get away. The ten-hour drive. My fear that Luke and I would be in an accident (and die) and I'd be a woman scorned. I'd gone through all that, and now I'd been rejected because I was twenty-three and past my prime. It was too much to take in.

That night, Luke and I sat in the balcony of the Shubert Theater and watched *A Chorus Line*. It was the story of a veteran dancer named Cassie who'd returned to audition for the chorus line because she couldn't find work as a soloist. At the end of the second act, the dancers were finally chosen, and the director asked each dancer what they'd do when they could no longer dance. The orchestra began to play, and Cassie began to sing.

Luke put his arm around me. I laid my head on his shoulder and cried.

We left Manhattan early the next morning and headed for Durham with the future heavy between us. We rode mostly in silence. When one of us did speak, it was to say something like, *I wonder how far it is to the next McDonald's?* or *Don't you love the lyrics to that new song by Steely Dan?*

Five hours later, we crossed into Virginia and were greeted by a sign that read, "Virginia is for Lovers." *Maybe Luke and I should move here*, I thought.

It was then I felt his eyes on me. I glanced over to see his face, raw with emotion. It was the first time I'd seen him like this, completely unmasked.

"Oh, my God," I whispered. "You were afraid you were going to lose me."

His lips pressed together in a silent *yes*.

"I knew they were going to sign you," he faltered. "That you'd move back. That it would be over."

The gravity of his words sank in. In the weeks leading up to our trip, I'd been self-absorbed—obsessing over my weight, my complexion, what I'd wear. I'd never allowed myself to think about what would happen to us if things actually *did* work out. But he had. And yet he'd never uttered a word. He wouldn't. He wanted my happiness, at any cost. That was just who he was.

"We'll figure it out," I reassured him. "I don't know how, but we will." It was the line I constantly fed myself, as though maybe, if I repeated it often enough, it just might come true.

But this time was different. As soon as I spoke the words, I realized they no longer held any meaning. We were just hours from home and on a collision course with reality. I wasn't sure we'd survive the wreckage, much less walk away unharmed.

I shut my eyes, took a deep breath, and tried to focus. The consolation prize for being turned down at Wilhelmina was that Luke and I were still together. Only we weren't. I was married. I knew nothing would get better between Troy and me. How could it? We were two people who shared very little except a last name. With Luke, I'd found my wings.

My chances of getting into UNC were good. After completing the next session of summer school, I'd have enough hours to enroll as a junior. I'd find a part-time position so I could attend classes in the mornings and work in the afternoons. As much as I loved my job at the music department, it had become difficult to work alongside Luke. Our frequent lunches and walks to my car were creating a buzz. It was time for a change. I'd seen in the internal job postings that there were a lot of part-time positions at Duke University Hospital. I'd start there.

"We have to talk," I said.

As we drove through rural Virginia, we devised a plan. We agreed that it made sense for me to move out when classes started. I'd look for an apartment in Luke's complex so we could be near each other. Troy could keep the house. Other than my clothes and a few family heirlooms, I didn't care about anything else.

The worst part, of course, would be telling Troy. I imagined his shock. The hurt. Our heated exchange. The coup de grâce would surely be some combination of words that would drive a stake through my heart. I dreaded it. Even talking it through with Luke didn't help. How would I survive?

Now, I told myself, *all you have to do is get into UNC, quit your job, land a part-time position, find an affordable apartment, and leave Troy.* My heart pounded. Who was I kidding? What if even one of those things fell through? What would I do then?

The months that followed were tumultuous. I was accepted at UNC in July—a lifelong dream finally realized—and started classes in late August. I got a job at the hospital working in the EEG lab at Duke North, transcribing test results and placing them in patients' charts. Next, I found a one-bedroom apartment in Luke's complex—just two buildings over from his place. The rent was more than I could afford on my modest salary, so he'd offered to help me out.

Everything was coming together. Then came the day I'd been dreading. It was a Friday in mid-September; the sky was bright blue, and there was a hint of fall in the air. I left the lab later than usual and made the five-mile trek home. I walked in and found Troy in the living room, sitting in his favorite overstuffed chair, reading the paper and smoking his pipe.

He looked up. "Hey."

"I'm leaving." For all my rehearsing, these were the only words to come out.

He gave me a blank stare as I watched the color drain from his face. "Now?"

"No, on Monday. I got an apartment."

His anger rose. "So you're just giving up? Walking out?"

Surely he wasn't surprised. Things between us had been deteri-orating for weeks. There'd been skirmishes, retreats, walls erected.

"It's not over," I lied feebly. "I just can't live here anymore."

His eyes pierced me. The words flew and I willingly endured his diatribe. Even though I never mentioned a word about Luke, I knew I'd been unfaithful. I stood guilty. His wrath was surely the punishment I deserved.

That night I slept in the guest room, tossing and turning and crying for hours. I woke with a pounding headache. Morning was just breaking when I heard Troy leave to get coffee. I was finally alone. I got up, walked down the hall, picked up the phone, and called Horace.

"You have told Mama and Daddy," he said, stating a question.

"I'm going to wait until I move out so they won't talk me out of it."

"You have to tell them now," he insisted.

"I can't. My head is killing me."

"It doesn't matter. Get in the car and go," he said firmly.

As much as I dreaded confronting my parents, I knew he was right. It would be harder on them to find out after the fact. I owed them that much. If they pushed back, I'd just have to stand my ground.

Still, I couldn't just show up unannounced. I hung up the phone, then picked it up again and called Mama and Daddy.

Daddy answered the phone. "Hey, sweetie." My father, always so tender toward me.

"Are you and Mama going to be around today? I need to see you."

"We're home. Come on."

Several hours later, when I pulled into their driveway, I thought I might throw up. How could I disappoint them again? I'd dropped out of college. Twice. Failed in New York. Rushed into marriage. Now, less than two years later, I was leaving my husband. I was their only daughter, and I'd been such a disappointment. What was wrong with me? Why couldn't I get anything right?

I walked through the kitchen door and heard the din of the TV.

"Hey!" I called out.

"We're in here!" answered Daddy.

I went into the den and sat down on the love seat beside Mama.

"I can't live with Troy anymore. I've gotten an apartment. I'm moving out."

Daddy had always been the passive one, letting Mama take the lead. Now he spoke up.

"Are you okay?" His tone was urgent.

I was his only daughter. Of course he was concerned.

"When?" Mama asked, worried.

"On Monday."

"That's two days," she said.

"I know. I was going to wait and tell you, but Horace said I should tell you now."

They looked at each other. My heart sank. *Here it comes.*

"It'll be expensive to live on your own. How are you going to manage?" Mama asked.

"I'll manage," I said weakly. "I have my job at the hospital. I'll figure it out."

I'd expected them to be angry; instead, they were responding with compassion. I was relieved.

Mama walked into the kitchen and came back with a glass of iced tea. I knew it was a peace offering; in the South, sweet tea heals everything.

We talked for a few minutes. They asked about Troy, wanted to know how he'd taken the news. When my glass was empty, I set it on the end table and stood. "I need to go."

Untethered

They followed me into the kitchen. Daddy gave me a lingering hug. Then I leaned over and kissed Mama on the cheek.

"I'm sorry, honey," she said, and I could tell she was.

On Monday, while Troy was at work, Luke and a few of his friends backed a small trailer into our driveway and loaded up my belongings. I took the guest room furniture, including the bed I'd slept in as a child. I took the rocking chair that had belonged to my grandmother Kate, the one in which Mama had rocked us and where Horace and I had held each other the night we discovered Lawrence had died. The piano stayed. It was one of my prized possessions and I hated to leave it behind, but it would require a professional mover and I needed to get out that day. I'd just have to get it another time.

I stood for a moment in our living room, staring at the hardwoods I'd polished with Johnson's Paste Wax until they gleamed. I glanced at the fireplace and thought of the bundles of wood I'd chopped and hauled inside. I considered the ruffled curtains I'd hung over the windows with care. Each recollection embodied a shattered dream. Then I walked through the dining room, into the kitchen, and out the back door.

I walked to my Beetle, got inside, and shut the door. As I sat there looking at our little bungalow, the sadness enveloped me. It had not been the happy home we'd envisioned.

Through my tears, I looked in the mirror and saw Luke backing the trailer down the drive. As I pulled away from the house and headed down Roxboro Road, I felt I was finally free.

166

Chapter Eleven

I found a seat in the lecture hall and waited for Basic Accounting Principles to begin. I hated this class. Dr. Rami would soon start droning on about supply and demand, and I had already checked out.

As Dr. Rami made his way to the podium, my thoughts turned to the mess that was my life. I had walked out on my husband and felt guilty yet relieved. Right now, guilt was winning. I knew because I was depressed and barely coping. I'd cry at the most inconvenient times: in the middle of class, on my way to work, sitting at my typewriter.

"When factors of production are allotted on criteria other than comparative advantage, inefficient production results," declared Dr. Rami as he paced the floor.

Who gives a shit about inefficient production? My life is falling apart. I shut my notebook, shoved it into my backpack, stood up, and made a beeline for the nearest exit. As I pushed open the door, I started crying. I walked into the marble entryway and down the steps of Carroll Hall to the brick wall below. I plopped down, pulled out a Kleenex, and tried to pull myself together enough to go back inside.

I was fragile, brittle. I'd become unmoored and I'd drifted far from my faith. I knew there was a shore, but I couldn't see a way back. I'd left Troy and gone back to college, but it felt as though I'd damaged my soul to get there. It was one of those junctures where you long for stability, for something that won't come undone at your bidding. I'd been reckless with my marriage—I'd hurt Troy and his family. I'd let my parents down. They'd never said so, but I was sure I had. The choices I had made—my affair and impending divorce—were choices I'd have to live with for the rest of my life.

There was a quiet restlessness stirring in me. I had the stability of school and Luke, but school would be short-lived. Then I'd be out in the world, making my way. And Luke? Even though he was a great guy, I'd been through one too many failed relationships to pin all my hopes on ours. No, there had to be something more lasting.

I wondered if finding a way back to God was my only hope. I considered that the one place I might encounter him was a church. But then I thought about facing a room full of saints and decided against it. I couldn't handle that right now.

There had been God moments over the past five years, I was sure of it. Moments when He had whispered to me in a still, small voice like he did to the prophet Elijah. In my case, that voice sounded urgent, more like, "Psst! It's Me!" Two of those moments—"God winks" as I'd once called them—came to mind: the first was that afternoon in 1975 when I'd stopped by The Circus Tent on the way to The Nags Header; the second, the Sunday I'd stumbled upon that Methodist church in New York. Since then, I hadn't heard a word.

I paused and let my ruminations settle.

Hey God, I could use a little whisper right now. Please?

Then it occurred to me: I was self-centered. And stubborn. Would I even hear Him if He spoke? Would I even listen?

Starting a new life had been harder than I'd thought. I was carrying a twelve-hour course load, going to school five days a week from eight to noon. After classes I'd rush to my car, drive the eight miles back to Durham, park at the hospital, and dash the half mile to the EEG lab so I'd get there by one o'clock. There, I'd sit for four hours in a windowless room the size of a large closet, transcribing EEGs.

After I'd finished typing my transcriptions, I'd walk the results around Duke North and Duke South and place them in patients' charts. At five o'clock, I'd gather my things, make the trek to my car, and drive to my apartment.

At home, I'd toss my backpack in the corner, check the mail, and freshen up before Luke arrived around six o'clock. Then we'd drive to one of our favorite restaurants—usually Café Monde, where the owner knew us by name. I was certain Troy wouldn't show up there—he was a steak and potatoes guy—so we were able to enjoy dinner in peace.

"Whisky sour, mademoiselle?" the owner would ask as he pulled out my chair.

"Yes, Henri, thank you," I'd say, offering my warmest smile.

Luke and I would sip our cocktails and share highlights from our day. I'd complain about my accounting homework; sometimes he'd reveal the name of the next hot performer coming to Duke.

"Elvis Costello," he said one night, then waited for my reaction.

I gasped. "Oh my gosh! I *love* him!"

"Well, I have to set up and run sound. Want to join me?"

"Are you kidding? Of course!" I gushed, and gave him a kiss.

After dinner each night, he'd drive me back to my apartment. Then he'd head back to the office to work. If he worked late, he'd crash at my place. If he finished early, he'd phone me when he was on his way home and I'd walk over to his apartment and spend the night there. In reality, we were living together. But I was still married, so we kept two apartments to keep up the facade.

I knew I was living a lie, and had been since starting my affair with Luke. And I was never more aware of that fact than when I woke up early in Luke's apartment and rushed back to my own in fear that my parents would call and discover I wasn't there.

Even in the short time since I'd moved out, it had begun to feel as though Luke worked all the time. There were the music department events where he was responsible for sound. Then there were the big-ticket events around campus. He was good at what he did, and I was proud of him. Still, he was gone a lot.

Meanwhile, I was in class and working all day; at night I did nothing but study. I was a morning person and had energy up until the two whiskey sours I enjoyed over dinner. Then I'd get home and open my textbooks, and for the next few hours, it would be a battle to slog my way through microeconomic theory and keep my eyes open while rectifying balance sheets. Sometimes, when I had a test to study for, I'd set my alarm and wake up, study for an hour, sleep for two, wake up and study for another hour, and so on, until the sun came up. Then I'd get up, dress, and head to campus.

We often make choices about the future in a vacuum. We believe that if we take the path we're compelled to take, things will work out. But it's a crapshoot at best, and we know it. Still, we plow ahead and hope for the best. That's certainly what I was doing. Who knew, given the bleak job market, if I'd ever even use my degree? At least I'd have one.

Throughout the fall semester, I'd often doubted my decision to major in industrial relations, a degree that would equip me for a management position in finance or personnel. I wanted desperately to follow in Lawrence's footsteps and study English. It had only been ten years since Lawrence had attended classes on this same campus. Many of his professors still spoke fondly of him, especially Dan Patterson, who had been a pallbearer at Lawrence's funeral. There was even a plaque in the English department with his name under an engraved gold plate that read, "Highest Honors in English."

My major had six math requirements, and I wasn't a numbers person. I loved words and literature and writing. For now, though, I'd decided to push that aside. I'd always followed my heart. For once, I was going to make a practical choice. I'd stick with my major and get a job in the financial sector, maybe become a stockbroker. My cousin's husband was a broker in Richmond. They had a beautiful home and drove nice cars. It was 1980, and the country was in the middle of its second recession in a decade. It was the smart thing to do, I reasoned. It would pay off in the end.

I told myself that things would work out for Luke and me—that Troy and I would divorce and Luke and I would marry one day. But I also knew better than to make assumptions. I'd gone to great lengths to leave Troy and go back to school to earn my degree. After my failed marriage and my missteps in New York, I couldn't take any chances. I had to look out for me. I had to plan as though I'd be single the rest of my life. Just in case.

Fall passed quickly, and my grades arrived in the mail in early December. I'd made it through my first semester, but barely. I'd never been a perfect student, but I'd always made mostly A's and B's. No longer. I finished the fall semester with three C's and a D in accounting.

The spring semester was only a little better. Overall, my grades improved, but when I started flunking my second accounting class, I knew it was time for a change. Economics interested me, and it didn't have the same accounting requirements, so I switched my major.

By spring I'd settled into my routine, and most of the time things felt normal. The hardest part was dealing with Troy. We spoke on the phone every few weeks. Sometimes he'd ask to see me so we could talk. We'd meet in a park or get together for coffee. The conversation was always the same.

"So, you happy?" he'd ask sarcastically.

"Yes," I'd say. "I'm glad to be back in school. And I like my job. The people are nice." Then I'd wait as the molten lava rose.

"I can't believe you just walked out."

"I'm sorry," I'd say, meaning it. "I know I've hurt you."

"But you won't come back."

"Things weren't good between us. You know that. We need some time apart."

And so it went. I kept him at arm's length, never using the words "over" or, God forbid, "divorce," even though I knew that was where we were headed. I was a good southern girl, and we avoided confrontation like the plague. We all spoke Avoidance, the cryptic language of our childhood. We'd only allude to uncomfortable subjects or use vague references, hoping all the while that the other person would figure out what we meant. I felt guilty about what I'd done to Troy. If I spoke it aloud, I'd be forced to confront it. *No, thank you.*

Over time, our meetings grew less frequent. Troy and I had been living apart for six months, and Mama and Daddy were pushing me to file separation papers. They knew Troy and I weren't going to get back together. They'd met Luke. They could see that I was happy and had moved on.

My parents' promptings surprised me. They felt that divorce would bring closure for both Troy and me. But I wasn't ready. I still couldn't get my head around the fact that I'd be walking through the world as a "divorcée"—a scandalous term, even in 1981. Instead, I chose to stay busy and hoped it would just all go away.

On a glorious Friday afternoon in March, Luke and I flew to New York for an audio convention at the Waldorf Astoria. I was excited to get away for the weekend and stay in such an elegant hotel.

We checked in, went to our room, and unpacked a few things. Then we headed downstairs to the exhibition hall. Everywhere I looked there were guys with lanyards hung around their necks, looking at the latest sound equipment.

A few minutes in, as we approached an impressive Bose display, Luke turned to me.

"You must be bored, young lady."

Does it show?

"Why don't you go do your own thing, and I'll see you back in the room at six?"

"You sure?"

He smiled.

"Thank you!" I said, relieved. As I turned to leave, my mind buzzed with possibilities.

In the end, I spent the afternoon walking around the city, along Central Park then down Sixty-Third Street to my old neighborhood. It was the first time we'd been back since our trip the previous summer, and things were different. I felt a mix of emotions: nostalgia for the old days, and a surge of excitement about my new life. I was proud of how far I'd come. As I looked up at my old apartment building, I realized that I'd survived that awful day when Cheryl had walked in on Brad and me. Now I was with a great guy who loved me, and realizing the dream of getting my degree.

On Saturday morning, Luke told me that he wanted to go out and shop for clothes. We walked over to Madison Avenue and found an upscale men's boutique.

"What do you think?" he asked, pointing to a brown hound-stooth jacket in the window.

"That would look great on you," I said.

Luke wasn't like the frat boys at Carolina. He was elegant; he had style. I'd met his mother once and knew he'd gotten it from her.

He paid for the jacket and told the salesman he'd pick it up that afternoon. Then we returned to the hotel.

Over dinner that night, he pulled out a small black velvet box and held it out to me. "Here."

I took the box and opened it. Inside was a pair of tiny diamond earrings.

"They're beautiful," I said. "Thank you." My heart swelled.

What was it about this man? He was attractive, witty, and playful. He certainly was romantic. But there was something more. It was his quiet, steady confidence—his ability to know what to do in any situation. It's what had drawn me to him most of all.

The wine and posh surroundings set our hormones in motion. That night, we made love with abandon. We'd always had a strong sexual connection; it was one of the things that had helped us push through the obstacles we'd faced thus far.

August brought record high temperatures. Summer school had been over for a few weeks, and I had nothing to do but sleep in and go to work—a welcome break. Luke decided to drive to Birmingham to visit his mother before Duke's school year—and the craziness— began. He left on a Thursday and planned to return Monday evening. It would be quiet without him around, but I knew I'd find something to fill my time.

That Friday, as I was about to walk over to Duke South to deliver the last of my reports, the sky unleashed a downpour. I stood just inside the door that led to the walkway between the hospitals and wondered how I'd make the five-minute trek to Duke South without getting myself and my reports soaking wet.

"Care to share my umbrella?" The distinctly baritone voice came from somewhere above my head. I turned around and saw a doctor, maybe six foot four or five, hovering above me holding a large black umbrella. In addition to his white lab coat, he wore glasses and a warm smile.

"Sure," I said, smiling back.

He pushed opened the door, opened his umbrella, and held it over our heads. "Mark Peters. Nice to meet you."

I looked up at him, avoiding his eyes. "Laura McConnell. I so appreciate this. I was totally unprepared." I glanced at the badge on his lab coat. *Cardiothoracic Resident.*

"I'm doing my residency in thoracic surgery," he offered. "I want to be a heart surgeon."

"Impressive!" I said. Clearly, the man was smart. I couldn't help noticing that he was handsome too.

He asked me what I did at Duke. I told him I was working in EEG to put myself through college at UNC.

"Good for you," he said.

We walked along for a few minutes without speaking.

"Hey, would you like to go to church with me on Sunday?" he said out of the blue. "Chapel Hill Bible Church. Ever heard of it?"

Is he asking me on a date? Sort of? I immediately thought of Luke, who was five hundred miles away. *He won't be back until Monday; he'll never know. Besides, it's church. What harm can that do?* I'd become aware of a widening distance between Luke and me. I wasn't sure if it was busyness or disinterest—but either way, the unexpected attention from Mark was nice.

"No, I haven't," I said. "But I've been thinking about finding a good church. So, yes. I'd love to."

As soon as the words came out, my pulse started throbbing in my ears.

"Great," he said, smiling.

What are you doing? You have a boyfriend, I reminded myself. *But this guy spoke to you for a reason,* I argued back. *And all he's done is ask you to church. Church, for Pete's sake. Maybe it's a sign.*

That night, the phone rang. I picked it up. It was Mark.

"Hey, I was thinking. How would you like to come over for dinner tomorrow night? I can show you my wine cellar. I'm digging one out under my kitchen."

A future heart surgeon who cooked and had a wine cellar? Well, that was intriguing. How could I resist?

So, the next night, Saturday, I drove to Mark's condo for dinner.

I'd told Luke I was spending time with a friend and he didn't ask any questions, so everything was good. Or was it? I kept telling myself that this was only a dinner invitation. That nothing would happen. That I could be cool. Besides, Luke and I both had friends of the opposite sex. What could possibly go wrong with a dinner that had started with someone inviting me to church?

Luke got home late Monday night. I'd gone over to his apartment to study and fallen asleep on the sofa. I woke up the moment he walked through the door, and immediately felt guilty.

I got up to greet him. "Hey, you!" he said, kissing me sweetly and pulling me toward him. As my chin rested on his shoulder, I closed my eyes. *What have I done?*

My dinner with Mark had been a lot of fun. He was smart and charming—definitely a catch. Just before dinner, he'd lifted the plywood board that covered the hole in his kitchen floor and led me down into the cave-like room that was his wine cellar. Luke and I drank wine, but this guy knew his stuff. As he pulled bottles out of their bins, Mark had talked about this vintage and that estate. He'd also proven to be an excellent cook, as I'd imagined he'd be. He'd served coq au vin and cheesecake for dessert—all homemade. When did a doctor possibly have time to cook? Much less dig out a wine cellar?

While we were eating dinner, the question I'd been dreading finally came.

"So, how has someone as pretty as you stayed single?"

Of course he assumed I was single. I hadn't given him any reason to think otherwise.

"I'm not exactly single. I'm separated. Getting divorced." I waited for the awkward silence.

"Oh," he said in a way that revealed his disappointment. "Were you married long?"

I knew anything I said would be inadequate. That it would be best to keep my mouth shut.

"Less than two years," I said, looking down. "We were young. We made a mistake."

As soon as I heard the words I'd uttered, I felt sick. I could wish my marriage away most days, but at times like this, the reality was inescapable. The shame flooded in.

His faint smile affirmed that he was trying to be kind. The rest of the evening we carefully stepped around the topic of my marriage. I definitely didn't mention Luke. Lord knows I'd given the man enough to ponder for one night.

The next day he picked me up at my apartment, and we made the twenty-minute drive to his church in Chapel Hill. On the way, we discussed his residency. He asked about my classes and my plans after college. I quickly surmised that Mark was the serious type, pleasant but not effusive. Was it his midwestern upbringing? The demands of his residency? Then it dawned on me: It wasn't any of those things. It was the fact that I was still married.

I suddenly felt uncomfortably self-aware. Oh well, there wasn't anything I could do to change that now.

As we pulled into the Chapel Hill Bible Church parking lot, I realized the time had passed quickly. We got out of the car and walked through the gravel parking lot to the front entrance. Just outside the door, people were buzzing around like bees. There was chatter and laughter, and I noticed that while there were some people my parents' age, the crowd was made up mostly of students.

"Hi!" said a redheaded girl in her early twenties who was obviously a greeter. She handed me a service bulletin. "First time?"

"Yes." I took the bulletin from her.

"Welcome! And be sure to pick up a loaf of freshly baked bread at the end of the service. Just inside this door."

"Thank you," I said. "That's kind."

We walked into the lobby and into a sea of fresh-faced students making their way into the sanctuary. I immediately sensed that there was something different about this place. Everyone seemed genuinely happy—joyful. It was unmistakable. I'd known that same joy many years ago, just after Lawrence died, in those days after I'd come to have faith in Jesus. He'd been my Joy.

Then I'd drifted away from all of that and tried to find joy in a land of my own making. And look how that had turned out. I'd lived a lie for so long. Keeping up a facade, hiding from my parents and the rest of the world, had left me exhausted. I wasn't sure I could do it anymore. I needed my life to match my values.

I caught a glimmer of something that Sunday morning, and I wanted more. It was one of those moments when you realize there's a huge gap between where you are and where you want to go, and there's nothing to do but start moving in that direction. I knew I couldn't make the mess I'd created just go away. I'd have to persevere to get to the other side. But now I had a glimpse of the peace and contentment that awaited me. It would be hard, but it would be worth it. And I believed I could do it, with God's help.

Mark called a few times after that. Then he stopped calling altogether. I knew it was all about Troy . . . and who could blame him? In Mark's eyes, being with me was the same as committing adultery, and he wasn't interested. Just as well. I had a boyfriend and an estranged husband, and I needed to figure out what I was going to do about both. But he was the reason I'd returned to church, and for that I was grateful.

I went back to the Bible Church Sunday after Sunday. There were so many people, I never worried much about running into Mark. I'd just walk in and sit in the second row and listen to Pastor Barber preach. I'd take notes and think about the dissonance I felt between my life outside the church doors and inside this nondescript room where I felt safe. I hadn't felt safe in years. Not in any of the places I'd called home. Not New York, or the beach. Or with Steve, who for the briefest of moments had felt like home. Maybe with Luke, a little, but even with him, the reality of my marriage constantly loomed over us.

Luke and I went on with our lives. We'd make love on Saturday, and then I'd go to church on Sunday. I felt like a hypocrite. I'd put on my good Christian girl face and greet fellow believers and think, *If they only knew*. It might be 1982, I reasoned, but this was the South, and living together before marriage was something that wasn't widely accepted. Oh, people did it, and everyone knew they did. But nobody talked about it. We all acted as though that kind of behavior just didn't exist.

And so I carried on, living at cross purposes with myself—wanting a clean slate with God while continuing my old way of life. I loved sex; I always had. Especially with a man I truly loved. But many of my sexual experiences had compromised my values. Maybe I didn't recognize it in the moment. But afterward, when I hated myself for what I'd just done and felt I'd give anything to take it back and knew I couldn't—then, I did.

That's when you feel the life flowing from you. It's a bloodletting—only worse, because it's your soul that's slipping away. You don't know how to stop the hemorrhaging, except to find someone with whom you won't feel that way. After so many mishaps, you know the search will prove futile. Still, you try.

I was now twenty-five. I'd been molested at ten, lost my virginity at eighteen, and married at twenty-one. In the past seven years, I'd been with dozens of men. I felt ashamed and disgusted. I couldn't change what had happened, but I desperately wanted a fresh start.

It wasn't that I was ready to give up sex—I just wanted it without the guilt.

Walking down the aisle seemed to be the only way, especially in my southern Christian culture. Luke and I had casually discussed getting married, and I'd assumed that if we stayed together, he'd propose. But I was just extricating myself from one marriage. Did I really want to fall into another one so soon?

In the few short weeks since I'd started going back to church, I'd realized I couldn't carry on this charade much longer. I was an imposter who'd grown weary. I had to try to find a way for my faith and my life to line up. I had a feeling it was just a matter of time before it would.

The fall semester was now in full swing. Since switching majors, my grades had improved. I was enjoying my classes, and with a year already behind me, I was beginning to feel as though I was actually going to get my degree.

Once again, I juggled work and school, with a little fun thrown in on the side. One day, between classes, I walked over to Franklin Street to grab an orangeade at Sutton's Drug Store. The campus was at its most beautiful; the leaves blazed in amber hues. As I waited at the counter to pay for my drink, I noticed that someone had torn off the latest cover of *Self* magazine and posted it by the register. "Chapel Hill Entrepreneur Starts Exercise Craze, pg. 43," read the headline. Underneath was a photo of a sweaty brunette flashing a radiant smile.

Curious, I went to the newsstand, picked up a copy, and began to read. Eleanor Nicholson, an Atlanta native and recent UNC grad, had just opened an exercise studio several miles from campus. *How did I miss this?*

I'd never really thought about exercise before. I'd loved riding my bike as a young girl. I'd taken the required gym classes in school. But I'd never thought about exercising for fun. Exercising to get healthier did sound like a good idea, though. I was intrigued, so I decided to check it out.

The next day, I drove my Beetle over to Village Plaza. I parked in front of a plain glass storefront with a sign overhead that read, "Nicholson Exercise Studio." It certainly didn't look like much. I wondered what all the fuss was about. There was only one way to find out, so I got out of my car and walked inside.

As my eyes adjusted to the light, I noticed that the "studio" was nothing but a large room with a wooden floor and a mirror covering the front wall. In one corner were a stack of exercise steps and a few oscillating fans. The furnishings were sparse. There was a card table just inside the front door scattered with note cards and copies of the *Self* magazine issue I'd seen at Sutton's, and a few chairs and a square end table with a lamp to my right.

"Hi! I'm Eleanor Nicholson!" called a friendly voice from the back of the room. I knew at once it was the woman from the cover of the magazine. She was short and shapely, and she approached me eagerly. "Hey there!" She stuck out her hand. Her smile stretched across her face and she exuded enthusiasm; I liked her immediately.

"Hi! I'm Laura." I offered my hand and she shook it with gusto, like I was a long-lost friend. Eleanor Nicholson looked about my age, but she was undoubtedly the most confident female I'd ever met.

"I saw the article in *Self* and wanted to stop by and see for myself." I paused. "Do you have a schedule of classes?"

"Sure do!" She handed me a piece of paper with a list of class dates and times. At the bottom was a list of prices.

Hmm, thirty dollars a month. I guess I could afford that.

"And your first class is free!" she said, as if reading my thoughts.

As I scanned the schedule, my eyes fell on words like *Step*, *Stretch*, and *Tone*. These everyday words suddenly seemed exotic and alluring. I looked up and took one last scan of the room. *This might be just what I need.*

I glanced at Eleanor. Her face was expectant.

"I'm in!" I said. "See you tomorrow at six!"

Pretty soon I was a regular at Nic's, as everyone called it. During the week, I'd drive back to Chapel Hill to take classes as soon as I finished up at the hospital. I stepped to "September," by Earth, Wind & Fire, and stretched to "Honesty," by Billy Joel, and little by little, I sensed a new confidence emerging—a confidence similar to the self-possession I'd admired in Eleanor that first day we'd met. Unlike modeling or sex, it had nothing to do with how I looked or performed. It was only about one thing: doing something for me without caring what anyone thought. When I pushed my body, I felt capable and self-assured and I wanted more. That, plus my emerging friendship with Eleanor, made it impossible to stay away.

Meanwhile, in early September, I joined the Bible Church choir. The director, Alan Jarrett, was a talented UNC grad who drew gifted singers. Every Wednesday night, about thirty of us would gather to practice in the sanctuary. We'd sight-read a piece, then run through the parts until we could sing them without hesitation. The result was transcendent. When we lifted our voices, Alan beamed, and we basked in his delight.

That semester, I made a new friend named Marty. Like me, Marty was an econ major. He was kind and he made me laugh. Best of all, he was a good listener. I thought back to the guy friends I'd had in high school. I could talk to them for hours and confide my deepest secrets without worry of judgment. Marty was that kind of friend, and I was grateful.

Sometimes on a whim we'd skip class and grab lunch at the counter at Sutton's. I'd talk to him about Luke and my faith and how I was torn over how to reconcile the two, and he'd always give thoughtful responses. We'd moan about econ, and then he'd tell me about some cute girl he wanted to ask out. We were buddies, nothing more, and it was effortless and good.

In November, Eleanor asked if I'd like to teach at the studio, and I immediately said yes. All I had to do was make a tape of music and commit to three or four classes each week. Best of all, I could keep my job at the hospital and teach after work and on weekends. I'd been working out regularly for three months now, and I was in great shape. I enjoyed toning and stretching, so we agreed that's what I'd teach. Besides needing a little extra income, I thought it would be fun—and it was. I soon made friends with the other teachers and drew a handful of loyal clients.

At the end of January, I finally gathered the courage to break up with Luke. I'd seen it coming for months, and had wrestled over my decision. Was I crazy to give him up? He was good to me and our chemistry was palpable, but he worked seven days a week and I felt lonely.

And there was the faith thing. I was a born-again Christian who had newly formed ideas about what a potential life mate should look like—someone who would read the Bible, pray with me, and attend church with me each Sunday. But I was with Luke, a lapsed Lutheran. In the end, our spiritual differences became a nonnegotiable for me.

It was one of those sad endings where nobody did anything wrong but you know in your gut that you're not well suited and it's best to say your goodbyes and move on before there's too much damage. When I told him how I felt, he agreed, reluctantly, that we should stop seeing each other. We'd both sensed it coming for months—there'd been a growing detachment between us. Still, it was bittersweet.

That night, I invited him to stay over. We slept curled up; I turned my face away so he couldn't see me cry. The next morning he kissed me tenderly, then walked out of my apartment and over to his own.

My newfound happiness revolved around Sam, a tall, blond, blue-eyed prelaw student who I'd started dating a few weeks after my breakup with Luke. It seemed that "all things had worked together for good," as we read in Romans 8:28. (That's the Bible verse people quote to you when something terrible has happened and they're trying to make you feel better.) I believed I had done the right thing in breaking up with Luke and God had blessed my efforts. Surely things had worked out for the best.

Sam and I had met at choir practice—he had a beautiful tenor voice. When he asked me to a Valentine's dance, I was giddy. We danced and drank punch in the basement of Cobb dormitory, and he kissed me for the first time. The next morning, we went to church. When he sat down in the seat next to me and took my hand and intertwined his fingers with mine, I knew we were officially a couple.

~9·6~

Chapter Twelve

March arrived, and with it my long-anticipated spring break. I decided to go to the Outer Banks to visit my brother and invited Sam to come along, mostly to show him off.

Horace, his wife, Emma, and their one year-old daughter, Olivia, lived in Kitty Hawk, in a house that had once been a gas station. You could see the ocean from their porch—or at least, you imagined you could as you stood there looking out across the beach road, past the majestic old cottages that had been built in the early 1800s, and over the windswept dunes that led to the sea. Horace and Emma had been married two years earlier behind one of those cottages, and Troy and I had sung. Nine months later, Olivia came along, a honeymoon surprise and a joy to us all.

Horace made boats and other things with his hands, and Emma grew sprouts and baked cheesecakes for a local restaurant. They had an organic garden and drank wine from pottery goblets. Olivia had just turned one, and she was bright and playful. I adored Olivia. She was the child I longed for, and everyone said she looked just like me. The three of them were happy, and I envied their simple existence.

Emma and Horace loved Sam right away. I knew they would. He was charming and engaging, and he was a natural with Olivia. Even though my breakup with Luke was still fresh, I was blissfully happy. My divorce papers had been filed and I'd soon be free and open to a new life, which I hoped might include Sam.

That night, Horace steamed fresh shrimp and we drank cheap wine and sat around the woodstove and talked until we were ready for bed. I insisted that Sam take the guest room. It was more private, and I was happy to sleep in the living room. We kissed good night in the dimly lit hallway and headed to bed.

In the middle of the night, I woke up on the sofa shaken to my core: *Holy shit. When was my last period?* At that moment, I didn't *think* I was pregnant—I knew it, as much as one can know it without a pink dot staring at them from a test stick. How could this have happened? I'd had an IUD for several years, so I'd never worried about this kind of thing. It had always taken care of itself.

I also knew that Luke was the father, since Sam and I had done nothing more than kiss—a refreshing change after so many years of failed relationships and perfunctory sex.

I thought back to an afternoon in mid-January. My apartment was being renovated, and Luke and I were making love in a sparsely furnished temporary space. The walls were bare, and the twin bed was too small for our tangle of flesh. Though neither of us knew it, it was the last time we'd be together that way.

Two months had passed since then. In the busyness of school and in the flush of new love, I'd overlooked one small thing: my period.

I woke Sam a few hours later, careful not to betray my mounting angst. We ate a quick breakfast, then packed our things in the car. I thanked Emma and Horace and gave Olivia a kiss. Then we got into Sam's Toyota, turned out of the driveway, and headed home.

The trip back to Durham was a blur. I moved through the minutes and hours in a state of shock, fighting back tears, barely saying a word. I kept glancing at Sam, praying he wouldn't pick up on the fact that I was upset—that something was wrong. As soon as he dropped me off, I called Luke.

"Can you come over?" I asked, my voice quivering.

"Of course," he said.

When I opened my door and saw Luke standing there, I broke the news, fell into his arms, and sobbed.

"What are we going to do?" I asked, gasping.

"We'll get married," he said nobly.

I pulled him closer and felt my stomach sink.

We'd parted ways for good reasons—and now I was with Sam. My being pregnant hadn't changed why we broke up, and being married certainly wouldn't fix it.

"I still love you," he whispered. "Everything's going to be okay."

I knew he would be a responsible, loving husband and a wonderful father, but it was too late. "I love you too," I replied—and realized the decision was mine alone to make.

I suddenly felt desperate. What was I going to do? I was graduating from college in just a few months. I'd worked hard to get this degree, and I wanted more than anything to get out and find a job. If I kept the baby, I wouldn't be able to finish school as planned. If that wasn't frightening enough, there was something that frightened me even more: telling my mother—the person in whom I rarely confided, the person with whom I'd chosen to wear a mask for much of my life.

I imagined the conversation: *Mama, I'm pregnant. Yes, Luke has offered to marry me.* Of course, she would want me to marry Luke and have the baby to avoid embarrassment for our family. I couldn't face her. It would be too hard.

Shame and fear twisted like a knife in my gut. If Sam knew, our relationship would be over, and I couldn't risk that. And what would the people at church say?

I regretted getting pregnant, and I was terrified of being found out. I grappled with my emotions as I pondered every possible scenario.

I emerged from my bewildered state to see Luke, who looked stricken. We'd been standing in the hallway, just an arm's length away from each other, for . . . how long? It seemed like hours, yet only a few moments had passed.

"There's only one thing to do," I said flatly. I met his eyes and saw a wrenching sadness.

I walked over to the kitchen counter, picked up the phone book, turned to the Yellow Pages, and looked under "A" for abortion, but it wasn't there. Instead it read, "*See 'Women's Health Services.'*" Even the Yellow Pages was too ashamed to print the word.

I ran my finger down the column and found the name of a clinic in Raleigh. It was Sunday night. I would call them in the morning.

I made an appointment for the following Saturday, and the week passed like ball bearings through a sieve. Luke asked if he could sleep over that week. He told me he wanted to be there for me, and I didn't want to be alone, so I said yes. Each night, we crawled into bed and held each other until we fell asleep. It felt strange but comforting, and I was grateful. I'd told Sam I was having a busy week and needed to focus on school. We lived ten miles apart—he was on campus; I was in Durham. So we chatted on the phone and he didn't seem suspicious. I was relieved.

I woke up and dressed each day and went to class and worked and tried to put Saturday out of my mind. Whenever the "A" word came to mind, I'd tell myself that I had thought through it, that I was making the best decision and there was no turning back. I confided in just one other person: Marty. We sat in the quad outside the econ building, and he listened and I cried, and he gave me a big hug and told me everything would be okay. I chose to believe him.

Saturday finally arrived. Luke met me at my place and together we stopped at McDonald's for breakfast. He brought my tray, and I sat and stared at the scrambled eggs and sausage on the Styrofoam plate and felt like I was going to throw up. We drove to Raleigh in silence and pulled into the clinic. I was numb, and I sensed that he was too.

I looked out through the windshield. There in the middle of the parking lot was a beautiful Bradford pear tree in full bloom. The contrast of beauty in that expanse of pavement struck me. It was March 20, the first day of spring.

I walked in and was handed a clipboard with lots of forms. I nervously filled them out and handed them to the receptionist, who smiled warmly. The waiting room was almost empty except for two other women, one middle-aged, the other slightly younger than me. Luke squeezed my hand and looked sad. Someone called me back to the procedure room and gave me a hospital gown to put on. I saw the instruments on the table. I was frightened.

It's not too late. I can still back out.

A young woman in her twenties walked me through what was going to happen and told me that she would be with me the entire time. She was soft-spoken and kind, and I was glad she was there.

The doctor came in and reassured me that it wouldn't take long, that it would hurt just a little, and that everything would be okay. *Why do people keep saying that?* I'd believed Marty when he'd said it, and Luke when he'd said it, but now it was different. I knew it wasn't okay. Not at all. I could stop right now and not go through with it. Then again, I'd searched my heart and found no recourse. Having a baby was not what I wanted, at least not now. And as much as I cared about Luke, I didn't want to be tethered to him for the rest of my life.

I was awake for the whole thing. I shut my eyes tight against the pain and consequence of my actions and escaped in my mind to someplace safe. Only a few random words spoken by the doctor broke through my semiconscious state: *Cramps. Tissue. Blood. Finishing up. Done.* That last word sounded so final. I immediately felt relief, then a deep sadness.

The doctor left the room and returned a few minutes later. He explained that there had been "complications"—my IUD had apparently lodged in my uterus, and it had made the procedure more difficult. Then, before I was discharged, more words: *Fever. Chills. Unusual bleeding. Emergency. Call.*

We drove home in silence. I felt empty, despondent. I hadn't dared ask the doctor, but I knew it was a girl. They'd repeatedly referred to her as "tissue," but I knew better—I'd been almost ten weeks along. Asking about the gender would have made her human, given her a heart, lungs, face, skin, fingernails. So I hadn't said a word. But I knew. I decided to name her Lily.

Luke dropped me off at my apartment that afternoon and offered to stay, but I told him no, I wanted to be alone. I called Sam and told him I had come down with the flu and needed to rest, and I would see him at choir practice on Wednesday, two days later. Luke called and stopped by to check on me a few times that next week, and then we went back to living as though it had never happened.

In early April, just a few weeks after my abortion, my divorce became final.

It was all I could do to push the ballpoint pen across the page to form the letters of my maiden name on the papers that had been sent to me in the mail. My signature equaled failure.

I signed it anyway. It was over. I was free. Free of Troy, free from the burden of raising a child. And yet, in both situations, I'd paid a price. I'd lost something in the process—vestiges of my innocence, pieces of my soul.

•••

A few weeks later, just as the spring semester was coming to a close, Eleanor convinced me to quit my job at the hospital and come work at her exercise studio. She'd outgrown her old location and had just rented a space on West Franklin Street, a large stand-alone brick building with a light-filled waiting area, two studios, and an ample dressing room.

Two months later, on an afternoon in mid-June, Sam called to ask if he could stop by and talk to me. When he arrived, he told me matter-of-factly that he was going to law school and didn't want to be tied down. I was hurt but mostly angry. Those things might be true. But what was also true was that his daddy was a pastor who didn't want his son dating a divorcée.

I told myself that it would never have worked out in the long run. For all my church-going, I was still the once-promiscuous girl whose marriage had failed. In Christian circles, I certainly wasn't virtuous.

Though I hid it well around my church friends, I fought a daily battle with the girl I used to be. My friends all seemed so spiritually together. Surely they didn't struggle this way. Then, one Sunday, I heard Pastor Barber read a passage from Saint Paul and realized I wasn't alone: "For I have the desire to do what is good, but I cannot carry it out. For I do not do the good I want to do, but the evil I do not want to do—this I keep on doing."

Whoa, that's me, I thought, squirming in my chair.

"Now if I do what I do not want to do," he continued, "it is no longer I who does it, but it is sin living in me that does it."

So it was sin's fault, not mine. Still, that didn't solve my problem.

"Who will rescue me from this body of death?" Pastor Barber's eyes swept the crowd. "Thanks be to God, who delivers me through Jesus Christ our Lord!"

I sat for a moment and let his words sink in. I knew in my head that what he was saying was true, but my heart was telling me a different story. Could God *really* deliver me? I wasn't Paul. And I certainly wasn't a saint. I was damaged goods. Surely I was too far out of the reaches of God's mercy to ever change.

I was groping my way back to faith, and I still had a long way to go. I wanted to believe I was worth rescuing, but I had my doubts. I was more convinced than ever that I'd wage this battle until I drew my last breath.

I graduated from college on a gray morning in mid-December. The small ceremony was held in a reception room at the Morehead Planetarium. My parents came, and Marty. It had been an intense two and a half years, and I was finally done.

Afterward, I walked to my car through the Old Chapel Hill Cemetery, passing gravestones dating back to the Civil War. I thought about Lily and pulled my collar up around my neck, chilled by more than the air.

~*⌒*~

Chapter Thirteen

On a Wednesday morning in May, I drove to Richmond, Virginia, to interview for a stockbroker position at Wheat First Securities. My cousin Brent, who was on the board of directors, had lined up the interview and put in a good word. I'd just finished talking with three VPs and I was hopeful. Now I was sitting in a windowless office, pondering my fate, while I waited for the personnel director to walk through the door.

I imagined what it would be like to live in Richmond and work for a prestigious brokerage firm. Enticing images filled my head—a brand-new car, posh apartment, stylish Brooks Brothers suits. *Don't get ahead of yourself. You don't even have an offer.* Still, I had my degree and felt more confident than I had in years. Whatever the day held, I knew I was ready to start making my way in the world.

After graduation, I'd moved back to Raleigh to live with Mama and Daddy until I could find a job and afford a place of my own. Mama had retired from teaching the year before, and Daddy now had a less demanding job at the paper. They had more time to work in the yard and watch TV, the two things they enjoyed most.

I'd been on my own for eight years, and it was strange to wake up in the four-poster bed I'd slept in as a girl. But I knew it was short-lived, and my parents weren't getting any younger, so I really didn't mind. I passed my days looking through want ads, sending out résumés, and taking classes at the new Nicholson Studio Eleanor had opened in Raleigh. I knew the perfect job was out there; I just had to give it time. But six months had passed since I'd graduated, and I was getting restless.

I heard a noise and turned to see Michael Parker, the personnel director, entering the room. He smiled, made his way to the desk, and sat down. He pulled up his chair, planted his elbows, and folded his hands.

The morning had gone well, and I allowed myself to believe he was coming to deliver good news.

"We'd love to hire you," he said, meeting my eyes, "but you're competing with two candidates who have just graduated with MBAs." He paused. "They're more qualified than you."

So my BA wasn't enough. *I* wasn't enough. It seemed to be the story of my life. It had been that way with Mama, with New York, and with most every guy I'd ever known.

"I understand," I said, finding my voice. "But I know I could do the job." *Stop. Now you sound desperate.*

"I'm sure you could," he said kindly. "But my hands are tied. That said, I think you'd be great in personnel. Any interest?"

In an instant, my lofty fantasies had crashed to the ground. Weeding through résumés in an airless office seemed like a dead end.

"I don't think so," I said as graciously as I could. "Thank you anyway."

I'd worked for two years to get my econ degree; I was going to be a stockbroker if it killed me. I'd been sidetracked enough. This time I was going to stay the course.

A few days later, as I was scanning the want ads, I remembered a conversation I'd had with Eleanor the previous summer. She was in transition, and I'd offered her my sofa for a few weeks. That afternoon, as we hung out, sipped Diet Cokes from bottles, and talked about life after graduation, she exclaimed in her typically boisterous voice, "Hey, Whitfield! You need a plan!"

She picked up the legal pad and pen that were lying on my coffee table, started making a list, and read it to me out loud. I'd thought her plan was ridiculous (for one, it involved moving to Atlanta—something I *did not* want to do). But I'd kept that piece of paper to remind me of our friendship, and of the fun we had together. And now that I'd hit a dead end with my job search and didn't know where to turn, I thought of her. Eleanor was always full of ideas.

She was in New York, staying with a friend from college, but she'd left a number where she could be reached. I picked up the phone and gave her a call.

"Hey, Nic!" I said when I heard her voice. "How's the Big Apple?"

"Great, darlin'! What's up?"

I told her what had happened at Wheat First and about my other unsuccessful attempts at finding a job.

"How would you like to work at McKinney?" Her question caught my attention.

McKinney was short for McKinney, Silver & Rockett; it was a prestigious Raleigh advertising firm where she had interned while studying journalism at UNC.

Advertising? Hmm, that could be cool.

"My friend Mary is pregnant, and she's looking for a replacement. Mind you, it's mostly a receptionist job. But it's a fabulous place to work, and you could get your foot in the door."

This wasn't finance, but it sounded glamorous. Certainly more glamorous than working in personnel. And I'd modeled for print ads. Surely that experience would help.

"Wow, that sounds amazing!" I said. "Would you be willing to call her?"

"Sure thing, sugar. I'm on it!"

The next day, Mary called and asked me to fax a copy of my résumé. Several days later, on a Tuesday, she called again and asked me to come in for an interview. I could hardly wait.

On Thursday, I drove downtown to the BB&T building. I took the elevator up to the fourth floor and entered an expansive lobby. Right in front of the elevator was a reception desk, and behind it a gorgeous blond with pale skin and bright red lips. I knew at once this was Mary, the person whose job I was applying for.

I gathered my confidence and walked over to her. "Hi, I'm Laura Whitfield." I offered her my brightest smile. "I'm here to see Mary Campbell."

"I'm Mary!" she said, beaming. "It's good to meet you!"

Mary had cornflower-blue eyes that danced with mischief. I liked her right away.

I imagined myself in her place, surrounded by an elaborate telephone system with lots of buttons and blinking lights, an electric typewriter, and a Rolodex, facing three elevators that constantly deposited and picked up an array of people—some visitors, some creative (it was easy to spot them), others in suits. We hadn't even discussed the job, but the atmosphere was lively and I sensed that I wouldn't be bored. I could totally see myself working there.

"Hungry?" she asked.

"Sure!" I smiled.

"Great. We can grab a sandwich and talk over lunch."

We went next door to the basement of Belk's Department Store, where we ordered sandwiches and Cokes from the grill. In the small lunchroom, Mary told me she'd been at her job for three years and loved it. Her husband, Phil, was an art director in the creative department, and they were expecting their first child.

"I want to come back after the baby is born," she said, "but I'll be moving into a new position. So you'll be working with Chick."

Charles "Chick" McKinney had started McKinney, Silver & Rockett back in 1969. Over the past fourteen years, it had grown into one of the most prestigious advertising agencies in the Southeast. The position was multifaceted; not only would I be the receptionist, I'd also be Chick's assistant—opening his mail, running personal errands, and screening his calls.

"Chick likes everything a certain way," she said, "but he's brilliant."

From the stories Eleanor had told me and everything I'd read, I knew he was a legend. I was anxious to meet him.

After lunch, we entered the sleek black building and took the elevator to Chick's office on the third floor. On the way, Mary explained that the agency occupied three floors: the account executives and media on the fourth, creative on the third, and the business office on the ninth. Chick had an executive office on the fourth floor, though he spent most of his time in the creative department with the writers and art directors.

"Creating is his first love," she said. "He wants to be right in the center of it."

We walked down a long hall with elegant black-and-white tiles and arrived at an unassuming office with an open door. I waited as Mary stuck her head inside.

"Laura's here," she said. She turned back to me, smiled, and motioned for me to go inside. "Just come upstairs when you're finished. Good luck!"

As I entered the room, the man sitting behind the glass and chrome desk looked up. Then he stood and walked toward me. Chick McKinney was just as Eleanor had described him: average build and height, with tortoiseshell glasses perched on the end of his nose and dressed in an impeccable (and, I suspected, custom) suit.

Resting in the corner of his mouth was a large cigar—unlit—which he promptly removed. "Chick McKinney," he said, holding out his hand.

I shook it firmly.

"Sit down," he said in a very refined southern accent.

"Thank you," I said, noticing at once that the room was messy—there were papers scattered on his desk and index cards scrawled with notes taped to the wall. Between the windows were large ad campaign posters. The headlines were eye-catching. I was enthralled—and suddenly nervous. I was sitting face-to-face with Chick McKinney, and all I knew at that moment was that I really wanted this job.

"I consider the receptionist position the most important one in the agency," he said with all seriousness. "You're the face people see when they walk off the elevator. Their first impression."

"I understand," I said.

"Can you keep a confidence?" he asked.

"Yes. Yes, I can."

"Good, because that's paramount. I get a lot of new business calls. A company may be thinking of switching agencies and exploring the possibility of working with us. One call could mean potentially millions in business. If word got out . . . well, you understand." He studied my face. "It would be your job to field those calls. Can you do that?"

That sounded like a lot of pressure, but now I was even more intrigued. "Yes, I can."

"Excellent. Do you have any questions?"

"No, I don't think so. Not right now."

"We're going to make a decision in the next few weeks. We'll be in touch." He stood up, walked around his desk, and shook my hand.

"Thank you again," I said. "It was a pleasure to meet you."

...

Exactly two weeks later, I got the call.

"Wonderful!" said Daddy when I told him my news. He and Mama were sitting on the screened-in porch drinking ice cream floats made with Pepsi and vanilla ice cream, a favorite from my childhood.

"That's great, honey," said Mama between frothy sips.

I knew they were relieved that I'd be able to support myself. And who could blame them? I was twenty-six and I'd spent the past eight years trying to find my way: first at the beach, then in New York, and finally in an ill-fated marriage. I now saw that marriage as a godsend. A wake-up call. I'd attached myself to Troy—and all the other men before him—like an IV line, then watched passively as my identity drained away. I couldn't let that happen again. I was done with unhealthy relationships. It was time to thrive on my own.

I began my job at McKinney on a sweltering Monday in early June. Mary's due date was only three weeks away, and we had a lot to cover before she went on maternity leave.

The first day, we walked around the agency and she introduced me to everyone—sixty-five employees in all. I was responsible for learning their names and the names of their family members, and our clients' names as well.

Next, we dove into the switchboard, which looked like a miniature spaceship from *Star Wars*. Over five hundred calls a day came through the switchboard, and it would be my responsibility to answer each one. "McKinney, Silver & Rockett! How may I direct your call?"

I listened and watched attentively as Mary showed me in great detail what I'd be doing. There were client calls to be directed and Chick's new business calls to screen. In between calls, it was my job to greet visitors, pass along messages from one department to another, review résumés, type letters and run errands for Chick, and open his mail.

In the three weeks between starting and Mary's leave, I quickly picked up my duties and began to feel at home. I'd been right when I'd sensed the job would be exciting. I was front and center for all the comings and goings at the agency. I loved the job and my days passed quickly.

Advertising drew a lot of interesting people. But my favorite person by far was Jack Braman, the account executive for Piedmont Airlines. Jack was classically tall, dark, and handsome in a Cary Grant sort of way—always turned out in the most stylish clothes, every strand of his jet-black hair slicked down in place. I was almost certain Jack was gay, and I loved gay men. I'd modeled with a few gay guys in New York and discovered they made the best friends. They were great listeners. And there was no competition or jealousy like there was with many of the females I'd encountered. Jack was playful and classy. He was also smart. The clients loved him, and so did I.

I soon became proficient at juggling several things at once; I could answer the phone, greet a visitor, and sort mail with ease. Around ten each morning, I'd ring my friend Robin to cover the switchboard. Then I'd head to Chick's office in the creative department to drop off his mail and see if he needed anything.

"Hey, old gal! How are you doing?" Chick greeted me this way each morning. One of the first things Mary told me was that Chick often called his employees "old gal" or "old boy" because he had a hard time remembering their names.

Surely he hadn't forgotten mine.

"Just fine!" I'd reply in my cheeriest voice. I'd hand him his mail, and then we'd go over his schedule for the day. He'd alert me of any calls or visitors he might be expecting, and I'd take notes.

After finishing with Chick, I'd take advantage of being away from the desk to walk around the creative department. I enjoyed going into the bullpen, as they called it, to see the latest ads the graphic designers were working on. Then I'd wander down to where the copywriters worked. Being a copywriter at McKinney was a coveted position. I'd begun to want more than anything to become a copywriter, to see my words in print ads and hear them on TV.

I'd walk past each office and poke my head in to say hi to Malcolm or Neal or Andy Benson. Sometimes they'd invite me to come in and chat. I'd go over to their desks and ask what they were working on, and they were always happy to show me. Whether it was a destination campaign for Piedmont Airlines, a brochure for Royal Caribbean Cruise Line, or a TV spot for North Carolina National Bank, I found it fascinating. I loved reading their catchy headlines and clever tags. Clearly, they loved their work and were good at it.

I imagined sitting behind a desk with a typewriter looking out over the Raleigh skyline. *I could do that.* But how?

Each of these writers had training. And they'd been at it a long time. They weren't junior copywriters just out of college. They'd worked at a number of agencies and had ended up here, working for Chick McKinney, at one of the most prestigious agencies in the Southeast.

I might be the receptionist, but I wasn't going to be one forever. I was determined to convince Chick that he should hire me as a writer. Obviously, I had to show him I could write. He also needed to see that I was collaborative and could work with clients. It was a long shot—like leaping over the Grand Canyon—but I was willing to take that risk. I just had to come up with a plan and execute it. I was confident my coworkers would help.

By September, I'd been with the agency for three months. I was getting on my feet financially and wanted to start doing a little decorating in my new home, a second-floor apartment in a two-story, very southern house in Cameron Village, the part of town where Mama and Daddy had lived when the boys were little—before I'd come along.

I had a Milton Glaser poster that Luke had given me when we were together. I'd never had it framed, so I thought I'd start there. A friend had told me The Print Shop in Chapel Hill did excellent work, so I decided to give them a try.

I hopped in my newly purchased Honda and sped down I-40 to Highway 54, which took me to University Mall. I parked behind the mall and walked to the entrance closest to The Print Shop.

The shop reminded me of a tiny art gallery. Every inch of wall space was covered with posters. In the middle of the floor were bins containing art prints. As I scanned the visual feast, I felt as though I'd finally entered adulthood. The thought made me smile.

I flipped through a few bins—Van Gogh, Picasso, Klimt—before making my way to the counter. Standing in front of me, smiling, was a charming young man about my age. He was maybe six feet tall with a mane of thick, sandy hair like a horse's tail and delectable brown eyes.

"Hi, can I help you?" he asked in an offhand way.

I'll say. I wasn't sure what it meant, but I detected a current passing between us.

"Yes, thanks. I need to get this framed." I showed him the poster.

"What did you have in mind?"

"Simple, I think. Silver."

"Ahh," he said, "we can do silver."

He took the poster, measured it, and showed me several options to choose from. Try as I might, it was difficult to focus. He was the cutest guy I'd seen in a long time. And in just a few minutes, I'd be making the thirty-mile drive back to Raleigh. I had to think fast.

I picked a simple silver frame. It would look good over my cream-colored love seat with the chrome trim.

"We can have this ready next Wednesday. Is that all right?"

"Yes, perfect," I said.

He slid the invoice across the counter and I looked at it. A little pricey, but hey, I was a working girl and could afford it. I pulled out my checkbook, filled in the amount, tore out the check, and handed it to him.

"Uh, would you like to go out for a drink when you get off?"

I immediately felt stupid. Why didn't I wait for him to make the first move?

He looked up at me. His lips slowly spread into a sly grin. "Yeah, I'd like that."

Whew. I was right about that current. "I'm Laura, by the way. Laura Whitfield."

"Yes, I saw your name on your check."

I blushed.

"Hugh Jenkins," he said. "Where should I meet you?"

"How about Pyewacket? They have a nice bar."

"Sure." He gave me a curious smile.

I looked at my watch. It was eight thirty.

"Nine thirty-ish? I have to close. I'll see you there." He smiled again, but this one was more relaxed.

"Great. See ya." I turned and walked out, feeling his eyes on my back.

That went well, I mused. It had been a long time since I'd gone out with a guy; I was eager to see where this current would lead.

I drove straight to Pyewacket, walked in, found an empty spot at the bar, and ordered an oaky California chardonnay. I glanced at the clock just above the liquors. It was 8:55. I'd have a bit of a wait, but I didn't mind.

I nursed my glass of wine for forty-five minutes. By 9:40, I was sure he'd stood me up. My face grew hot. Who could blame him?

I was a complete stranger who'd walked into his shop and asked him out for a drink. Maybe he was worried that I was just another neurotic female and decided to stay away. *Give it five more minutes*, I told myself.

At 9:45, he walked through the door. I was reminded at once of how attractive he was—boyish, like Robert Redford's character in *The Way We Were*. He scanned the room and our eyes met.

"There you are," he said as he made his way toward me. He pulled out a barstool and sat down.

"Scotch and water," he told the bartender.

"That was my drink in New York," I said.

"New York?"

"Hmm," I said, thinking a little mystery might be just the thing to balance my initial come-on.

"Sounds intriguing," he replied, smiling ear to ear like a Cheshire cat.

"I'd rather talk about you," I said.

He told me he'd gone to UNC and majored in journalism at the "J-School," as it was called. As an undergrad, he'd been a writer and editorial cartoonist for the student newspaper, the *Daily Tar Heel*. He'd graduated a little over a year ago and thought he might want to go into advertising. For now he was working at The Print Shop and doing some freelance writing on the side. He lived in an apartment on Ransom Street, near campus, with two other guys.

"I've also done some professional bike racing."

A biker. Sexy.

"I shave my legs," he added. "All the pros do it."

"Ahh," I said, pretending I knew all along.

I told him about working for Chick and how I hoped to become a copywriter one day.

"So you work at McKinney," he said with reverence. Every J-School student knew about McKinney. Getting a job there right out of school was the Holy Grail. A few UNC grads were hired as junior copywriters each year, but the competition was tough.

We chatted about my time in New York. I briefly mentioned my marriage, which now seemed in the distant past. He appeared completely unfazed. We talked about our families; his mother was from the eastern part of the state and had the same maiden name as my grandmother.

"Whoa, you don't think we're cousins, do you?" He chuckled nervously.

"I hope not!" I said with conviction.

After we paid for our drinks, he asked for my phone number.

I wrote it down on a cocktail napkin. "Here you go."

He picked up the napkin and studied it as though it contained some ancient code. Then he looked up and gave me an impish grin. "So, Laura Whitfield, mind if I give you a call?"

"Yes, please," I said with delight.

Hugh and I talked until eleven thirty, and then I made the forty-five minute drive home. I crawled into bed at twelve thirty, exhausted.

At six thirty my alarm sounded. I had to be at work by nine. My foot hit the floor with a thud; I'd had too much to drink and too little sleep the previous night. But thoughts of Hugh infused my brain like shots of espresso and quickened my movements. As I showered and dressed, I imagined him calling, our conversation, and when I might see him again. I knew I was jumping ahead of myself, but last night had gone well and I felt certain that he wanted to get to know me better.

He called me after work that evening. I'd been running on adrenaline all day, and just hearing his voice calmed me down.

We went out a week later. Soon, we were inseparable. Every once in a while, I'd meet him on a weeknight for dinner. Mostly, we spent weekends together. When five thirty rolled around each Friday, I'd silence the switchboard, grab my purse, and head for the elevator. I'd dash to my apartment, check the mail, pack a change of clothes, and head straight to Ransom Street.

As soon as dinner was over, we'd go upstairs and lock ourselves away from his two roommates. That's where we stayed pretty much all weekend, coming up for air only to go to the bathroom, shower, and eat. (I hadn't found a new church since my move, and suddenly finding one didn't seem so urgent.)

Sometimes we'd lie in bed after making love and talk for hours. We had so much in common. We'd had similar upbringings, attended the same college, and had many of the same interests. I was especially impressed by his artistic skills; for my birthday that November, he drew and framed a caricature of Woody Allen because he knew I was a huge fan. I loved *Annie Hall* and *Manhattan* because they reminded me of my days in New York.

Things went along smoothly until one Friday night in mid-December. The holidays were quickly approaching, and I was looking forward to showing Hugh off to my extended family at our yearly Christmas gathering. I arrived at his place at the usual time, around six thirty. I walked in and there he was, standing at the stove, making dinner.

"Fried eggs?" he asked.

I guessed that the refrigerator was nearly empty and we were "making do," as Mama always said. "Sure. How are you?" I walked over and kissed him on the neck.

He looked over at me with a spatula in his hand. "Not bad." He gave me a faint smile.

Something was wrong. I looked down at the two eggs in the pan, like two continents situated perfectly side by side, pre-continental drift. It was an omen.

Over those fried eggs and coffee, he told me he was moving to

Chicago to pursue a job in advertising. I felt an odd mix of happiness and dismay. I'd known from the moment I'd met him that he might not always be around. He'd said as much that first night at Pyewacket. He was extremely talented, and his best shot at a job was in Chicago or New York. I wanted that for him. Still, things were good between us. I hated to see him go.

We spent the weekend making love with urgency, knowing our time together would soon come to an end. Mostly, we lay side by side in his twin bed and gazed at each other. We had an almost telepathic relationship. We spoke so often without words, though we both loved them. With us, they weren't necessary. It was just one of the things I would miss.

We briefly discussed whether we wanted to keep seeing each other after he'd moved away. After all, we'd done a pretty good job of managing a long-distance relationship. But the eight hundred miles between Raleigh and Chicago would make it nearly impossible. He was barely getting by financially, and I certainly couldn't afford the airfare back and forth. We finally decided it was best to let it go.

I stopped my weekend visits to Chapel Hill—a weaning away of sorts—and for the next three weeks, we only spoke on the phone. On the first Friday of the New Year, he left.

Everything about that day was cold. My heart felt numb, like fingers needing gloves that I'd lost.

It was one of the few times in my life when I'd experienced that kind of paradigm shift where the way you used to think doesn't work anymore and you suddenly see things in a new light. I'd gotten into the habit of driving to see Hugh every Friday, and I didn't know what to do with myself. So I sat on the sofa in my living room as night fell and let my thoughts drift. I thought about Hugh. In many ways, ours was the most mature relationship I'd ever had. We genuinely liked and respected each other. We enjoyed being together but both valued our space.

Then I thought about Steve, Troy, and Luke. Each of those relationships had been born out of insecurity—and Steve in particular out of sheer lust. I'd made a string of bad choices; now I regretted how careless I'd been. I sat there in the dark, hugged my knees to my chest, and cried, quietly at first, then loudly, from a place deep inside. It had been months since I'd cried, and it felt good.

When I was in New York, I thought I'd be twenty forever. That I had all the time in the world to make things right. I was now twenty-seven. I'd wasted so much time—floundering, groping—and there was no getting it back. All I could do was move forward and try to do better. But I couldn't do it alone. I knew that now. I'd pushed God aside for years, and look where that had gotten me. If I was going to turn my life around, I'd need His help. I'd need to figure out what I wanted.

What do I want?

A deep connection. Chemistry, of course. But also someone who shared my faith. I knew it seemed counterintuitive; finding that combination in one man was a long shot. Still, I could hope. I wasn't in a hurry to date. And while I hoped to remarry, I wasn't ready for a serious relationship, much less marriage. Not yet. I needed time to get over Hugh. For now, I was content to be alone.

In the days and weeks that followed, I turned my attention back to work. I went in each day and did my job. But Hugh's absence did more than just leave me lonely; it left me thinking. If he could make it in advertising, why couldn't I? Yes, he'd studied copywriting in school; he had that advantage. But why couldn't I learn?

And why not now? With Hugh in Chicago, I could focus on this one thing with nothing to distract me.

I began brainstorming ways to position myself for a junior copywriting job at McKinney. I was already friends with the copywriters.

Laura Whitfield

I could learn a lot from them. I also needed to study great copy. I'd start reading our ads, especially the headlines. I'd take home copies of *Communication Arts*, which featured the ad industry's best of the best. It was a start.

Chapter Fourteen

March came and brought relief from the long winter. The official softball season had kicked off at the agency, and there was a buzz in the air. After work I attended games, pulled for my colleagues, and went out with the gang to Players' Retreat to enjoy a few beers.

I was still taking a break from dating, except for a few dinners with a guy I'd known back in college named Chase Reynolds. We'd met just outside Carroll Hall the spring semester of my senior year and quickly become friends. He'd just completed his MBA and had landed a job at AT&T in Washington, DC. He was smart and polished–the quintessential preppy. I found him handsome, in a clean-cut sort of way. He'd already moved to DC and was living in a townhouse in Georgetown. I decided to stay open and accept his invitations when they came.

I'd just returned from lunch on an uneventful Monday and was settling back into my typing when the elevator opened. A group of creatives stepped off and walked past me on their way to meet with the Piedmont team. That's when I saw him: a striking guy with dark brown hair, wire-rimmed glasses, and a full mustache.

Who's that? I thought, trying not to stare. I had the entire agency roster in front of me; surely I knew his name.

I scanned the list. *Ah, Drew Wagner.* He was a graphic designer who stayed holed up in his office. I knew I'd seen him at the softball games, but I'd never given him a second thought. Until now.

Twenty minutes later, he sauntered by my desk, stepped up to the elevator, and pushed the down button.

"Hey," I said, "I'm Laura. I don't think we've formally met."

"Drew," he said, walking over. "Drew Wagner. But you probably knew that."

"Yep, that's my job," I said, hiding the fact that I'd been clueless until a few minutes earlier.

The elevator pinged.

"Nice to finally meet you," he said before walking to the elevator and getting on.

When the door closed, I sat for a moment, smiling. What was it about him? He certainly was attractive. But he was also quiet and unassuming. Appealing qualities.

On my break, I went straight to Jack's office to do a little sleuthing.

"Drew? Oh yeah, nice guy. Really talented. He's doing some great work on our new campaign."

He gave me a knowing look and asked, "Why?" He raised his eyebrows as his mouth broadened into a grin.

"Just curious. And he's cute."

"Oh, I see," he teased. Jack was like a big brother to me by now.

"Is he dating anyone?" I asked.

"I don't know, but you could probably find out."

McKinney resembled a small village. If you wanted to know anything, all you had to do was ask a few key people. I decided to approach Malcolm, my favorite copywriter, who played on the softball team with Drew. Maybe he'd know.

"I'm not sure," Malcolm said. "I've seen a girl with him a few times, but that's all I can tell you." He smiled at me. "He's a great guy."

I didn't see Drew for a few days. Then, on Wednesday, the elevator opened and he walked out.

I was ready. "Hey, would you like to have lunch sometime?"

"Sure," he said. I thought I caught a slight smile behind his mustache. "What'd you have in mind?"

"I like Side Street," I said, "and it's easy to get in and out."

"Sounds good. I can't get away today. How about tomorrow?"

"Tomorrow's great," I said, relieved. "Noon?"

"I'll meet you here. We can take my car." He smiled, then walked past my desk to the Piedmont hall.

I liked his understated manner. I couldn't wait.

Our lunch was fun. Side Street was an old turn-of-the-century building that had once been a grocery store. With its white tablecloths and scattering of antiques, it was charming and cozy. We found a table and sat down. He ordered the Moby Dick and I got the Holey Hen with chips.

Drew immediately made me feel comfortable. He told me he'd been born in Orlando and had moved to Raleigh when he was nine. That his dad was a wholesale news distributor and his mom had a part-time accounting job. He had two brothers; he was the middle child. He'd studied graphic design at East Carolina University—the college Horace and my parents had attended and where Daddy had later served on the board of trustees. ECU was known for its exceptional arts program. I was impressed.

I told him about my family, a little about Lawrence, about my adventures at the Outer Banks and in New York. That I was a UNC grad. And that I'd been married and divorced.

"No children," I said, knowing that might be a deal breaker.

He was quiet. I realized it was a lot to take in.

"I'm a Christian," he said, out of nowhere.

Uh-oh. It's my divorce. Is that his way of telling me I'm not good enough?

"Me too," I said. I certainly hadn't been the poster child for righteous living. But I did understand faith, and it wasn't about my being good. It was about grace. And forgiveness. No matter how big a mess I'd made of things.

He shared how in college he'd hit a low point emotionally. He was sitting in his living room one Sunday, feeling depressed and hopeless. He turned on the TV and heard a televangelist give a call for people to accept Jesus as their Savior. So he prayed the prayer that flashed on the screen—and after he became a Christian, his life turned around. He started going to church, and not long after became president of a Christian organization on campus called InterVarsity.

I listened with rapt attention as images of televangelist Jim Bakker and his heavily mascaraed wife, Tammy Faye, swirled through my mind.

"Wow. That's some story," I said. I guess God really used those gospel hawkers after all.

"Do you go to church?" he asked. From his question, I guessed he knew, as I did, that being a Christian and church attendance didn't necessarily go hand in hand.

"I did growing up. And when I was at Carolina. But not much in between." I paused, realizing I hadn't really answered his question. "So, no. But I want to go back."

"I go to a great church. Asbury Methodist. You'd like my pastor, Joe Merritt."

"I grew up Methodist," I said. "Maybe I can come with you sometime."

"That'd be great!" he said, sounding pleased. For a few minutes he didn't say anything. Then he looked up. "Just so you know, I'm seeing someone. Her name is Angie."

Whoa. That came out of nowhere. I thought of Chase, my friend in DC. "That's okay," I said. "So am I. Nothing serious. We've just been on a few dates."

"Same for Angie and me." He glanced down, then back up at me. "So, you free next weekend?"

213

"Yeah, sure!" I said, thinking he must not be too involved with Angie if he was asking me out.

"Would you like to come to my place in Cary?" Cary was a suburb of Raleigh, about fifteen minutes away. "I'll make dinner and show you my garden. You can meet my cat, Shep."

"Shep?" I chuckled. "That's a funny name for a cat."

"I know. My crazy roommate, Craig, named him. If he's around, you'll get to meet him too."

"Perfect," I said.

Our dinner date was, indeed, perfect. Drew served sautéed scallops and fresh green beans from his garden. I met Shep. And Craig. Everything felt so natural—like I didn't have to try and be anyone other than myself. I liked that he was creative and had a great sense of humor. For me, there was nothing better than being with a man who could make me laugh.

A week later, we went on our second date. He brought me home after a nice dinner at Irregardless Café and stepped inside my apartment to kiss me good night, and I took him by the hand and led him to my bedroom. One thing led to another, and before I knew it we'd fallen on the bed and melded together.

Our lovemaking was urgent yet constrained. When it was over, we were both quiet.

"I'm sorry," I whispered. "I didn't see that coming." Who was I kidding? I'd initiated it. Still, I sensed that maybe it had been too much, too soon.

We chatted casually while we dressed. Then we walked into the living room, which was dark. Without saying a word, he kissed me tenderly and left. I closed the door behind him and let the full weight of my body fall against it. *Here you go again. Rushing in.* In that moment, I felt like that nineteen-year-old girl peering into Steve's bathroom mirror the night I lost my virginity. What was wrong with me? I'd been reckless then and I was reckless now. Hadn't I learned anything?

I walked to the kitchen, opened the refrigerator, and reached for a half-finished bottle of wine. I pulled it out, found a clean glass, and filled it. Wine would still that voice. Or at least calm my nerves. I took a sip. *You're not that girl. You've learned a lot.*

That was more like it. A voice I could live with.

I wasn't a bad person. I'd pulled myself together after New York. I'd survived a divorce. And an abortion. I'd completed college. And I was working on becoming a writer. Yes, I'd been impulsive when it came to men. And I was trying to change that.

March turned to April, and Drew and I went out every other weekend, like clockwork. On alternating weekends, he'd see Angie. She stopped by the agency once and they went out for lunch. She was younger than me, and pretty, and meeting her was awkward.

Sometimes, when we were together, I'd get up the nerve to ask about her. She was the proverbial elephant in the living room, but I couldn't help it. He never said much, just enough to keep me wondering.

On the Saturday nights when I sat at home, knowing he was with her, I was jealous. I tried not to be, but I couldn't help it. I'd imagine them together—laughing, holding hands, kissing. I'd sit down at my piano and play Gershwin tunes to try and push it away. But it never helped.

How long was I willing to keep this up? I wasn't sure. Still, something told me he was worth it. This felt different. It wasn't just about chemistry or sex, though that certainly was part of it. I was comfortable around Drew. He seemed steady and reliable, two things I'd recently begun to seek out in a man. Once, at church,

I'd seen him playing with a little boy; I thought he'd make a great father. He was kind and gentle and loving. I wasn't sure where this was going, but I was willing to wait and see.

One Sunday morning in late April, Drew and I went to church together. I'd been with him twice and really enjoyed the service. His friends were nice and treated us as though we were a couple, which I liked. But during the sermon I felt restless and distracted by thoughts of him being with Angie. Even though I'd agreed to it, I didn't know how much longer I could live with our arrangement.

The following Friday, Chase called. He sounded excited. "Hey, whatcha doin' next weekend?"

"Not sure, why?" I asked, curious.

"I wanted to know if you'd like to come to DC?"

My mind reeled. A weekend in DC could be fun. But what about Drew? Driving almost three hundred miles to spend a weekend with someone implied commitment. What would he think? It was an "off" weekend for us—he'd be seeing Angie. I could go and not say anything. But I didn't want to do that. I needed to be transparent if I wanted this to work.

I thought about Chase. If I went, what message would I be sending him? Was I just using him? Did I really think we had a future? Except for a kiss on the cheek, we hadn't engaged in any kind of physical intimacy. Surely if I went to see him, we'd end up sleeping together. Did I want that? I really liked Drew. And in my heart I was hoping he'd choose me. Did I want to risk losing Drew for a weekend with Chase? I wasn't so sure.

"That sounds great," I said. "But I may have plans . . . I've been seeing someone."

"Really? Who?"

"His name is Drew." I told him that we worked together, that we'd only been going out for a few weeks.

"I'm inviting you to DC, for Pete's sake!" he said, emboldened. "You *have* to come. You can stay at my place in Georgetown. I'll show you around. Take you to a couple of nice restaurants. It'll be fun!"

It was tempting. Still, I hesitated. I needed time to think. "Can I let you know in the next few days?"

"Sure," he said.

We chatted for a few more minutes.

Right before we hung up, he made a final plea. "Blow him off! Come! It would be great to see you."

One thing about Chase: he was persuasive. And Drew was still seeing Angie. Why shouldn't I go?

I hung up the phone and spent the rest of the evening and all day Saturday wrestling with what to do. I finally picked up the phone and called Drew.

"A friend from college invited me to come to DC for the weekend," I said as casually as I possibly could. "A guy friend."

"DC? Are you going?" His voice sounded compressed.

"I don't know. I mean, you're still seeing Angie. Why shouldn't I?" I'd acquiesced for weeks. Now I felt defiant.

"That's true." His tone softened. "But it's different now. I'm starting to have feelings for you."

"Really?" I'd never been quite sure, given his sometimes guarded demeanor. This changed everything.

"Yeah," he said.

"I really like you too. But I don't want to get hurt. I mean, Angie is younger than me, and she's pretty."

"So are you," he said. "You need to decide what you want. If you go to DC, I'm afraid it'll be over with us."

I couldn't believe it. *An ultimatum? Where did that come from?* My anger started to rise. "You need to decide too," I countered. "It's not fair to lay it all on me." I was putting up a tough front, when all I wanted to do was cry.

"You're right. I'll let you know."

"When?"

"Tomorrow. I'll stop by after church. Will you be home?"

"Yeah, sure," I said.

I hung up the phone. What a conundrum. Drew? Or Chase? In so many ways, my fate was in Drew's hands. I felt strongly that I should stay in Raleigh and not ruin things with Drew. But what if he chose Angie over me? At least by tomorrow, I'd know.

Around one o'clock the next afternoon, Drew appeared at my door. I'd put on a white eyelet skirt and top and made sure my makeup was perfect. I wanted to look my best.

"Wanna go for a ride?" he asked.

"Sure," I said.

As we walked down the stairs, out of my apartment, and over to his car, I was nervous.

We got into the car and I put on my seat belt. Though I'd made my decision to decline the invitation from Chase and hold out for Drew, I couldn't handle the suspense. I turned to him. "So, did you make up your mind?" I braced myself for the worst.

"Yes, I told Angie I want to be with you."

"You did?" I reached over, put my arms around his neck, and buried my head on his shoulder. He gave me a big hug. We stayed that way for a few moments before I pulled back and looked at him.

"I'm so happy!" I gushed.

"Me too."

Drew and I soon fell into a comfortable rhythm of being together. With Angie no longer in the picture, our every-other-weekend dates became weekly.

While we'd navigated the choppy waters of Chase and Angie, however, we were still treading water at work. We wondered if there was a company policy about dating coworkers. We had no clue, and we were afraid to ask. We'd just started seeing each other. What if we were told we had to stop?

We discussed the fact that Mary, the former receptionist, had met her husband, Phil, when they were both working at McKinney. They'd dated and eventually married. As long as we kept our relationship out of our work, we told ourselves, it would be okay.

In addition to our weekly dates, we continued attending church together. Everything about Asbury seemed familiar from the beginning. Drew's friends were cordial, his pastor welcoming. I soon felt right at home.

After a service one Sunday, the youth pastor, Nate Daniels, came up to us and asked if we'd like to work with the twenty or so teenagers who attended the church.

"It's easy," he said. "You just show up on Sunday nights. Hang out with them, play games. Be available if they need to talk."

It sounded easy enough. And we liked that it was something we could do it as a couple, so we agreed. I'd attended MYF (Methodist Youth Fellowship) growing up, and fondly remembered a youth pastor named Ed. After Lawrence died, I'd felt lost, and he'd been especially understanding and kind. Maybe we could make a difference too.

Sunday nights soon became the highlight of our week. Drew was a natural. He was funny and easygoing, and the quieter kids felt comfortable around him. The girls were sweet and chatty and self-conscious. A group of five middle-school girls—Rachel, Joy, Abby, Kate, and Gracie—would cluster around me the moment I arrived. They reminded me of myself at that age—naive, full of hope. It made me smile. Sometimes they'd ask about my modeling days, and I'd tell them the glamorous parts.

"It was hard to support myself," I'd add, sprinkling in a bit of reality. "I had to wait tables to make ends meet." But I left out the rest. The things better left unsaid.

In those moments, I'd think back to that awful afternoon in New York when I'd stood in front of my bathroom mirror and gazed at my reflection. If eyes truly were a window to the soul, mine had revealed a cache of secrets, failure, and shame. I'd known I was destroying myself and had to stop. That was the moment I'd decided to go home. I knew now that decision had probably saved my life. Thank God I hadn't turned away.

The things I'd done were part of me and always would be. But I was beginning to see that there was more to me than the sum of my choices. I wasn't a victim. I had the power to change. With Drew and with the kids at church, I was being given the chance to make a fresh start, to be someone other than the person I'd been for so long.

I'd begun to share sordid fragments of my past with Drew, a little at a time. And he'd done the same with me. We'd each made mistakes; we both had regrets. But Drew didn't hold those things against me. He knew he wasn't perfect and he didn't expect me to be. It was freeing to know that with him, I could just be myself.

Sunday after Sunday, Pastor Merritt preached of God's unconditional love. *But what does that even mean?* When I'd first encountered Jesus, I'd embraced His relentless love. I'd been passionate for Him, on fire. Then I'd moved to the beach and exchanged that Truest of loves for a six-foot, one-inch counterfeit. Steve had caused me to divert my eyes from the Divine. I'd fallen, tumbled into a pit of my own making, and over the past eight years, I'd been with dozens of men. Sex had become my god.

Surely I'd incurred God's wrath. It felt as if Lawrence had abandoned me, and I was convinced that God had too. Why shouldn't He? I'd cut myself off from Him, and there'd been a cost: I'd been left to fend for myself. It was just like the six hundred dollars Mama had given me when I'd headed off to New York. "When it runs out, you're on your own," she'd said. It had begun to feel that way with God too. I knew I'd spent every last dime of His mercy.

But since returning to church, I'd realized I was wrong about that. I was beginning to see that it never ran out.

Spring came on slowly, then burst into all of its glory. The daffodils seemed more vibrant, the sun more radiant. *Can it be that I'm in love?* I wasn't sure; we hadn't yet used those words. I just knew that Drew and I were happy, that things were good with us. Our common thread was work; the rest we wove together, one day at a time.

We lived for the weekends. Most Fridays, we'd make the ten-minute drive to The Rialto to catch an art film or old black-and-white movie. We'd head to the concession stand and order a large buttered popcorn and two Diet Cokes—the perfect dinner after a taxing week at work. On Saturday night, we'd usually go out to eat or make dinner at home. After dinner and a glass or two of wine, we'd almost always end up in bed.

Our lovemaking was impassioned and deep. We definitely had chemistry. But being with Drew was different than with anyone before. It felt solid. I wasn't sure what the future held for us, but I sensed we might have what it took to withstand the hardships most couples face over time. For now, we enjoyed each other's company. And that was enough.

"How would you like to go to the beach?" he asked out of the blue one Saturday. We were strolling through Cameron Park. It was late April and the weather was turning warm.

My face lit up. "Do you even have to ask?"

"I was thinking Wilmington. It's only two and a half hours away."

"Sounds wonderful!"

Wilmington was a beautiful town along the Cape Fear River, best known for its antebellum homes set off by vibrant azaleas and gnarly trees draped with Spanish moss like long, gray beards. The boardwalk along the river was dotted with trendy restaurants and bars. And Wrightsville Beach was only a fifteen-minute drive away. It was the best of both worlds.

"Andy Benson told me about a nice B&B. Said it's romantic," he added in that dry way of his. "I thought I'd check it out."

"Ooh! I like romantic! When?"

"How about next weekend?"

"Why not?" I was suddenly giddy.

I liked his spontaneity. In fact, I liked Drew, period. He was cute and easy to be with. He was a gifted illustrator—an all-around good guy. Plus, it hadn't escaped Mama's notice that he was the reason I'd returned to church. In my twenty-seven years of life, I'd learned that it was never a bad thing to have Mama on your side.

A few days later, I was sitting at my desk at work when Drew emerged from the stairwell to the right of the elevators. He was smiling from ear to ear. In his right hand was a full-color brochure. He walked over and dropped it on my desk. I looked down, curious.

Anderson House B&B, Wilmington, North Carolina. On the cover was a photo of a huge white two-story house with a wraparound porch dotted with rocking chairs and giant ferns.

"Is this where we're staying?" I asked, delighted.

"Yep!" He beamed.

I picked up the brochure and opened it. "Beautiful in-town B&B on a quiet street. Stately home on historic register. Enclosed garden. Romantic guest rooms with sitting area, queen bed, private bath." I looked up. "Thank you," was all I could muster.

"We can drive down on Saturday morning, come back Sunday night." He paused. "The owner asked for my wife's name. I guess he assumed we were married."

He'd gotten my attention. "What did you say?"

"I went along with it." He shrugged. "What else could I do?"

I chuckled nervously. "Yeah, I guess you're right."

We were doing a dance that was so wildly popular in the South—the dance of deception. You take your partner's hand and twirl around the uncomfortable thing that's between you, which is almost always sex. You do the dance, but Lord knows you don't admit you're doing it.

We knew what we were doing was wrong. Call it want you want—in God's eyes it was sin.

Our trip to Wilmington was even better than I'd imagined it would be. I made it through check-in at our B&B, averting my eyes as Drew signed us in at the register as "Drew and Laura Wagner." We quickly put our bags in our room, then walked into town for lunch. Drew had brought his camera, and we stopped by the river to take pictures. I stood next to a bridge and posed, remembering a few tricks from my modeling days. My smile came naturally—I was spending a weekend at the beach with an attractive man whom I loved being with. Why wouldn't I be smiling?

That afternoon, we went back to our room and made love. This trip had deepened our connection; there was a spark, an energy that hadn't been there before.

When we finished, Drew looked over at me and smiled. "I love you," he said simply.

It was the first time he'd spoken those words.

"I love you too," I whispered.

May came, and suddenly the agency was buzzing with the excitement of two new business pitches. Chick and the VPs were thrilled. But Drew and the other creatives were working long hours, pulling all-nighters over several weekends, to get everything ready for presentations the following week—so our date nights went out the window.

Drew was exhausted from the extra hours. More and more, he

talked about quitting his job at McKinney and becoming a freelance illustrator.

"My friend Rob from college, he freelances," he told me on a rare date night. "He says there's a market in Raleigh. He's making good money, and he gets to work at home."

I knew Drew wanted more than anything to be an illustrator. He'd studied art in college and still took life-drawing classes from time to time. I'd seen his work. No doubt about it, he had talent.

"Aren't you nervous about giving up your job?" I asked. "The steady paycheck and all?"

"Yeah, I know. It's risky. But Rob has some leads. I think I can make it work."

He sounded confident. And he'd proven himself at McKinney. Why not?

A few days later, I headed to the gynecologist for my annual checkup. Having my girl parts checked definitely wasn't my favorite thing to do. Still, since that botched IUD, the one found lodged in my uterus the day of my abortion, I'd tried to be more careful. I couldn't go through that again.

I walked into the waiting room, checked in, and found a seat by the window. On the table next to me was a magazine with a cover line that read: "Sexual Abuse and Promiscuity: Is There a Link?" *That's interesting.* I picked it up, flipped through the pages, found the article, and began to read.

My stomach churned. My eyes fell on phrases like "difficulty forming and maintaining relationships," "compulsive or addictive behaviors," and "adult promiscuity." And finally, the sentence that sent me reeling: "Keeping promiscuous behavior secret reinforces the original abuse pattern and leads to guilt, shame, and isolation."

My mind flashed back to that day in the storeroom at my aunt's house. The hum of the deep freezer, the acrid smell of fertilizer, my cousin's face. Then I thought about the past eight years. My obsession with men and sex. My overwhelming shame. Suddenly, I felt sick. *The storeroom.* Could that be the reason?

Since that night at The Nags Header with Steve, I'd equated sex with love. It had defined my self-worth. If a man found me attractive and desirable, I must be worthy. Time after time, I'd exchanged my body for that silent affirmation: *You are enough.* I'd convinced myself that my insatiable sexual appetite had been about numbing the pain caused by Lawrence's death. Certainly that was part of it. Now, however, I realized it was about so much more.

On a Monday morning in early June, I walked down the hall to get a Diet Coke and check on Jack.

I poked my head into his office. He was at his desk working away, oblivious that I was there.

"Hey," I said quietly.

He looked up, a beleaguered expression on his face. "Oh, hey."

"You okay?"

"Yeah. Just crunching first quarter numbers. Client wants them by noon." Piedmont was the golden calf, worth millions. Jack felt pressured not to screw up.

"I'll leave you alone," I said. "I just wanted to say hi."

"No, no, it's fine," he said apologetically. He put down his pencil. "Hey, my mom and dad and Barb are in town this weekend. I thought I'd host brunch on Sunday. Are you and Drew free?"

"Yeah, I think so," I said, pleased that he'd asked. "Can I check with Drew and get back to you?"

"Of course!" he said. "I can't wait for you to meet Barb. I've told her all about you." Barb was Jack's younger sister. She was about my age and worked as a travel agent in DC.

Drew was happy to accept Jack's invitation, even though it would mean we'd have to skip church. We both liked Jack, and we were honored that he'd included us.

On Saturday, Mama called to tell me that Daddy had been admitted to Raleigh Community Hospital for observation.

"He complained about his heart, so I took him in. They said he'd had more of those TIAs," she explained. "Mini-strokes."

My breath went shallow. "Oh my gosh!"

I adored Daddy. I was worried. He'd had these before, but they'd never put him in the hospital.

"He's okay," she reassured me. "They just want him to stay for a few days so they can monitor his heart. Maybe you and Drew can stop by and visit him. He'd like that."

"Of course," I said. "We're going to Jack's tomorrow. The hospital is on the way. We'll stop by on our way back."

The last thing I remember about that Sunday was me lying on a gurney in the ER of Raleigh Community Hospital with the room pulsing in and out and words like *shock* and *ruptured* and *stat* swirling around me. Drew's ashen face and his hand squeezing mine and a doctor standing over me, saying, "We're taking you to the OR, young lady. It's going to be okay."

Then everything went black.

I woke up in a hospital bed six hours later, light-headed, groggy, and confused. My body felt heavy against the mattress, my head like it was in a sort of vise grip.

As I came to, I saw Drew sitting next to me. I managed a smile.

A look of relief spread across his face. "Hey," he said softly. He took my hand and squeezed it, careful not to disturb the IV line attached to a bag of fluid dangling above my head.

I began to recall fragments: Jack's face, flutes of champagne, a young woman with black hair, a tiny bathroom, strains from a Michael Franks tune, and me curled up in a ball on Jack's bed . . .

Then I remembered Daddy.

"Daddy. Is he okay?"

"Yes, he's fine. He's on the fifth floor. I went up to see him while you were asleep."

"I can't believe we're in the same hospital. That's so weird."

"Yeah, I know. Your mom told him what happened."

"What *did* happen?" I asked through my fog.

Before he could answer, a doctor in blue scrubs walked in. He reached over and shook hands with Drew. It was obvious they'd already met. He looked at me. "I'm Dr. Butler." As he removed the surgical mask covering his face, I could see that he was in his late thirties and handsome. "You're one lucky girl."

My eyes searched his face.

"Your left ovary ruptured. By the time I opened you up, there was so much blood I could hardly see what I was doing." He inhaled deeply. "We almost lost you."

I let the weight of his words sink in, then looked at Drew and saw that his eyes were filled with tears. I looked back at Dr. Butler. "Thank you," I said, though it hardly seemed enough.

He smiled warmly. "I was on call, playing tennis, when I got beeped. I made it to the hospital just in time."

Just in time.

Then it clicked. I'd almost *died.*

Surely we all live on the edge of our final breath.

I saw Lawrence tumbling through the darkness, like an angel falling from heaven. It was an image I could call to mind at will. Now I'd had a near miss. But, unlike Lawrence, I had survived. Why? I was sure I'd never know.

What I did know was that life is made up of gossamer moments, mostly undetectable, until a foot slips or a car skids out of control.

Then, for a fleeting second, you see it—that wisp of a curtain separating life from death. You either pass through it or you don't. I was still here, lying in a hospital bed, talking to Drew and the doctor who had saved me. Surely God had given me a second chance.

"You're going to have to take it easy for a few weeks. But you'll be okay." He looked at Drew. "Think you can keep an eye on her?"

I liked him. Not only had he saved my life, he also seemed to be a genuinely nice person.

"I'll do my best," Drew said.

"Good." He turned to me. "You'll need to stay put for a few days so we can monitor you."

"Okay," I said. "Thank you again."

He smiled, then turned and left the room.

I looked at Drew. We sat for a moment in silence. Then Drew got up from his chair, sat down on the bed, and kissed me.

"I thought I was going to lose you," he said, tears trickling down his cheek. "It made me realize . . . I don't want to live without you." He drew in a breath. "Will you marry me?"

"Yes, yes I will," I said, breaking into a smile.

Wait a minute. Did he just propose? And did I just say yes? I certainly wasn't expecting a proposal, at least not so soon. And this definitely wasn't the setting I'd imagined—not a dimly lit hospital room.

He reached down and hugged me. His body next to mine felt comforting and warm.

"Let's get married in December," he said suddenly. He pulled away and waited for my response.

"That's six months from now. It's too soon." I remembered my hurried first wedding, and my divorce. "No, I want to wait a year," I said firmly. "Besides, they say you need to see a person in every season to know them. And I've only seen you in two." I winked at him.

I loved this man and I was ready to commit to him. I knew a year wouldn't reveal anything that would make me change my mind. Still, I'd rushed into so many relationships. I wanted to be careful and slow things down.

"Okay, then," he said. "A year it is."

"We'll have to set a date," I said.

"I have my checkbook. It has a calendar."

He pulled it out of his back pocket and handed it to me. I took it, opened it, and flipped past the checks. I found the calendar, 1985. I dropped my finger down on June.

"What's today?"

"June tenth."

"How about June fifteenth? It's a Saturday."

"June fifteenth. Sounds good!"

We'd set out that morning for brunch with friends, and it had turned out to be a day that would change my life forever. I was happy to be alive—and to know I was going to marry someone I loved deeply, someone with whom I could envision having a life and family of our own.

Almost a week later, I left Raleigh Community Hospital and moved back to Mama and Daddy's. I knew Mama and Daddy were relieved I'd made it through my ordeal; I could see it on their faces when Drew and I walked through the door.

Daddy had returned from the hospital just a few days earlier. He looked older to me, and frail, but the doctor said he would be fine.

"It was so hard not being able to visit you." I released a weighty sigh.

"I felt the same way," he said, his face soft.

While I regained my strength, Mama waited on me—bringing trays of her delicious home-cooked food with a dish of peach cobbler or a piece of pound cake thrown in for good measure. I marveled at her cooking. She'd cooked for her family of eight when she was just a teenager. Her mama had taught her, and she'd tried to teach me. But we'd never found peace in the kitchen. Was it my stubbornness? Her determination not to be outdone? Whatever the reason, I'd come to understand that every dish she prepared had one common ingredient: love. I'd never be the cook Mama was, and that was okay. I'd learned enough to get around the kitchen, and for that I was grateful.

I stayed with Mama and Daddy until I was strong enough to move back to my apartment—about two weeks. In early July, I returned to work. Now I faced a dilemma: when to break the news of our engagement to Chick. For months, I'd been haunted by the same questions: *What will Chick say? Will one or both of us be fired?*

For a few weeks, we kept it a secret. Finally, unable to keep it to ourselves any longer, we decided to tell him.

"That's great, old gal!" He removed the expensive Havana cigar from between his lips and broke into a smile. "Drew Wagner, huh?" He tilted his head, scrunched his brow, and looked at me, perplexed. "Oh, yes. Drew! Nice fella. I'm sure the two of you will be happy." He picked up his cigar, put it in his mouth, and began to chew. "Well, he's a lucky guy!"

I chuckled. Chick was bright, but he could also be forgetful.

Over the past two years, I'd come to love Chick McKinney. He'd grown up in a mountain holler in Spruce Pine, North Carolina, raised by his mama. He'd dug his way out of poverty and put himself through college. He'd ventured into advertising and had phenomenal success. Even on Madison Avenue, they knew his name. Chick was quirky and eccentric, and most people didn't understand him. But I did. Behind that rough exterior was a kind man—at least, if he liked you. And I knew he liked me.

The news spread quickly. Everyone at the agency was happy for us, especially Jack. "I want to throw you and Drew an engagement party!" He and I had been close before that fateful Sunday, but we'd grown even closer since.

The months that followed flashed by like fields on a rushing train. There were honeymoon plans to make. A photographer to hire. Invitations and flowers to order. A reception venue to book. Foremost in my mind, of course, was my wedding dress. I'd worn an antique dress for my first wedding. This time, I wanted something different. With Drew, I was making a fresh start. I knew this would be a true marriage, one that would last.

"I want a long, white dress," I announced to Mama as we sat at her kitchen table one Saturday in October. I'd asked her if she'd like to go wedding dress shopping, and she'd agreed. I'd stopped by the house to pick her up and found her finishing a cup of coffee.

"Brides usually wear cocktail-length dresses the second time. In blue. Or cream," she said very matter-of-factly.

"I know. But I want a full-length. I want to treat this like a first wedding."

We took my car and drove the twenty minutes to Person Street Bridal Shop. We got out of the car, walked inside, and started to browse.

I found the smalls and began to flip through the dresses. A simple white satin caught my eye. I immediately tried it on. It was elegant. Definitely a contender.

Then I saw another dress, the complete opposite of the first. I envisioned Scarlett O'Hara surrounded by beaus at the picnic at Four Oaks. It had a scoop neckline with large, puffy sleeves made of organza, a fitted bodice, and a full, tiered skirt. Every inch was embellished with lace; intricate appliqués were scattered everywhere.

I took off the first dress and tried the second one on. When I looked in the mirror, I felt like a princess.

Which one should I choose? Simple? Or southern?

"What about a veil?" the woman asked.

No veils. No more covering up. I looked around and saw the perfect accessory: an English riding hat. I picked it up and placed it on my head.

"This," I said to Mama as I glanced at the young girl in the mirror.

"You look beautiful," she said.

I studied her face, indelibly marked by the landmarks of her life, including the heartache of losing Lawrence. It had been years since Mama and I had gone shopping together, and there was something about it that was comforting, like warm bread. I thought back to the time right after Lawrence died. I had no desire to leave my room, much less go back to school. It was the early seventies, and no one in Raleigh went to therapy; instead, we went to the mall. Mama and I got into her Pontiac sedan and took the beltline to North Hills, where she bought me two skirts and a vest with expensive labels.

I'd felt self-conscious in those designer clothes—we were middle-class, and they'd seemed extravagant. But Mama had grown up during the Depression, and appearances were important to her. We might have lost Lawrence, but we hadn't lost our dignity. I thanked her profusely, hung them in my closet, and wore them with a mix of embarrassment and pride.

Then there were the things she'd sewn by hand. Mama had always been an exceptional seamstress; she took pride in each carefully installed zipper and pristine seam. My freshman year at UNCG, she'd made me a white ball gown to wear to my first formal, not unlike the classic dress I'd just tried on. When I went to New York, she'd made pants and a matching top from gorgeous, cream-colored silk. It was the outfit I'd worn for my first studio shoot. I'd never given much thought to those outfits. Now I felt a little ashamed that I'd been so unaware of the care she'd taken with each one.

I'd make it up to her somehow. I'd find a way.

...

I moved out of my apartment on West Johnson Street at the end of May and moved in with Mama and Daddy. My wedding was in two weeks, and there was still a lot to do. It was nice to be home. My parents were both in their sixties, not getting any younger. I was happy to have that time with them.

When our wedding was just a week away, Mama and I were out in the backyard together. I was getting a little pre-wedding sun; she was gardening. She stopped, put down her trowel, and walked over to my lawn chair.

"I want to show you something." Her tone was solemn.

"Okay," I said, curious, and a bit concerned.

She turned, walked to the house, opened the screened porch door, and headed straight into the kitchen. I followed close behind. When she got inside, she stopped and pulled up her tube top, exposing her right breast.

"I wanted you to see this," she said. Her voice was shaking.

Her breast glared back at me with horrifying clarity. Her nipple was dark, rippled. Deformed.

Oh, my God.

I'd never had an encounter with cancer. Now it was staring me in the face.

She pulled her top back in place. I stood there looking at her, silent.

"I found a lump about a year ago," she offered weakly. "I was afraid to go to the doctor."

Her words hung like a readied guillotine.

She's known for a year? Why did she wait?

The image of her shriveled nipple gripped me.

"I'm going in to have it looked at," she said, as if reading my mind.

"Yes. You need to call the doctor. Today," I said in the most adult voice I'd ever used with her.

"I will. Right now." She turned and walked out of the room.

I stood there, incredulous. I was getting married in one week, and I was almost certain that my mother had advanced breast cancer. Could we go ahead with the wedding? If we did, would she even be there? It looked bad. Really bad. Would she be all right? I wasn't sure.

~~~ꝏ·ꝏ~~~

Chapter Fifteen

We were married on a Saturday in the middle of June, and Mama was there to celebrate with us.

She was a walking miracle: she'd been diagnosed with stage 3 metastatic breast cancer on Monday and undergone a radical mastectomy on Tuesday, and she was the first to arrive at our rehearsal dinner Friday night. Her surgeon said he had never seen anyone recover so quickly. Mama said it was our prayers. Her doctor was sure our wedding had been the catalyst.

Stage 3 breast cancer certainly wasn't good news. With chemotherapy, Mama's prognosis was about five years. I hated that she had waited and let her breast turn into a cesspool of disease. *What was she thinking?* In the days that followed our initial conversation, I traversed between anger and fear. Mostly, I lived somewhere in between. I told myself that maybe she'd beat the odds. That it wouldn't be as bad as they'd predicted.

Daddy was upbeat and positive, as always. He was being strong for Mama, who was worried enough for all of us. I knew he must be frightened, but it rarely showed; I saw it only on occasion, when I caught a somber look akin to the ones I'd seen when we lost Lawrence. I pushed Mama's prognosis aside and busied myself with wedding details. I'd deal with the cancer later, once the wedding was over. I had faith she'd be okay.

On Saturday morning, I woke to the sun filtering through

the curtain that hung like a veil across the window in my room. I pried open my eyes, sat up in bed, propped my pillows against the headboard, leaned back, and smiled. *Our wedding day is finally here.* I couldn't remember ever having been this happy. I believed with all my heart that I'd made a thoughtful and considered choice. Drew and I had been through weeks of pre-marital counseling with our pastor, and we were ready for this. He'd be a loving husband and a wonderful father someday.

But there was something more. I sensed that God had carried me through the loss and heartache of the past fourteen years to bring me to this day, for this reason—to be this man's wife. After Lawrence's accident, I'd embarked on a journey. My odyssey had taken me from the Outer Banks to Manhattan and home again. I'd frantically searched for love. I'd sought solace in flesh and forgiveness from God as a way to purge my pain. I'd encountered potholes, detours, and dead ends along the way. Somehow, I'd survived. Today, I was setting out on a new journey, unencumbered by the burden of my past. I couldn't wait to begin.

That morning swirled around me like a waking dream. I was poignantly aware that this was the last time I would be in my parents' house in just this way. I clung to every word, every interaction, knowing this sliver of time would soon come to an end. It was bittersweet, especially because of the uncertainty of Mama's cancer and the stinging awareness of Lawrence's absence, though I sensed somehow he was there.

Horace arrived promptly at noon to escort me to the church.

"At your service, ma'am," he said as he opened my door and helped me into the back seat of Mama's freshly washed navy sedan. I pulled my voluminous skirt inside the car, and then he leaned down and kissed me on the cheek.

"You look beautiful, sis," he said, his eyes twinkling with pride.

We drove across town to the beltline and took the Creedmoor Road exit to Asbury. As we pulled into the gravel parking lot, I saw my bridesmaids arriving, some with curlers in their hair, all carrying dresses the color of peacock feathers in their hands.

Our church was small, so the girls dressed in the kitchen; Drew and his groomsmen took the loft upstairs.

For the next hour, there was a flurry of activity—makeup, dresses, photos. I glanced over and saw Mama chatting cheerily with Drew's mom. The two of them couldn't have been more different: Fran was a smoker who enjoyed her five o'clock cocktail; Mama was a tee-totaler who had never smoked a day in her life. But none of that mattered today. We were going to be family.

All at once, I was jolted out of my musings.

"The florist forgot your kneeling bench," my aunt Delores announced.

The service started in thirty minutes. Panic spread across my face. "What'll we do?" I fretted. We couldn't get married without a kneeling bench.

"You can kneel on the floor," she said calmly. Aunt Delores was married to Phil, Mama's oldest brother. She was jovial. And smart. In my eyes, there was almost nothing she couldn't do and do well.

Her comment reminded me why I had asked her to direct our wedding: from my earliest memory, she'd been my champion. That was especially true today.

I took a deep breath to still my nerves. Then I glided across the kitchen, cracked the door, and peeked through.

The foyer was bustling with excitement—childhood friends greeting one another; aunts, uncles, and cousins embracing. I spotted a few friends from McKinney, and Chick McKinney himself. They'd all come to celebrate *us*. My heart swelled with gratitude and pride. It was almost more than I could take in.

At that moment, there was a thunderous boom, and the sky opened up with a torrential rain.

"Rain on a wedding day is good luck!" said a cheerful voice.

I closed the door and found Mama, so pretty in her aqua dress with a rose corsage pinned just above her missing breast, standing behind me.

I knew that old superstition—that rain on your wedding day represented cleansing. And fertility. Today, however, all it represented to me was a ruined reception, the one we'd planned for outdoors.

"Oh, well," I said, close to tears. "Good thing we ordered that expensive tent!"

In less than an hour I would be Mrs. Andrew Wagner, rain or not. I smiled as I pondered my new name for the hundredth time, only mildly aware of the commotion all around me.

"Places, everyone!" ordered Aunt Delores. "It's time!"

I looked around at my friends, who gave me a collective smile as we exited the kitchen and entered the foyer, where Daddy stood waiting. When he saw me, he broke into a grin. He looked so elegant—and fragile—in his gray tux. As I approached him, I felt a wave of tenderness. He seemed so childlike. And now he had to care for Mama. Would he be okay?

"Hey, sweetie," he said. "You look beautiful."

His face was serene; his eyes shone. I slipped my arm through his, leaned close, and kissed his wrinkled cheek. In a few moments, he would give me away. This had been the happiest day of my life, and yet it felt bittersweet. I wanted to be Drew's wife, but I also wanted to make time stand still—to stay here, by his side.

"I love you, Daddy."

"I love you too."

The thick wooden doors opened, and I heard the lilting strains of the wind ensemble playing "Jesu, Joy of Man's Desiring." My bridesmaids began processing to the front of the church. I clung to Daddy's arm, watching as though in a dream. My wedding day. Drew. It seemed so perfect. And so surreal.

"Now!" whispered Aunt Delores.

As Daddy struggled to get in step, my heart sank. In all my busyness, I'd hardly noticed. He was different, somehow. Altered.

"Right . . . left," I whispered.

Our steps finally aligned, and I suddenly noticed all the people looking at us—heads nodding with approval, women dabbing at their tears. My line of vision moved to the front of the church, where Drew was waiting, composed and incredibly handsome. His eyes never left mine as I made my way to him.

For the next forty-five minutes, it felt as though time were expanding and contracting. Moments when time stood still and everything around us fell away. As Pastor Merritt pronounced us husband and wife, a jolt of electricity passed through me. I knew in that moment that we had been sealed by God, inextricably one. I felt it to the very core of my being. Our union had forged us like steel. Nothing could destroy us or tear us apart.

Our lips melded together in a long, lingering kiss. Then Drew took my hand and we walked down the aisle to the strains of Vivaldi's "Spring." As my eye caught the large, circular window at the back of the sanctuary, I saw the sun breaking through.

We returned from our honeymoon in St. Thomas and settled into a little two-story condominium on St. Mary's Street. It was small, just right for the two of us, with a kitchen barely large enough to turn around in, a dining room, and a cozy living room. The upstairs had two bedrooms, and Drew used the smaller one for his office.

I returned to work at the end of June a married woman. Everyone told me I practically glowed. I felt it too. After so many failed attempts at happiness, I'd finally gotten it right. Drew was a good man. We shared the same beliefs and wanted the same things in life—to use our talents, travel, have a family one day.

But in my newfound contentment, I felt restless. Drew was finding success as a freelance illustrator—he was gaining notoriety and his drawings were in demand. Sometimes he'd work late into the night finishing an airbrush project while I sat at the dining room table and cranked out a short story. I didn't have a burning desire to write fiction; I just wanted to write, and I'd heard short stories were a good place to start. What I really wanted to do was write copy—to create clever headlines and see my words on the printed page.

I'd dropped a number of hints to Chick about the possibility of copywriting, but they'd gone unnoticed. So I decided to take my campaign to Bob Doherty, the head of Piedmont. I knew Bob liked me; he was kind and warm and always treated me with respect. I knew he'd not only listen but also come to my aid.

"Of course I'll put in a word for you," he said without hesitation.

I waited several days, then gently nudged Chick. We were sitting in his office, going through his mail.

"Bob? Yes, yes, he talked to me. Told me you're interested in copywriting." He pulled off his glasses and took a bite off his Havana cigar.

My heart almost leapt from my chest. *This is it.*

"You know that receptionist position is the most important one at the agency. You're the first impression, and you do a damn good job."

I blushed, flattered.

"Truth is, I like you right where you are."

At those words, I heard the slam of a heavy door, one I was sure I'd never be able to open. I forced a smile. "Thank you," I said through pursed lips. "Well, I'd better get back upstairs." I stood up to leave.

"Okay, ol' gal!" he said.

I turned and walked out. Time for plan B.

In July, Chick hired a senior copywriter named Caroline Richards. And that's when my fate began to change.

"I need your help with Caroline," Chick said one day during our morning check-in. "I want you to be her point person. Assist with her move, introduce her to folks, help her settle in. I want her to feel welcome."

I didn't know much about Caroline, just that she was getting a large corner office. Still, I sensed from the intensity of Chick's directive that her arrival was a big deal.

The first time Caroline walked off the elevator, I was awestruck. She had the appearance of an angel and carried herself with great aplomb. She had alabaster skin, flawless makeup, beautifully coifed golden hair, and eyes that twinkled with delight. I was sure I'd never met anyone so lovely.

I showed her to her new office. Then we walked around creative and I introduced her to the gang. It didn't escape my notice that everyone spoke to her with the utmost respect.

"Please let me know if you need anything. Anything at all," I said to her as we headed to Chick's office.

"You're so kind; thank you."

Caroline and I hit it off right away. She had an easy manner. She was elegant yet gracious and approachable. She loved a good laugh, especially at herself. But what I was drawn to most was the fact that she was strong. I was captivated by strong women; the ones I'd known had shaped the person I'd become.

There was Mama, of course. While we'd had our bumps over the years, I admired how she spoke her mind and pursued her passions—teaching, gardening, flower arranging. Then there were my aunts, a handful of church ladies, and the women who'd cleaned for Mama and helped raise me. In my eyes, all these women were forces of nature.

Caroline was no exception. I believed she would be the perfect mentor. I wanted a career as a freelance writer, something I knew little about. I'd never had a mentor, but it seemed like a smart thing to pursue. Caroline was talented and accomplished. She'd made a name for herself in a male-dominated profession. She had expertise, and clout, especially with Chick. I could learn a lot from her.

On a sweltering day in late July, I got up the nerve to ask Caroline if she'd read one of my short stories. My hope was that she'd see some promise. That she'd encourage me to keep writing. I'd worked hard, polishing it until it shone. Still, I'd wrestled with the idea of approaching her. She was a senior copywriter and her job was demanding. What if she said no?

That morning, I printed out a copy at home and brought it to work. When she stepped off the elevator, I seized my chance.

"Of course. I'd be happy to," she said. Her voice evoked the scent of wisteria.

"Thank you!" I said, delighted.

"But you need to know"—her tone grew serious—"I'll be honest. It won't do you any good if I sugarcoat my feedback."

"Of course. I understand."

Now to wait.

A few days later, Caroline called me at the switchboard to tell me she'd finished my story.

As I rounded the corner to her office, voices of self-doubt went off in my head.

What if she says it was terrible? What if she says you can't write?

I stopped just short of her doorway and sighed. *Here goes.*

As I walked in, Caroline looked up from her desk.

"Come in!" she said in her cheery manner. "Have a seat!" She pointed to a chrome director's chair.

I lowered myself into the chair. She picked up my short story, then pulled her glasses down to the end of her nose. She looked me square in the face. "It's not a bad first effort," she said pointedly. "You used a lot of adjectives, but that's fairly common for someone starting out. I've marked a few places. Go through and get rid of those wherever you can. And keep writing. Your work will improve."

She reached across her desk and handed me the stapled copy.

"Thank you," I said. My face flushed with embarrassment and relief.

We chatted a bit more before I left. As I headed back upstairs, story in hand, I felt relieved. It wasn't the most flattering critique, but it could have been worse. I was grateful. And more determined than ever. I might never have my short stories published. Or be a novelist. But I believed, with practice, I could be a good copywriter. I knew I had to try.

So much of my life had been a puzzle, but now I'd found my missing piece. Drew and I enjoyed the ins and outs of daily life, and we laughed easily and often. On Sunday, we'd attend church, then go to Mama and Daddy's or his parents' apartment for lunch. It was rewarding to see Mama and Daddy get along with Drew; I could tell they loved him like a son. While he couldn't replace Lawrence, he seemed to fill a void, and that made me happy.

We'd kept up our work with the youth group; it was something we could do to make a difference. I'd especially enjoyed getting to know some of the girls, and we'd grown close. They looked up to me. From time to time, they'd call me during the week to ask for advice.

In August, after talking it over with Drew, I asked several of the girls if they'd like to be part of a weekly group. We'd meet together on Wednesdays to discuss things like dating or how to get along with their parents, do a brief Bible study, and the rest of the time we'd talk and pray. I'd never seen myself as a role model before then—far from it. Still, I'd learned a lot from the mistakes I'd made and felt I had a lot to share. Maybe I could help these girls make better choices than I'd made. I hoped so.

On a Tuesday afternoon in late August, I was sitting at my desk rifling through a stack of résumés when the elevator doors opened. It was Drew.

What is he doing here?

"I couldn't wait to tell you." He was beaming from ear to ear.

"Tell me what?" I asked. He had my attention.

"I signed us up for diving lessons!"

"Diving lessons?" I asked in a tone somewhere between skeptical and excited.

"I thought it would be fun."

My mind instantly swirled with images of tropical islands and colorful fish. But wasn't diving for wealthy people? We certainly weren't that.

"Remember how much we enjoyed snorkeling in St. Thomas? And how we want to travel?"

I couldn't deny those things were true. But what about sharks? A large mouth with bloodied teeth flashed before my eyes. "Yes, I remember," I replied timidly. "The lessons . . . aren't they expensive?"

"They were pretty reasonable. The equipment can be pricy, though. And the trips."

My stomach tightened. We'd just gotten married and we were saving for a house. Were we being careless? Should we be doing this at all? Still, I was intrigued.

"It'll be fun!" he said, sensing my hesitation. "I signed us up with a local instructor—a woman named Shirley. The classes run six weeks—part classroom instruction, part of the time in the water. Then we get certified."

"Certified?"

"Shirley will take us to Florida with the rest of the class. We'll do our checkout dive at a state park in Key Largo. After that we can dive anywhere we want!"

"Wow!" I said, still torn. I loved his adventurous spirit. But this whole thing was overwhelming. What if I couldn't master the skills? What if I didn't pass and Drew did? What then? I needed time to think.

He looked at me expectantly. I could see he was excited; I didn't want to spoil it for him. So I rallied some enthusiasm. "Sounds great! When do we start?"

"Thursday night," he told me.

We still had forty-eight hours. Maybe he'd change his mind.

That September, Drew and I encountered our first real challenge as a couple: caring for my parents. Daddy had several more "mini-strokes," as Mama called them. He was sixty-nine, but he seemed vulnerable and old. Mama, meanwhile, had finally healed enough from her surgery to start chemotherapy.

It was difficult for me to take time off from work, so Mama's sisters took her to appointments. I felt guilty. Mama assured me she was okay. But okay didn't last for long.

First, I noticed it in her face—the dullness, the lack of expression. Then in her voice, which had become flat and robotic. That's when it hit me: This was the same Mama I'd known those five years after Lawrence died. The despondency. The daily naps. I'd been sure that her depression had disappeared forever. Now it had returned.

On a golden day in mid-October, I got a call from Mama. Drew and I had just gotten home from Key Largo—relaxed, tanned, and with our newly issued diving certificates in hand.

"I'm going to Holly Hill," Mama announced in a monotone.

Holly Hill was the psychiatric hospital just a few miles from Mama and Daddy's. I hated the name. It sounded so cheery. It was anything but.

Mama explained that her depression hadn't improved, and her doctor had told her it was probably the effects of the chemo. She'd decided to check into Holly Hill for a week; her sister Karen would take her. She would attend group therapy sessions with other people who were struggling to make sense of things. Her doctor said it might help.

"You'll need to come stay with your father," she continued. "He's been having hallucinations. I'm afraid he'll wander off."

Her words jarred me. *Daddy? Hallucinating? My brilliant father, who supported our family and carried us all through Lawrence's death?*

"Yes, of course," I said. "We'll stay with him. Just feel better. And don't worry about a thing."

I hung up the phone. Who was I kidding? I was only twenty-eight. I didn't know a thing about taking care of parents who were depressed and imagining things that weren't there. All of my friends had healthy parents; my parents had *issues*, embarrassing ones. I couldn't just go around telling anyone that Mama was having psychiatric problems and that Daddy appeared to be losing his mind. It wasn't that I didn't love them; I did. But I was frightened.

All at once, I had a million questions. *Who can I talk to? Where can I go for help?* I had no clue.

For the first time in a long time, I felt all alone. I knew I wasn't; I had Drew, thank God. And Horace. But he was five hours away, and busy with work and a young family. There was Caroline, of course. But we were new friends, and I wasn't ready to confide in her. I had my church, Pastor Merritt, and the friends we'd made there over the past year. I knew they would be there to pray for and support us. But right now I needed a manual telling me step by step what to expect and how to react, though I was pretty sure one didn't exist. I didn't know where to turn.

Right now, I had to keep my promise to Mama. I called Drew and asked if he could go over and stay with Daddy until I could get there. I left work, drove home quickly, and packed an overnight bag with my toothbrush and a few things. Then, just as dusk began to fall, I headed over to Mama and Daddy's.

As I drove down New Bern Avenue, I felt anxious, wondering what it would be like to see Daddy as someone other than the person I'd always known him to be. I could barely allow myself to think about Mama being at Holly Hill. Or how difficult it must have been for Daddy to see his wife of forty years go to a place like that.

I turned off the avenue at King William Road and crept along until I spotted the familiar mailbox perched under a towering pine. I inched up the driveway, pulled in front of the garage, and turned off the engine. I sat for a moment, unable to move. Daddy had always been my rock, the one whose faith in me had been unwavering. Now, with Mama in the hospital and Daddy so lost, I felt lost too, and disoriented. I wanted to make it all go away, but I couldn't.

I had to be the grown-up. I knew Drew was there for me. We were a team, and knowing that gave me strength.

When I walked into the kitchen, Daddy was sitting at the table in his usual spot, his elbows propped on an orange straw place mat. He was staring at a vase of artificial daisies on the lazy Susan. Drew was sitting beside him, his face fraught with worry.

Daddy looked up. "Be careful out there!" he said, as though I were a stranger. I noticed that his eyes were glassy and wild. "There are SS agents hiding in the bushes. I saw them!"

I froze. *Oh, my God.* This was far worse than I'd imagined. I hardly recognized him at all.

"It's okay, Daddy," I said, trying to reassure him, and myself as well. I walked over to the door I'd just walked through. "Look, I'm locking the door. They won't bother us."

"They're out there, all right. I'm glad your mother's not here to see them."

Drew and I exchanged a look. What were we supposed to do?

"C'mon, Daddy," I coaxed. "How about we watch a little TV?"

He got up and dutifully followed us into the den. This den had been the heart of our family life. It was where we'd cried through John Kennedy's funeral and witnessed Bobby's assassination. Where we'd sat, breathless, waiting to see if Lawrence's number would be drawn for the draft. Where, fourteen years ago, Daddy had broken the news to Mama and me about Lawrence's accident. There had been lots of happy moments in that room since that fateful day, but it was that moment I remembered most clearly.

That night, Drew and I lay in my old four-poster bed and spoke in whispers.

"What are we going to do?" I asked as a tear slipped from my eye.

"It's going to be okay," he said.

"I know, but I hate this. We just got married, and now we have to take care of my parents."

"Our parents," he said without hesitation.

My tears began to fall, gratitude comingled with grief.

Our parents. He'd never once complained about this disruption to our lives. He was like Daddy in that way. It was something I'd seen in him early on. One of the reasons I'd wanted to marry him.

I leaned over and kissed his cheek. "Thank you."

Sleep began to nudge. I was exhausted. I was also a light sleeper. I knew I'd wake up in an instant should Daddy decide to wander from his bed.

...

By Thanksgiving, things weren't much better. By mid-December, they were worse. Daddy's hallucinations had stopped, but the strokes had left him weak; he was a more childlike version of himself. I wondered if he could care for the house, much less care for Mama, whose condition had continued to decline.

The week at Holly Hill didn't seem to help. I was frustrated by the whole group therapy thing. Mama didn't need to sit in a circle and listen to other people's problems; she needed someone to listen to hers. She'd lost a beloved son. She'd been through cancer and was going through chemo. Now her husband of forty years was quietly slipping away. That was a lot to cope with, and she wasn't coping well.

By Christmas, she was back at Holly Hill, this time for an extended stay. It was the twenty-third of December—a still, frigid day—when I helped her pack a small suitcase, eased her into my Honda, and drove her the two miles from their house to the hospital. I hated that place, its red brick facade and sterile interior. The staff tried to mask what lurked inside, but you could feel it in the air—all that hopelessness and despair. It tumbled down the hallways and crept under the door and drifted through the lobby like a chilling fog. I sensed its presence even as I stood there at the reception window, filling out paperwork for Mama.

I stopped what I was doing and turned to see Mama sitting in a fake leather chair. Her head was bent slightly; her eyes stared off into who knew where. I didn't want to leave her there. Not for anything. But I had to. She was despondent and needed help, and I didn't know where else to turn. This was one of only two mental health facilities in Raleigh. The other was Dorothea Dix, the old pre–Civil War state mental hospital that looked more like an asylum. I'd heard about Dorothea Dix all my life—from Mama, of all people. "If you and Horace keep up that bickering, I'm going to end up at Dorothea Dix!" she'd snapped time and again during our tumultuous teens. It had been her go-to phrase when she was fed up with us. I'd heard it so often, I'd come to ignore it. And while Horace and I hadn't been the cause of this breakdown, it seemed prophetic.

I finished the paperwork, then checked Mama in. A nurse escorted us through a locked door and down a dreary corridor to her room: a sterile box with a standard-issue bed, dresser, and chair. There was no phone, of course. They didn't want patients calling family members to implore them to take them home. The only TV was in a common room. I imagined everyone sitting together, staring blankly at the screen.

I numbly hung up Mama's clothes and made sure she was settled before I left. Mama sat on the side of the bed, her drooping navy-blue sweater matching the expression on her face.

I leaned down and kissed her soft cheek. "Bye, Mama. We'll take care of Daddy. And check in on you. You're going to be fine. I love you." My lip quivered as my eyes filled with tears.

"I love you too, darlin'," she said without looking up.

With hesitation, I brushed away my tears, turned, and left the room.

On Christmas Eve, Drew and I sat together on the orange corduroy love seat in Mama and Daddy's den. Daddy sat across from us in his worn La-Z-Boy recliner, the same one he'd sat in for as long as I could remember. We'd just finished supper and turned on the radio to listen to *A Prairie Home Companion* with Garrison Keillor. I loved the tales he spun about Lake Wobegon and never missed a show.

"Live from scenic Northfield, Minnesota, the St. Olaf's College Choir performing an old sixteenth-century German hymn, 'Lo, How a Rose E'er Blooming,'" he said in his homespun midwestern accent.

There was an anticipatory silence as the invisible conductor raised his hand. The next moment, the radio emanated a sound so ethereal that it pierced me to the core. The poignancy of that moment didn't escape me—the voices of an angelic choir set against the stark, bleak reality of the present: Mama exiled to a psychiatric hospital and Daddy adrift in his own world, and on this Holiest of nights. I sat, unmoving, as the strains dipped and swelled, fixating on every note until the last one was sung and it was silent once more.

We started the New Year hopeful. Mama was home and seemed less despondent. Every once in a while I'd even detect the glimmer of a smile. Daddy's hallucinations hadn't come back, and Mama mentioned in passing that they might have been caused by cross-medication—one medication counteracting another. *Cross-medication?* Over the past few months, I'd become my parents' caregiver, and this possibility was something I'd never considered. I made a mental note: *Stay on top of Mama and Daddy's meds.*

In the middle of January, Drew and I slipped away for a five-day diving trip to San Salvador. Dealing with my parents had been hard; it would be good for us, we reasoned. And it was. We found a few exotic locations and swam through habitats swarming with creatures of every imaginable color. It was exhilarating. And addicting.

A few weeks later, late one Saturday afternoon near the end of January, Drew and I were hanging out at home when the phone rang. It was Horace, calling to tell me Mama had been talking about moving into the Methodist Retirement Home in Durham, thirty miles away.

My body tensed. I shut my eyes. The words "retirement home" rattled like loose bolts in my head. "Are you serious?"

It had been less than a month since Mama had been hospitalized for depression. There was no denying she was better. But was she well enough to make this kind of life-changing decision?

"They'll have to sell the house first," he said, trying to console me.

His words whizzed like an arrow and lodged in my heart. *Sell the house?* Our childhood home? She wouldn't sell it; she couldn't. It was all we had left of Lawrence. If she sold it, that remnant would be lost to us, just as surely as he was.

"She's never said a word to me." I was stunned.

"Ask her yourself," he said calmly.

"I will." I was hurt—not that Horace knew before I did but that we were having this conversation at all.

I said goodbye, hung up the phone, and stood there for a moment, gathering my thoughts.

Then I picked up the phone and dialed my parents' number. Mama answered.

"I thought I'd stop by for a visit. It's been a while," I said, searching for an excuse to see her.

"Sure, come on. I'm just simmering some butter beans."

I ran upstairs and briefly told Drew what was going on. "I'll be back in time for dinner," I said. I kissed him, collected my coat and purse, and headed out the door.

I pulled into the driveway and parked beside Mama's blue LeSabre. I clipped up the sidewalk to the back door and turned the knob.

"Hey! I'm here!" I called out.

"I'm in the hall!" Mama replied.

I walked through the pine-paneled den. Daddy, usually glued like a fixture to his recliner, was nowhere to be found. As I reached the hallway door, I saw Mama standing in front of a bookcase she'd recently refinished, so lost in thought she didn't notice I'd come in. In that moment, I felt a wave of tenderness toward this woman I'd taken for granted for so long.

I followed her index finger as it ran across the row of spines sitting on the top shelf.

"Horace told me you're thinking about moving to the Methodist Retirement Home," I said abruptly.

She turned around, and we looked at each other as if for the first time. Her brown eyes danced, and her lips pressed together gently in an almost undetectable smile. Her once auburn hair, now a soft dove gray—an unexpected surprise after the chemo—framed her angular face. Her youthful skin, which I'd inherited, effortlessly hid her sixty-six years. She'd been a beauty as a young woman and she still was.

"It will be good for us." Her voice was childlike and resigned.

Her words shook me out of my reverie. So it was true. I took a breath and tried to let it register.

Without saying a word, she turned and walked into the den. A few moments later, she returned with a brochure. "Here." She handed it to me. "I'm working on the application."

Daddy's mini-strokes had left him unable to handle their everyday affairs. Mama was now in charge. She'd always been more assertive than Daddy, a natural-born leader; the role suited her.

On the cover was a brick building with towering Tuscan columns. I opened it up and saw photos of happy white-haired people—eating together in a dining room, engaging in activities.

"The yard has gotten to be too much for your father," Mama said.

She was right, of course. Daddy was seventy and still mowing the acre of land they owned. But what about Mama? She'd never admit it, but caring for the house—and Daddy—was too much for her.

"They will get all our money." She paused to consider my reaction and the weight of what she'd just said. "But they promise to care for us the rest of our lives, no matter how sick we get. Even if our money runs out."

Her words took me aback. Giving up all their money seemed extreme. Then I thought about Mama's cancer and Daddy's declining health and the fact that they would be cared for. Maybe it wasn't such a bad idea after all.

"That sounds good, Mama," I said weakly.

I could tell she was trying to convince me—and herself—that this was the best course of action. As hard as this was on me, I knew it was harder on her. This was *her* home, the one she'd built with Daddy. It held the wealth of memories they'd shared together. It was too much to take in that they might not live there anymore.

"We'll need to sell the house, of course. I've contacted a realtor, a friend of ours, Betsy Clarke. She's going to list it next month."

All at once I wanted to run away and hide under the sweeping magnolia in the front yard. It had been my hiding place as a child. I'd gone there when I needed to think or when the world and all its messiness got to be too much for me. It had been a sheltering friend, a place of safety.

I'd leaned against the large, sturdy trunk and closed my eyes, and I'd sat there until I felt restored and at peace once more.

I was no longer a child, but I could go there in my mind. And that's where I was now, hiding.

In February, 113 King William Road went up for sale. Losing that house, for me, meant losing the last shreds of my innocence—and there seemed so little, if any, innocence left after the choices I'd made. And yet I could still recall those happier times before Lawrence vanished into thin air. Surely that must count for something.

Within a few days, Mama and Daddy's next-door neighbor, Mr. Campbell, bought the house as an investment property for his daughter, Mandy, who planned to rent it out. Mama was relieved that their house had sold so quickly; she felt it was an answered prayer.

As I'd imagined it being inhabited by a nice, young family, I'd finally been able to accept the inevitable sale of the house. I could live with that. But renters? Strangers inhabiting our rooms? Mama seemed indifferent about renters; the very thought made me wince.

That tumultuous event left me restless, like a ship without a harbor to return to. In desperation, I clung to my faith. I sensed God was with me, with us all. And yet there was so much uncertainty. Six months had passed since my talk with Chick, and I was still tied to that U-shaped desk. It wasn't that he didn't believe in me; he did. He was just old-school when it came to women. He wanted to keep me in the place that best suited him. But that arrangement only worked for one of us. More than ever, I was ready to quit my job and try my hand as a freelance copywriter.

That would be risky, of course—I'd never written a word of copy. But there were two things in my favor: I'd spent the past few years studying ads and reading headlines, and my dad was a gifted writer. Surely I'd inherited a few of his genes.

Good copywriting was all about being clever and concise. I believed I could do it. But right now I had more pressing things on my mind. Horace and I still needed to pack up Mama and Daddy's house. It was full of books and furniture, and the attic was crammed with keepsakes that had accumulated over thirty years. The whole task felt daunting, even though I knew we'd get through it, one step at a time.

It helped seeing Mama and Daddy settle into their new accommodations. Mama had a one-bedroom apartment in independent living. Daddy required skilled nursing care, so he lived in a separate building. After breakfast each morning, a nurse walked him across the parking lot to Mama's room. They spent the day together and ate their meals in the cafeteria. After dinner, another nurse walked Daddy back to his room, where he spent the night. It was the best of both worlds: Mama got to spend her days with Daddy, but she didn't have to worry about his care.

When I asked them how they were doing, they said things like, "pretty good" or "We're fine." Still, they'd gone from a 2,500-square-foot home they'd inhabited for three decades to living in two tiny rooms. Daddy seemed content. It was Mama I worried about. Even though she'd never admit it, I heard an unfamiliar meekness in her voice and knew giving up everything that was precious and familiar to them had been particularly hard on her.

In early March, just before Mama and Daddy's closing, I took a week off from work. Chick had been understanding about my new caregiving role and was happy to give me the time. Horace drove up from the beach on a Monday so we could begin the arduous task of emptying out the house.

As I made my way up the driveway that morning, grief enveloped me like a blanket still damp from the dryer. As I pulled up into the spot where Mama had always parked her car, tears fell down my cheek and onto my old Carolina T-shirt.

I turned off the engine and wiped my eyes on my sleeve. *I just can't do this. It's too hard.*

I inhaled deeply and let out a sigh. Like it or not, we had a house to empty. I didn't have time for tears.

Horace started in the basement, and I tackled the master bedroom. I walked down the hallway and entered the pale green room. I stopped for a moment to take it all in—the series of framed black-and-white photos of Lawrence as a little boy—maybe two years old?—hanging over their mahogany chest. The matching Queen Anne bed and dressing table where I'd stood and watched Mama put on her makeup a hundred times.

I meandered over to the dressing table and sat down on the stool. There were crisp linen doilies covering the table and hints of powder—blush, perhaps—everywhere. My eyes scanned the items before me: makeup and perfume bottles of various shapes and colors, a gold jewelry box with a glass lid that revealed an array of necklaces and earrings. This still life of my mother's earlier existence evoked a sense of sadness. Why couldn't things just return to their former state? Before Lawrence was killed and I'd lost my way and Horace wasted so much time dodging Lawrence's shadow, which was larger than life?

I wondered when Mama had last sat here and what she'd been thinking. Was it about her next hair appointment? Or which slip she should wear under her stylish new suit? Perhaps she'd had weightier things on her mind, like Daddy's dwindling health or her cancer and whether or not she'd survive.

"I have something to show you."

I'd been so lost in thought I'd forgotten about Horace.

I rose from the dressing table and followed him out of the room and down the narrow hall into the living room. I watched curiously as he stopped in front of Mama's cedar chest, the one her daddy, Melvin, had bought her at the age of eighteen. He bent down and opened the lid, releasing the distinct, woodsy smell that permeated the items inside. He reached into the chest and picked up a thick stack of pale blue envelopes, held together with a red satin ribbon.

"These are Mama and Daddy's love letters," he said, offering them to me.

I took the letters and examined them carefully. I recognized the envelopes as Air Mail, with their signature striped borders and Par Avion stamp. I also knew the handwriting—my father's illegible scrawl and my mother's elegant script.

I pondered their contents. *How did this all start?*

My father grew up in a tiny two-bedroom shotgun house in Greenville, North Carolina. His father was a carpenter, his mother a homemaker. Determined to be the first in his family to go to college, he sold apples on the street corner and delivered newspapers to pay for his education.

Mama grew up on a tobacco farm, the oldest of six. While she helped her mother take care of the family, she dreamed of being a teacher and someday attending East Carolina Teachers College.

That day came and she left the farm and headed to ECTC, as it was known.

Daddy chose the same college. Always a high achiever, he quickly made his mark: News editor and head writer for the Greenville daily paper. Correspondent for the *Raleigh News & Observer*, the *Norfolk Times*, and United Press. Assistant editor of the college newspaper. Founder and president of the Young Democrats Club.

As Mama told it, he was out of her league. She'd often watch him from her dorm room window—sauntering across campus, chatting it up with a young coed, rushing off to class. Then the war broke out and Daddy was drafted. He left the comfort of college, enlisted in the army, and was sent to South America to protect the Panama Canal.

One of the skills my mother had learned on the farm was sewing. She belonged to a sewing circle, and she and her friends decided they would take part in the war effort and write letters to servicemen. My mother drew my father's name. That's when it began: the letters. Three years of their budding friendship, their declarations of love, and Daddy's proposal of marriage were all right here in pen and ink.

"I don't think we should read them," Horace said with conviction.

"No, I guess not," I answered dutifully, though I wasn't so sure.

Wouldn't these letters give us some insight into the people who had raised us? The ones who were growing older before our very eyes? I longed to see a younger version of my mother, to get a glimpse into a gentler time. Maybe I'd uncover some secret that would help me understand her. Maybe I'd discover that she, in some way, had been like me.

I was now twenty-nine. I'd spent countless Sundays and weeks of summer vacation on my grandmother's tobacco farm where Mama had grown up. I'd had overnights at Karen's and Diane's—Mama's sisters—and endlessly played with my cousins. And yet there was so much about my mother I didn't know. Increasingly, I was aware of a huge gap in my knowledge. Was it her illness that had brought this feeling on?

Then I realized it was because Horace and I were emptying out and closing up the last vestiges of our nuclear family. I wanted to know as much as I could about the people who had built this home and inhabited it for thirty years. That window of discovery was shattering, and I was desperate to grab onto even the tiniest shard of insight.

"What's in these letters is between Mama and Daddy," Horace insisted. "We don't have any right to pry."

I was weary and there was no fight left in me. Horace was my big brother. Maybe he knew best.

"Okay," I finally conceded.

We'd just let go of so much. I told myself this was just one more thing.

It took us weeks to box up and throw away everything that had lived so long in that house. When we were done, I hugged Horace goodbye, then got in my car and crept down the driveway for the last time.

About halfway down, I stopped to look back. I took in what had once been our ranch-style home, set back from the street, high on a hill. I nodded to the magnolia, smiled at the crepe myrtles, and ran my eyes along the sloping front yard where I'd once sledded with my brothers. A mixture of sadness and joy overwhelmed me. I let out a sigh, took a right out of the driveway, and drove down the street.

The next week, Drew and I were set to go on a diving trip to Cayman Brac. It had been planned for a while, and the timing couldn't have been more perfect. There were nine of us altogether, including

Shirley and a guy I'd known in high school named Doug Hayes. Doug was a prominent criminal attorney in Raleigh, and his wife, Terri, was in private practice. They were the kind of people you would expect to find diving; they lived in a large house and drove BMWs.

Drew and I, in contrast, were an anomaly: he was freelancing and I was about to quit my job, and we had a sizable IRS bill looming over our heads that arrived a few days before our trip.

I stood in the middle of our living room, holding the notice in my hand.

"Shouldn't we pay this instead of going away?" I asked, concerned.

"We can take care of it when we get back," he said nonchalantly.

I thought back to the conversation I'd had with Lawrence the morning he'd left for Edinburgh. The one where he promised he'd return home. How I'd known deep in my gut that everything was about to change forever.

I had that same instinct now, that same sense of foreboding. Was I being unreasonable?

This was my husband. I trusted him implicitly.

"Okay," I said.

Years later, I'd look back on that moment and wish I'd said more.

Spring broke through the barren winter. Daffodils popped up out of concrete planters on the downtown pedestrian mall. April displayed its colorful brilliance, which spilled into May. The days grew increasingly warmer, and sweaters gave way to short sleeves.

Drew and I discussed things at length and agreed that I'd give a two-week notice and quit my job at the beginning of June. It was now the middle of May.

Sometimes I was energized by the thought of freelancing, sometimes scared. Wasn't this just like running off to New York to model without any idea of what I was doing? No, I told myself. This was different. I knew I could write. I just had to prove it to my clients—the ones who would pay me. For now, Drew's business was doing well. We'd be okay.

That long-awaited day finally arrived. I was nervous that morning as I took the elevator down to creative to talk to Chick. Even though we'd hit an impasse, I wanted to end things well. As I walked down the familiar black-and-white-tiled hallway, I felt nostalgic. This had been my first job out of college, and it had been amazing. I'd met Drew there. And some of my dearest friends. Surely that wasn't a coincidence. Still, there was no opportunity for growth here. It was time to move on.

As I pushed open the door to his office, I lifted a silent *Help* and *Thank you* to God.

Then I told Chick the news.

"That's wonderful, Laura."

Laura? Not ol' gal?

I'd worked for Chick McKinney for three years and knew him pretty well. This was his softer side, the one most people rarely got to see. He had just given me his blessing. There was no doubt about it. This was an answered prayer.

Chapter Sixteen

A few days later, on a deliciously warm morning, I was sitting at my desk, staring at the gold elevator doors, when a call came through the switchboard.

"McKinney, Silver & Rockett!" I answered in my best singsongy voice.

"May I speak with Laura Wagner?" It was a man's voice.

"This is Laura," I said, curious.

"Hi, Laura! It's Rich Evans." I immediately recognized the name. Rich and his wife, Lisa, owned a little design shop in Cary, just outside of Raleigh. Rich had hired Drew to do a few illustrations, and Drew spoke highly of him.

"Drew tells me you're doing some freelance copywriting. I may have a little job for you."

Job? Me? I quickly gathered my thoughts. "Yes, that's right," I said hesitantly.

He explained that he was doing a brochure for a local roofing company. Drew had agreed to do the illustrations, but he needed someone to write the copy.

"What do you charge per hour?" he asked.

Charge? I hadn't written a word of copy; I didn't know what to charge. I thought for a second.

"Twenty-five an hour," I said. Surely an hour of writing was worth that.

"Great! Could you stop by after work tomorrow? I'll need to go over the material, give you some copy points."

"Of course!" And just like that, my freelance writing career began.

My last day of work was a Thursday in early June. Chick gathered the VPs, account executives, and creatives to wish me goodbye. We congregated in the area outside of Chick's third-floor office. There was beer, laughter, and lots of well wishes. I would miss this place, especially the close friends I'd made. I was in a Bible study with Caroline and Robin, though, and Jack was one of our closest friends, so I wasn't worried about losing touch.

While I wouldn't miss the monotony of my job, I'd miss that ol' boy, Chick. He might be eccentric, but he was a good person. And smart. Except when it came to helping me realize my dream. Now that was up to me.

The first thing I did after quitting my job was set up my office in a corner of our postage stamp–size dining room. One sweltering Sunday after church, Drew and I drove to the State Fairgrounds flea market near our apartment to hunt for a writing desk.

We browsed for about an hour before finding the perfect one: a small, antique oak with a central drawer. Now all I needed was a typewriter, and I wanted an electric, of course. I splurged on a beauty, the latest model: a tan Smith Corona with auto-correct tape. I brought it home from the office supply store, pulled it out of the box, set it on my desk, and plugged it in. I fed it a piece of paper, then pressed the power switch and waited. The quiet whir of the engine and the sight of a blank sheet of paper awaiting a keystroke made my heart pound.

Drew put out the word about my business to small design firms and agencies he'd worked for. Soon calls—and freelance work—began pouring in. It felt strange to work from home after going to an office every day. But Drew and I enjoyed being together doing what we loved. Writing copy was challenging and energizing; it was reward-ing to see my words in print. For the first time in my life, I felt a sense of purpose. I had a creative, supportive husband. We had a good marriage, despite our growing debt. And I was finally writ-ing—the thing I believed I was born to do.

Mama and Daddy seemed happy with their new life in the Method-ist home. Daddy was at peace with the world, as always. Mama was leading a women's Bible study and making new friends.

What they'd done seemed extreme. Most retirement commu-nities allowed you to move in and rent from month to month. But Mama had been worried about the future, and the decision she'd made meant they'd be cared for—for life. Given Daddy's fragile con-dition, I was more convinced than ever that they'd made the best choice.

On a cool, rainy day in early September, out of the blue, Daddy pulled me aside while I was visiting. "Will you take me to the mall?" he asked. "I want to buy your mother a new wedding ring, one with sparkles on it."

By sparkles, I assumed he meant small diamonds similar to the ones on the wedding band he'd given her when they'd married forty-two years ago. One of the diamonds was cracked, and the band was thin from years of wear. I smiled, wondering what had prompted this sudden interest in surprising my mother with some-thing sparkly.

Mother knew about our little trip—with their daily routine so carefully measured, it was impossible to keep something like that from her. I took him to a jewelry store at South Square Mall, fifteen minutes away. We walked to the counter, and I told the eager sales-person that Daddy wanted to look at wedding bands for my mother.

The salesman was warm and generous, and Daddy picked out the second ring we looked at—an eighteen-carat gold band with four small diamonds across the front. I helped Daddy pay for the ring, and the salesman placed it in a black velvet box and slipped it into a bag. As we headed home, Daddy didn't say much, but I knew he was thinking about the ring. And Mama.

"We're back," I announced as we walked into Mama's tiny room. She seemed more upbeat than usual.

"Well." She posed, smiling. "What have you two been up to?"

Daddy stood there sheepishly holding the bag with the name of the jewelry store printed on the side. "Oh, nothing," he replied, playing along.

Mama deftly excused herself and went into the bathroom.

"I know it isn't really a special occasion," he whispered, "but I want to give it to her now."

I looked into his face and saw a young man nervously getting ready to propose. He pulled out the box and handed me the bag.

A few minutes later, Mama emerged from the bathroom. Daddy went over, stood awkwardly in front of her, and opened the velvet box. "Will you marry me?" he asked.

Mama lowered her gaze. Then she lifted her head and looked at him, and her lips spread into a smile. "Yes," was her tender reply. Their eyes locked, and everything around them seemed to fade away.

I watched as Daddy gently slid the gold band onto Mama's ring finger. She accepted it without hesitation. I blushed to witness such an intimate moment between my parents.

At that moment, I thought back to the tiny parsonage in Burlington, North Carolina, where they'd said their vows on December 21, 1944. In their wedding photo, Mama is wearing a powder-blue dress with lace at the neck, a pillbox hat, pearl earrings, and an orchid corsage. Her skin is like porcelain, her cheeks flushed. She is breathtaking. Daddy is in his dress army uniform, just returned from the war. Every hair is in place, and he is wearing the same glasses I now keep on my desk. Their gaze is so direct, I feel that any second they will speak. *Yes, we are young,* they might say, *but the future seems so bright!* Oh, that they could have held on to that moment forever. Little did they know the heartbreak that was to come.

A time of settling came for all of us. In the months that followed, Drew and I stayed busy working on new ad campaigns. When I wasn't writing or going to see Mama and Daddy, I volunteered to do phone banking and fundraising for presidential candidate Gary Hart. He reminded me so much of JFK—young, vibrant, inspiring. I'd never thought of myself as political, but his new vision for America stirred me to get involved.

Just a few days after Valentine's Day, I was working at my typewriter when the phone rang. I jumped up and walked into the kitchen to answer it.

"Hello?"

"Laura, this is Nan Davis at the Methodist Retirement Home."

"Oh, hi, Nan!" I said, still deconstructing the last sentence I'd typed. Nan was the head nurse with whom I'd spoken several times about Daddy's care.

"It's your mother. She's . . ."

A sense of dread swept over me. Whatever she had to say next couldn't be good.

"She's not doing well."

"What's wrong?" I asked, not really sure I wanted to know.

"She's had a breakdown."

Breakdown. My thoughts instantly flashed back to the previous Christmas, when Mama had been hospitalized at Holly Hill.

"Where is she?" My words sounded small, like a child's.

"In her room. She needs to go to Duke. To the psychiatric ward. I think it's best that you take her."

My stomach lurched and my hands started to tingle. *Not again.*

"I'm afraid it's urgent. You need to come right away."

I shut my eyes and let out a weighted sigh. "I'll be right there."

Drew was having lunch with a friend, so I'd have to go alone. Mama lived in Durham. It would take thirty minutes to get there, maybe twenty-five if I pushed the speed limit.

I picked up a pen, dashed out a note to Drew, and left it on the table. Then I threw on my jacket and walked out the door.

Some twenty minutes later, I pulled into a parking space outside of Mama's building. I turned off the engine and sat there for a moment. My brain felt as if it were filled with a gray soup. For the life of me, I couldn't remember the drive, only getting into my Honda and putting the key in the ignition. I felt numb, but I had to shake it off. Whatever awaited me, I'd have to deal with it.

I took a deep breath and exhaled.

Here goes.

I got out of the car and walked down the sidewalk that led to Mama's entrance. I opened the heavy door, which was left unlocked during the day, and walked inside.

The hallway was narrow and poorly lit; the linoleum looked more yellowed than usual. I walked at a clip towards Mama's room and paused just outside the door. *Room 108*, read the gold numbers. Underneath was the framed cross-stitch I'd made of her name just after she'd moved in.

I put my trembling hand on the doorknob. The last time I'd visited Mama, she'd asked about Drew and wanted to know how my freelance work was going. She'd seemed fine, at least as far as I could tell.

I turned the doorknob and walked in.

I took one look and shuddered. There was a stranger lying in Mama's bed, curled into a fetal position, rhythmically rocking back and forth.

That can't be her.

And yet, the soft gray hair, the birthmark in the middle of her neck . . .

I was pierced by a million tiny needles. An emotional acupuncture. Had I been so caught up in own my life that I'd failed to pay attention to what was right in front of me?

I walked over to the bed, reached out my hand, and put it on her shoulder. "Mama, it's me. Laura."

At my touch, the woman slowly opened her eyes and glanced up at me. In that moment, I caught a glimmer of Mama, an unmistakable look of terror in her eyes. "Laura," she whispered.

Recognition. But then she shut her eyes and resumed her rocking.

"Mama. Mama, listen," I urged, frightened to see my mother this way. I sat down on the rumpled bedspread and started stroking her hair. "Mama, the nurse called me. I'm taking you to Duke. You need help."

The rocking stopped and she looked at me once more. Her face was flushed, her gaze vacant. Her eyes were tinged with a distant madness. And yet, when I looked closely, I could see tiny fragments of the woman who had given me life.

"No!" she protested. "I can't! I can't afford it!" Her voice trailed off and she began to cry.

A sharp pain ran through me, as if a predatory bird had swooped down and punctured my throat with its talons.

She drew herself into an even smaller ball and began rocking, this time with more urgency.

My heart beat wildly as the severity of her condition began to sink in. "You don't have anything to worry about," I reassured her. "Your insurance will cover it."

"No. It won't," she insisted. "You and Drew will be out on the street."

I froze at her words. Where had that come from? What was this fixation on money?

Now I was terrified. This wasn't just depression; it was more insidious. A devouring monster, unleashed. I stood up and stepped away from the bed to get some distance.

What was I going to do? I took a deep breath like a wordless prayer. "Mama," I said calmly. "My car is outside. I'm going to drive you to Duke. It's a wonderful hospital. They can help you."

The rocking slowed. She drew her head out of its shell and glanced at me with narrow eyes. Now all semblance of the mother I knew was gone. Something or someone had taken her from me. "Okay, honey," she said meekly.

I recognized that voice, heard her resignation. Mama had always been a fighter. Now her defenses had crumbled.

I helped her sit up and slip on a pair of shoes. Then I walked to the closet, found her coat, and grabbed her purse from a chair sitting next to the TV.

"Here, let me help you," I said as I lifted her up from the bed. She was limp like a rag doll, as though the life had been drained from her.

I helped her put on her coat. Then I put my arm around her, and we shuffled to the door. I opened the door and shut it firmly behind us. We walked down the corridor to the exit and out into the frozen February day. With every step, I was afraid she would push me away and turn back or, worse, collapse in a heap at my feet. It was only a few hundred yards to the car. I just had to get her into the passenger's seat, buckle her in, and drive away.

A few moments later, she was in the car. A miracle.

Duke Hospital was just a few blocks away, on the other side of Erwin Road. It was one of the best hospitals in the country, so familiar to me from my days working in the neurology department. I knew from my time there they had an excellent psychiatric hospital and that she would get the best of care.

I pulled onto Erwin Road, followed the emergency signs to Trent Drive, and took a right. I glanced over at Mama, who was staring straight ahead, silent and still as death.

Stay strong. You have to stay strong.

I pulled into a small parking lot outside the emergency room. As I got out of the car and made my way to the other side to help Mama, I felt a glimmer of hope. If I could just get her to walk through those glass doors, she'd be fine.

That's when I realized: God was, and had been, with me. On the drive over, in Mama's room. Now. I was sure of it. There was no way I could have done this alone.

"Mama, we're here. Let's go inside." As I helped her out of the car, I looked up and saw an orderly in dark blue scrubs coming toward us with a wheelchair. His kind eyes offered reassurance.

"Here, let me help you," he said, and I took my first real exhale since Nan's phone call. He pushed the wheelchair up to the car door and lowered the footpads.

"Here, ma'am," he said, helping her into the wheelchair. "Let's take a little ride."

Dutifully, she sat down in the black vinyl seat, raised her feet, and placed them on the metal plates.

"Here we go," he said gently. I retrieved Mama's purse from the car and followed him up the ramp to the platform that led to the ER.

We walked past the emergency check-in on the right and continued down a hall that led to a spacious lobby filled with people. The orderly pushed Mama over to a spot where there were two empty chairs.

"You'll need to go to that desk and get her paperwork," he said, nodding to my left as he helped Mama into a chair.

"Thank you," I said. I glanced at his nametag. *Eric.* "Thank you, Eric. I appreciate it."

I walked over to the desk labeled "Admissions" and told the receptionist that my mother was there for psychiatric help.

"She has to admit herself," she said. She handed me a clipboard with forms and a pen attached. "Page three." Her tone was perfunctory. "There's a place for her signature. Without that, we can't take her."

"Right," I said, feeling defeated.

I turned around to join Mama and noticed the sea of faces in the room—addled, exhausted, contorted with pain. Everyone here was in crisis. I spotted Mama through the crowd and focused intently on her, ignoring everything around me.

How long had it been since I'd walked into Mama's room and found that stranger lying in her bed? Thirty minutes? Ten minutes? An hour? I had no clue. All I knew was that my reserves were depleted; soon, there'd be nothing left.

Then I looked at Mama, sitting there defenseless and vulnerable, her head bowed. No matter what I was feeling, I had to set it aside. I had to be there for her. She was all that mattered right now.

I sat down beside her and started filling out the first sheet.

There were so many questions, many I wasn't sure how to answer. Had anyone in her family died of cancer? If so, when? Had her mother been diabetic? I once again realized there was so much I didn't know about Mama or her family.

Finally, I came to the third sheet, which had the words "Permission for Treatment" printed across the top. I quickly read through it, checking each box. Then I glanced at the bottom. There was a line for her signature and the date. That was all that was left to do.

"Mama," I said, turning to her. "You need to sign this." I was aware that I was speaking to her as a mother would to a child. "Right here." I pointed to the blank space.

"I can't."

My stomach knotted.

"You and Drew will be destitute."

There it was again. Her fears about money.

I reached back in my memory to find something, anything, to help me understand. Mama had been the eldest daughter of a farmer during the Depression. Times had been hard and material things had been difficult to come by, and precious.

For as long as I could remember, she'd enjoyed surrounding herself with nice things: a silver tea service, the finest wool carpet, an expensive oil painting to hang over the mantle. Had giving up those things triggered this breakdown?

"Drew and I won't be destitute," I said as firmly, and kindly, as I could. "You have insurance. Lots of it." I was speaking in snippets she might possibly understand.

"No," she insisted. "You'll be ruined! I can't do that to you!"

I knew she believed with all her heart in what she was saying, but it simply wasn't true. She'd given me power of attorney, and I handled all their finances. I filed her insurance and paid her bills. I knew her chemo and Daddy's extra nursing care was depleting the money they'd handed over. Still, the retirement home had made good on its promise to care for them. I knew they'd be okay. Convincing Mama in her current state, however—that was another matter.

I fought back tears. I'd give anything for Drew to be there. Or Horace. But he was hundreds of miles away.

"Mama, look at me." She slowly raised her eyes to meet mine. I looked into brown pools of tears. "Mama, you have to trust me. Drew and I will be fine. You need to do this. Please."

I slid the clipboard into her lap and placed the cheap Bic pen in her hand. She looked down at the paper. I knew she had no intention of signing it.

"Mama. Please."

"I can't, honey," she said in the faintest voice.

My heart sank. I didn't know what else to do. I'd tried to reason with her. I'd pleaded. She wasn't going to sign. She couldn't go back to the home; they didn't have the resources to help her. This was the only hope I had for her. She certainly couldn't go on this way.

Without even thinking, I rose from my chair and knelt down in front of Mama. I could feel people staring at me, but I didn't care. I closed my eyes and did the only thing I knew to do. I prayed.

God, please. I need your help. I need Mama to sign this paper. Help. Please.

As I said those words silently, time stood still. Everything fell away–Mama, my anxiety, the room full of strangers. I felt an inexplicable peace wash over me. I opened my eyes and lifted my head to see Mama, pen in hand, signing her name.

Since losing Lawrence, nothing in my thirty years had been as difficult as what happened that day. After signing the admission form, Mama was taken to a locked unit on the psychiatric ward at Duke South. I knew it well; I'd frequently delivered lab results there when I worked in EEG during college. What I hadn't fathomed then was that my mother would one day be a patient there, one of those people whose mind had come to a crossroad and taken the wrong turn.

I tried not to think about her being in a locked ward–a place in my mind that was for crazy people. (The doctors weren't worried she would hurt herself, but they were concerned she'd try to escape.) I told myself she would get better; she was just going through a hard time. Deep in her distraught soul, she trusted God, and I did too. He'd brought us through so many things; He wouldn't stop now.

I tried to stay busy so I wouldn't think about Mama, but it was hard to focus on my writing. I prayed for her when she came to mind, and for Daddy. But I couldn't let myself dwell on the fact that she'd had a breakdown, that she was under psychiatric care, and that the future was unclear. It was too much to take in.

A week after she was admitted, I went to see her. I would have gone sooner, but her ward had a policy that visitors weren't allowed the first week to make the adjustment easier. *Easier on whom?* I wondered. It certainly hadn't been easy on me.

It was dusk when I pulled up to the hospital. The pastel sky set off the large Gothic cathedral that towered over Duke South. I checked in, then took the elevator up to the third floor. I got off, walked over to the locked door, and pushed a red button. A moment later, I was buzzed inside. I made my way to the nurses' station and told them I wanted to see Mama.

A young, redheaded doctor in a lab coat—thin, with freckles and bright blue eyes—turned around when he heard her name. "Are you Mrs. Whitfield's daughter?" he asked.

"Yes, I am."

"Dr. Larson." He reached out his hand. "I'm your mother's doctor." His smile was warm, and I could see in his eyes that he was kind.

"How is she doing?" I asked with trepidation.

"Not so good today, I'm afraid. She's quite agitated." He shook his head. "She's a sweet lady. She told me she and your father sold their home. That he's had some health problems. And there's her cancer, of course. That's a lot for someone to deal with. I think those things plus the chemical effects of her chemo have taken their toll. We're trying ECT, electric shock therapy. I know it sounds scary, but clinically, we've had great results. I believe it will help."

I stiffened. It had never occurred to me that electric shock would be part of her treatment. I'd seen *One Flew Over the Cuckoo's Nest*. Wasn't that for people who were certifiably insane?

I looked into his eyes and saw only compassion. I had to trust him. What else could I do?

"Thank you," I said. "Can I see her?"

"Yes, I'll take you. It might be best to keep your visit short. She's had a long day."

Together, we walked through a secured entrance and proceeded

into a sterile hallway with rooms on either side. I followed nervously
behind the doctor as he entered the second room on the right. There
was Mama, lying in a hospital bed with metal railings. Her bedsheets
were pulled tight across her body, as if she were a mummy.

The last time I'd seen her, she'd looked sad and vacant. Now
she seemed fidgety. Her pupils were dilated—the effects of the drugs,
I assumed.

"Mrs. Whitfield? Hi, it's Dr. Larson. Your daughter, Laura, is
here to see you."

Your daughter, Laura. His introduction reminded me of how far
gone she was.

"I'll leave you two," he said, looking at me. "We'll talk soon." He
smiled, then turned and walked out of the room.

"Mama, hey. How are you?" I bent over her bed and gave her
a kiss. Then I stroked her hair and looked into her eyes, longing to
see some sign of improvement.

"Get me out of here," she said. There was anguish in her voice.

An invisible fist landed in the space just below my diaphragm. I
closed my eyes against the crippling blow.

"Mama," I said, opening my eyes. "I know you want to go
home. But you need to stay here for now. You have a nice doctor.
He's going to help you. I'll come to visit . . ."

I stopped short. I couldn't bear to see her so vulnerable.

I looked up at the clock, the only object on the otherwise bare
pale green wall. I watched the second hand make its painful way
to the end of a minute, and then another, my eyes darting back
between the two faces—the clock's and Mama's—until the silence
was too much to bear.

My throat tightened. I felt the room shrinking, closing in on me,
as though it were choking off my air supply.

"I love you, Mama," I said, my voice quivering. A tear ran down
my cheek, pooling inside the corner of my mouth.

I thought of all the mean things I'd ever said to Mama, all the heartache I'd put her through. She'd lost Lawrence, her perfect, first-born son. That was pain enough for a lifetime. Then I'd inflicted more—running off to New York, getting a divorce. It had been years since we'd exchanged harsh words, but I was filled with regret. I promised myself that when she got out, I'd be a better daughter. More attentive. And more patient.

I took her hand and squeezed it before leaning over to kiss her forehead, which tasted salty and warm. "I have to go now," I said, measuring my words carefully. I'll be back soon."

I slowly pulled back. The face looking back at me was stricken with fear.

"Don't go," she whispered.

On hearing those words, my heart wrenched. I knew I couldn't stay, but I didn't want to go. All I wanted to do was reach down, swoop her up, and carry her away—somewhere, anywhere she might escape this personal hell.

"It's okay, Mama. It'll be okay."

But would it? Would she ever get better? I wasn't so sure.

"Please," she begged. Her tone was desperate.

Now all I wanted to do was run away.

I let out a heavy sigh and the tears started to flow. Not knowing what else to do, I started walking toward the door. One step forward, two back, as if a chain was tethering me to her heart. My resolve was weakening. I had to leave quickly, or it would be impossible to leave at all.

"Bye, Mama," I said, looking over my shoulder. "I love you."

I made my way out of her room and walked quickly down the hall toward the locked metal door. If I could just get on the other side, I'd be okay.

"Laura! Don't leave me here!" I heard a voice call after me.

I shut my eyes and pressed the button.

"Don't leave me!" she called again. This time it was more insistent.

The door opened with a click and I walked through, shutting out the voice as the door closed behind me. I stood motionless. Everything around me felt cold and opaque. I'd been dropped into a dark, murky ocean, miles from shore, with no sense of how to find my way back.

Sometime in March, the fog began to lift. Mama started getting better. She was more talkative during my visits, and she seemed less depressed.

A month later, Dr. Larson told me she was ready to go home. It felt like a miracle. It had been a long, tedious journey, carrying the weight of Mama's illness and worrying about Daddy. Then there were the hospital visits, which, due to Mama's altered state, had become nearly unbearable. As the weeks stretched on, I clung to hope like a climber grasping a piton, afraid to let go and lose my footing. I prayed more, trusted more, believed far more than I'd thought possible. If God and I had once been strangers, we were no more. I clung to him like a lost child. And I was. I knew it. And I surrendered.

It was a balmy April day when Mama was released from the hospital. The grass was bright green, the dogwoods were in bloom, and a band of yellow forsythia wrapped itself around Duke Chapel, a contrast to its gray, volcanic stone. I felt lighthearted, even joyful, as I drove Mama home.

The day was only matched by Mama's beauty. Her chestnut eyes were bright, her face expectant. Everything about her was alive. She was talkative, excited to see Daddy and be back in her room.

As we headed down Erwin Road, it didn't escape my notice that she was going home three days before Easter, Resurrection Day. There was no doubt in my mind: Mama had been resurrected too.

...

In the midst of Mama's hospital stay, Drew and I had decided to rent an office with a friend. A graphic designer named Denise Sanders was looking for someone to share a space in a quaint old brick building on Glenwood Avenue, not far from downtown. The timing wasn't great; between work deadlines and trips to Durham, we had all we could handle. Still, it was a good opportunity, and something we'd dreamed of doing. Denise would be taking financial responsibility for the renovation of the space. Other than furnishings, we wouldn't have to put in a lot of money.

After talking it over for several days, we'd signed the lease.

The new office meant Drew would have a large workspace with a small conference table for client meetings. Adjoining that room was a small space that would serve as my office.

We moved in after the renovations were completed, about a month after Mama came home. I bought a bigger desk and placed it in front of the large, airy window overlooking the brick courtyard. Then I added bookshelves and an overstuffed chair. It was sparse and charming, and I felt as though I had arrived.

If nothing else, that year had been a year of change. I'd quit my job and started freelancing. And then, in late July, we started the search for a house. Our businesses were doing well and we'd outgrown our small apartment; it was time. We somehow pulled together a down payment—quite a feat, since we were still going on diving trips and struggling to stay current with our taxes. The truth was, I'd grown desensitized to our debt. In typical Scarlett O'Hara fashion, I pushed it aside, telling myself everything would work out.

In September, we found the perfect place: a one-story brick ranch on Brooks Avenue, a ten-minute drive from our office and just a few blocks from Caroline. It was a starter house in an upscale neighborhood, and just what we could afford. There were three bedrooms—one for us, one for guests, and one for a nursery, since starting a family was foremost on our minds.

We put down every penny we'd saved and signed a contract. In early October, when the oaks and maples were blazing with color, we moved in. There was painting that needed to be done and a kitchen sorely in need of new flooring and cabinets. But we'd pushed ourselves to the limit to get in this house. I bought a few rugs and a new comforter for our bed. The bigger-ticket items would have to wait.

I woke up in our bed the first week in our new house and knew I was ready to start a family. Not tomorrow but right now. Somehow, after Mama's breakdown, it seemed urgent. As hard as it was to face, my parents were getting older, and I wanted to have a baby so they could experience the joy of another grandchild before they died. Plus, I was turning thirty-one in one month, at the end of November.

I called my ob-gyn that same morning and went in for a checkup the next week. My blood work, along with everything else, looked fine. We were good to go.

The idea of being a mother filled me with anticipation and excitement. We were young and healthy. Surely getting pregnant would be easy. I figured all we had to do was have sex around the time I was ovulating.

Friends who'd already gone through this told us it might take a few months. With a little luck and good timing, I reasoned, we'd be parents by the end of the next year.

I bought a thermometer and took my temperature each morning, watching anxiously for the slightest rise in mercury. A spike in red meant conditions were optimal—it was *time*. Sex began to feel mechanical. Still, if this is what it took, we told ourselves, it was worth it.

As our focus turned to babies, Lily was more often on my mind.

I added up the years; she'd be five now, almost to the day. I envisioned her angelic face, her corn silk–colored hair. And bachelor button eyes, blue like mine. She'd appear as I drove to the grocery store or penciled in my morning temp.

I'd gotten pregnant once; I was confident I could do it again. But along with that reassurance came mounting shame over having ended my first pregnancy. Drew knew, of course. But it was a secret I'd hidden from everyone else for fear of being judged.

I'd recently joined a large community Bible study of almost five hundred women. We'd been meeting weekly since early fall, teaching and then breaking off into small groups. I enjoyed making new friends and challenging myself in that way. One day, as Christmas drew near and the semester came to a close, my small group leader called.

"I wanted to know if you'd like to be part of our ministry group at the women's prison."

"Really?" I knew I'd heard her right, but I was amazed. The women's prison ministry was a big deal; not just anyone was asked to do it.

"Would you mind playing the keyboard and leading worship?" I'd been playing the piano and singing in the choir at Asbury since Drew and I had become members, and it was something I enjoyed.

"I'd be honored," I told her.

Going to the prison became the highlight of my week, and increasingly it was a nice distraction from our unsuccessful attempts to conceive. Not that going to a maximum-security prison for women was easy; it was anything but. Our group of seven women met in the parking lot outside the prison each week before going inside. We'd pile into Linda's large blue cargo van, which looked like something out of a B-grade bank heist movie, and once inside, we'd pray for an hour—for wisdom and protection, and for God to use us to minister to the women there. When we finished, we'd gather our things and walk down the sidewalk to the security gate, where we'd go through pat-down and show our visitor IDs.

The prison buildings were ominous—dark red brick structures surrounded by several layers of barbed wire fence. Each week, we'd pass the most menacing of all the buildings, maximum security, which held the worst of the worst—those who'd committed murder. We all knew about it because our Bible study leader, Anne Lotz, had received a lot of attention for her friendship with Velma Barfield, better known as "Death Row Granny." In 1984, Velma had been charged with poisoning her fiancé and three other people. While in prison, she'd made a profession of faith in Christ. While many were skeptical, Anne believed her conversion was real.

Twenty-five or so prisoners attended our Bible study each week. We never knew how many other "Death Row Grannies" were among us, or what the women had been charged with, whether it was larceny, grand theft, assault and battery, or homicide. We knew them only by their first names. I grew to love these women, and I looked forward to seeing them each week. They knew we were there to love, not judge, them. And who were we to, anyway? Lord knew I was no saint. If not for the mercy of God and a different upbringing and circumstances, it might have been me in their place.

With everything I had on my plate, that fall flew by. Christmas came and went, and soon we faced a new year. It had been four months since we'd started trying to get pregnant, and I found myself teetering between hope and despair.

When my period arrived in March, I considered once again that God might be punishing me. After all, I'd broken the fifth commandment: I'd murdered my precious Lily.

In the weeks that followed, remorse became my constant companion. I knew I needed to keep stress at a minimum in order to get pregnant. But how? The more time that passed, the more anxious I became. What if Lily had been my one shot at being a mother and I'd blown it? What if my abortion—or that IUD lodged in my uterus—had made me infertile? I increasingly regretted that decision, though there was nothing I could do to alter it now.

The following week, as daffodils were popping out of the ground and the trees were starting to bud, our Bible study group marched through the doors of the Correctional Institution for Women and began to set up for the evening. Several of the prisoners who'd been assigned to assist us passed out hymnals. I pulled out my keyboard and began looking through my songbook, considering which pieces I might play.

The remaining prisoners, nondescript in their khaki pantsuits, filed in slowly, chatting quietly as they moved down the improvised aisles to find an empty seat. After everyone had gathered, Linda, our leader, opened with a prayer. As she said, "Amen," I began to play the first stanza of an old Baptist standard, "And Can It Be, That I Should Gain?"

"Long my imprisoned spirit lay, fast bound in sin and nature's night," the women sang as I began the second stanza.

"My chains fell off, my heart was free."

I looked up and saw two women singing fervently, their faces streaked with tears.

"I rose, went forth, and followed thee."

I looked again. This time they were smiling, their eyes tilted toward heaven. These women knew what they'd done. And yet, in that moment, they knew forgiveness in a way I couldn't possibly understand. I thought about my abortion. If they could feel that forgiveness in their souls, surely I could know it in mine.

~ↄ·ↄ~

Chapter Seventeen

Another couple months passed, and I woke up on June 8 just like any other day. Drew and I chatted over coffee and Wheat Chex. He had a meeting mid-morning, so he left early for the office.

As I stood in my closet, figuring out what to wear, the phone rang. It was a few minutes after eight, early for anyone to be calling, though I didn't think much about it.

"Hello?"

"Laura." My breath caught in my chest. It was Uncle Matt, Mama's youngest brother. Why would he be calling?

"It's your daddy. He's at the hospital."

"What's wrong?" My throat constricted like a tightly wound violin string.

"A nurse went in to check on him this morning around seven thirty and found him unconscious."

Unconscious. The word entered my ear and began boring its way into my brain. I glanced at my alarm clock. It was seven minutes past eight.

"They rushed him to Durham General. He's in the ER. Your mother is with him."

This was just another of his mini-strokes, I told myself. He'd come around.

"I just need to get a quick shower and call Horace," I said.

"I just spoke with Horace. You need to leave now. It's not good." I heard the gravity in his voice.

With those words, the newly painted walls of our bedroom began to close in. I drifted to the bed and sat down, not saying a word. My eyes closed and I saw Daddy's face, beaded with sweat, unmoving, pale for lack of oxygen. I longed to magically transport myself there and be by his side.

"I'm on my way," I muttered. I hung up and paused for a moment to brace myself. "Lord, help," I whispered—and there it was—that inexplicable peace I'd experienced hundreds of times before, especially in crisis.

I called Drew and told him what was going on.

"How soon can you get home?" I asked, anxious to see him.

"I'm sorry," he said, "but I have an important client meeting at nine. You'll have to go without me."

Really? This isn't more important? I told myself I shouldn't get upset with Drew. That I was making too much of this. Daddy would be okay.

"Call me and let me know how he is when you get there," he said. "I'll come as soon as I can."

"Okay," I said, deflated yet resigned.

I hung up the phone, pulled on a dress, and headed out the door. It was a beautiful morning. The sky was pale blue and dotted with clouds tinged in pink. Though it was early, the temperature was rising and the air was laden with humidity.

I turned right onto Wade Avenue, which merged into I-40. It was now eight twenty. I estimated that I'd arrive by nine. Would that be too late?

As I drove, I deliberately numbed myself to what might lie ahead. Along with a strange peace, I also felt a disquieting déjà vu. I reflected on the morning Nan Davis called to tell me about Mama. It hadn't been that long ago, really, and the memory of it was still raw. That story had ended well, but not without a lot of heartache and pain.

I thought of Daddy's face, slack with age. His hair—no gray, only the gleaming dark brown I'd always known—had escaped the ravages of time. Finally, his twinkling eyes and infectious smile. It was his eyes, those adoring eyes, I saw most clearly. I was his only daughter and still his little girl. He had loved me unconditionally my whole life. That love permeated every cell of my being, even now.

I pulled into the emergency entrance at Durham General, parked, and entered the ER. As I walked over to the information window, it felt as if I were stepping into a nightmare.

"I'm here to see James Whitfield. He was brought in about an hour ago. I'm his daughter."

The woman behind the window looked down and began to scan a list of hand-printed names with her finger. She stopped about two-thirds of the way down. "He's this way, on the left." She pointed. "The middle set of curtains."

The peace I'd felt earlier was gone. I steeled myself against the overwhelming panic that now swept over me—my breath shallow, my hands sweaty, a rhythmic pounding in my chest. I walked across the scuffed tile squares and stood for a moment outside the brown-and-yellow-striped curtain separating me from my father.

My eyes tightened. I whispered a silent prayer.

I pulled back the curtain and took in the tableau before me: Daddy lying on a stretcher under a blanket, his eyes closed, his face pallid. Mama sitting next to him in a chair, holding his hand. A monitor beeped monotonously to the left of Daddy's head.

Mama turned. Her eyes were pools of sadness, not the eyes I'd seen since her recovery, which had been full of hope and light.

"Hey, honey," was all she said. Her voice sank like an anchor somewhere inside her.

"Oh, Mama."

I walked over and wrapped my arms around her. I pulled her close, and she felt airless and fragile. I buried my head in her hair and looked over at Daddy, vacant and lifeless.

"His heart stopped twice," she said in a half tone.

Her words took me back. I knew she was being careful, not wanting Daddy to hear.

"They tried to revive him with paddles, but it didn't work. He's breathing, but just barely." She stopped and looked at me, her head motioning toward the curtain where I'd entered.

She rose and I took her cue and followed her out of the makeshift room.

"The chaplain drove me here," she said as we walked together toward the waiting room. "I want you to meet her."

As we entered the waiting area, a young woman who looked to be in her early forties stood up and walked toward us. She had dark brown hair and glasses, and she looked like someone who was skilled at saying just the right thing. Mama introduced her to me as Patricia, and she gave me a sad smile.

At that moment, I knew I couldn't go through this without Drew. Or Horace. But my brother was at the beach, more than four hours away.

I glanced at my watch. It was eight fifty-five; Drew's meeting hadn't started. He could cancel and be here before ten.

I walked over to the pay phones on the wall next to us and dialed our office number. Drew picked up after two rings.

"Hey, it's me. Things aren't good," I said, as calmly and as firmly as I could. "I need you to come."

"Okay. My client is on her way. I'll keep it short and come as soon as I'm done."

He doesn't get it. But how can he? I'd deliberately avoided the word *dying,* afraid that saying it would make it so. I still believed the doctors would revive Daddy, that he wouldn't die. But what if he did die before Drew got here? How could I go through that alone?

"I'll be there soon," Drew said, breaking through my thoughts. "I love you."

My anger began to soften. "Hurry. Please. I love you too."

I hung up the phone and returned to Mama and Patricia.

"Your father and I have living wills," Mama said. "He doesn't want to be hooked up to a machine." Her voice shook as she spoke.

As the agent of their power of attorney, I'd reviewed their living wills and knew their wishes well. I didn't want to have this conversation, not at all. All at once, I was heading into a dark tunnel on a runaway train, with no way to escape.

I knew what her words meant. The doctors had come to the end of their options. We would need to release Daddy, let him go.

Patricia went to find Daddy's doctor. The four of us formed a circle, and I stood by Mama's side as she told the doctor what she'd just told me. The young doctor put his hand on Mama's shoulder and gave her a knowing look.

"You should go be with your husband."

Daddy would surely be gone within the next few hours. Not knowing what else to do, I turned to my faith and prayed. I knew the moment Daddy stopped breathing, he'd be with Jesus. I wasn't afraid of death, but I was afraid of losing my father. Losing Lawrence had been unbearable. How could I possibly bear up under this?

Mama nodded at the doctor. "I appreciate all you've done. Thank you."

She turned, walked over to the curtain, pulled it back, and walked in. Daddy was waxen, the mask of death already seeming to harden on his face. Mama sat down in the metal chair and reached across the bed for his hand. I stood just behind her, my eyes darting between his face, the beeping monitor, and the back of Mama's head.

Hurry, Drew. Please. Hurry.

I glanced at my watch. It was ten after ten. I did my best to calculate Daddy's last heartbeat. There was no way Drew would make it. For some reason, God wanted me to go through this without him. I didn't understand, but I had to trust.

As I stood taking in this final act of my father's life, I felt utterly alone. Mama was there, but her attention was fully riveted on Daddy. I watched her gazing at him, focusing all her love on him like a laser beam. In that moment, I understood for the first time the depth of their love. They were so different, and yet they had made a commitment and kept it, something I'd been unable to do until Drew and I had taken our vows.

What I was witnessing was so incredibly intimate, their final moment. I felt like an outsider. And yet I made myself stand there until the monitor began an incessant *beeeppp* and I knew it was over.

Mama sat for a moment, unmoving. Then she stood up, leaned over his bed, and kissed him on the lips. "I love you, Jimmy."

In that instant, my heart shattered into a million jagged pieces.

I stood immobile, not wanting to alter that moment in any way. Then I took two steps forward and stood beside her. I looked down at my father, once so full of life. I knew he wasn't there, not really. Still, that body was the only physical reminder I had of him, and soon they would take even that away.

I leaned down and gently kissed his forehead. He felt cold and clammy without the life coursing through him.

Mama's beloved husband and my precious father had just slipped away. We would never be the same.

I immediately called Drew and Horace and broke the news. As I spoke, my voice sounded as though it belonged to someone else. Daddy's death had happened so quickly; I hadn't even begun to process it all. And I was worried about Mama. I begged her to let me drive her back home, but she insisted she was fine, that Patricia would take her back and stay with her.

I looked into Mama's eyes, the eyes I'd come to know so well during her illness. She seemed deeply sad but strong. I had to believe that somehow, she'd be all right.

Once that was settled, Mama urged me to go home and start getting ready for the funeral. Horace was driving from the beach, so we agreed that he would pick her up the next day and bring her to our house.

At Mama's prodding, I'd pre-arranged both my parents' funerals several years earlier. As hard as that had been, now I was glad. The major decisions had already been made. The visitation would be at our house, the funeral at Brown-Wynne Funeral Home just a few miles away. Daddy would be buried beside Lawrence, in a plot they had purchased when he died.

Less than half an hour later, I exited the hospital into the glaring sunlight. I had just entered the land of walking, breathing human beings going about their day, doing ordinary things, unaware that my life had been inextricably altered. A huge piece of me had just been ripped away, though no one could see the vacuous crater it had left behind. I looked up at the sky. It was a vibrant blue, cloudless. How could such a glorious day be so shrouded in death?

I willed one foot in front of the other through the parking lot, located my car, and got in. It was approaching noon, and the heat inside was stifling, making breathing even more difficult. As I eased myself into the driver's seat, the vinyl scalded my legs. I was shocked back to reality, but only for an instant.

My emotions were in overdrive. Heat hotter, light brighter, sounds more jarring. Was it shock? Or just grief wreaking its insidious havoc? I started the engine, pulled up to the pay station, and handed the attendant my ticket.

"That'll be three dollars," he said, smiling.

As I handed him my money, I realized he was clueless. I felt both angry and resigned. When I'd entered this parking lot, Daddy had been alive. Now he was gone. Like that. In a matter of just a few hours.

My father just died! I wanted to shout. Instead, I remained silent and drove by the mechanical arm that lifted to let me through.

I'd always imagined that, after Lawrence, the hardest thing I'd have to go through in life would be losing Daddy. But nothing had prepared me for the reality of it. Over the past five years, I'd pieced together this beautiful mosaic: a happy life with Drew, my freelance business, our new home. Now all the pieces lay scattered, indistinguishable as a whole.

I thought back to that day long ago when I was living at the Outer Banks. I'd driven over to take a walk on the beach and dropped my keys in the sand. I didn't have a spare key, and retracing my steps had proven futile. Not knowing what else to do, I called Daddy.

"I'll be right there," he said cheerfully. Then he hung up the phone.

Horace had picked me up and driven me back to our house in Manteo. Daddy arrived five hours later, in the middle of the afternoon.

He got out of his car, walked toward me, and gave me a big hug. I pulled back and looked at him, expecting a lecture.

"Here you go!" he said, smiling, and dropped the spare set of keys into my hands.

That's it? No lecture about being more careful? About keeping a spare key so he won't have to make this drive again?

He walked back to his car and opened the door.

"It's a nice day for a drive," he said. He told us he loved us, and then he got in the car and drove away.

There hadn't been a second that I hadn't felt loved and adored by my father, and that was a prime example. I knew most people couldn't say that—many of my friends bore the scars of neglect, abuse, or abandonment at their fathers' hands. I knew the relationship we shared was rare, and I recognized and treasured it until the moment he took his last breath. Even now, that deep well of love and acceptance filled me. It was something I would draw from every day for the rest of my life.

In the days immediately following Daddy's death, I floated through each second, detached from reality, swimming through sorrow. I spent the first day meticulously cleaning our house. It was something I'd always found cathartic, especially now.

The next evening, our tiny house filled to overflowing with family, old friends from our Methodist church, colleagues from Mama's teaching days, and Daddy's coworkers at the paper. My father was beloved. Everyone who spoke to me that night said he was one of the kindest, gentlest, and most generous men they'd ever known. I'd always been proud to be James Whitfield's daughter. That had never been truer than it was now.

Daddy was buried next to Lawrence after a brief service at the funeral home Saturday morning. As Mama, Horace and his family, and Drew and I climbed the hill at the cemetery that warm June morning, I thought of the stark contrast to Lawrence's service that blustery March day years earlier. Both had died suddenly. And yet Lawrence's death had seemed more profound, with his life still so full of possibility—marriage, divinity school, teaching at a university someday. He'd lived such a short time; Daddy had lived to age seventy-two, three times as long. Standing there, listening to the pastor recite the words of Psalm 23, I felt comfort knowing they were together and regretted that I'd been unable to give Daddy a grandchild before he'd died.

Our third wedding anniversary fell exactly a week later. Things had pretty much gotten back to normal—on the outside, at least. I'd go to bed each night hungry for sleep to quell my lingering melancholy. The next morning I'd open my eyes, only to realize Daddy was gone. Then the process of navigating my grief would start all over again.

Our anniversary reminded me that life goes on. That love is what matters and sustains us. In many ways, it was like any other day—we were still exhausted from the aftermath of Daddy's passing and weren't up for a big celebration.

Drew's parents sent us a card. Several of our close friends called to congratulate us. I'd expected to hear from Mama, but by the time we went out to dinner, I hadn't heard a word. I tried not to let it bother me, but it hurt. I felt abandoned. Surely she hadn't forgotten. I needed her to remember, especially now that she was the only parent I had left.

When we returned from dinner, I walked into the kitchen and saw the light on our answering machine blinking red. I pressed the button and heard the automated voice announce that we had one message.

"Laura, Mama." Her voice was unusually quiet. She sounded weary. "I've been finishing up my thank-you notes for Daddy's funeral. I'm going to put everything away and go to bed. I'm tired." There was a long pause. "Happy anniversary, darling. I love you." And, then, ever so faintly, she said, "Mama," as if she were signing her name.

I was sure I had never heard anything so sweet and tender. In the midst of her grief, she had given me a great gift, an acknowledgment of her love. I wanted to wrap my arms around her and tell her I loved her, that I was here for her, that everything would be all right.

I pressed the lid of the answering machine until it popped open. I removed the tiny cassette and closed it shut. Then I walked down the hall and into our bedroom. I went over to our closet, reached up on a shelf, pulled out a box of keepsakes, and placed the tape gently inside. Something in Mama's voice had nicked the still-raw wound that was my heart. Mama had battled cancer. She wouldn't be here forever. When she was gone, I'd have this little piece of her, safely tucked away.

A few weeks after Daddy's funeral, Linda, the leader of our prison ministry, called to see if I'd be interested in signing on for a second year at the prison. Not wanting to make a hasty decision, I told her I'd pray about it and check in with her the next week.

A week later, the phone rang.

"Well? Have you decided?"

"Yes," I said. "It might sound strange, but for some reason I feel like God is saying no. It doesn't make sense. I've only been part of the team for a few months. And I really enjoy it. Still, I need to follow this instinct. I guess the answer is no."

All my life I'd heard the phrase "God works in mysterious ways." I was about to find out just exactly what that meant.

Seventeen years had passed since Lawrence's accident, and yet my grief still felt the same—a dull ache in the chest, an inexplicable sadness at the strangest moments, a lingering memory that pierced the heart. I began to experience how grief was cumulative—how the grief of the past piggybacked on the grief of the present, somehow. Was it familiarity? Maybe it was simply because there were two people missing now, not one. Two-fifths of our family was gone, leaving just Horace, Mama, and me.

I remembered reading a book by Elisabeth Elliot, a missionary to the Auca Indians in eastern Ecuador. After several years of living among these Indigenous people, they brutally attacked and murdered her husband, Jim. After his death, someone asked her how she got through each day. "I just do the next thing," she said. It was one of the simplest and wisest pieces of advice I'd ever heard.

So that's what I did. I got up. Kissed my husband. Made coffee. Showered. Dressed. Went to the office. And worked on my assignments. Whenever I'd come face-to-face with that gnawing sense of loss, I'd stop. Then I'd go through the motions of doing the next thing. It became my salvation in the weeks and months that followed.

Back in the spring, Drew and I had made plans to go to Ocracoke Island for a week in July with our friends Ben and Molly. Ben and I had met in college, when I was teaching exercise at Nicholson. He'd met Molly shortly after Drew and I were married, and the four of us had hit it off. We desperately needed a vacation, and they were easy to be around. It would be good to get away.

On a Saturday morning in mid-July, we headed to the Outer Banks.

The four of us quickly settled into our rickety but charming cottage, Wit's End. Ben and Molly would go for a run every morning while Drew and I had breakfast on the screened-in back porch. We spent our days walking around the island or biking from one end to the other. In the evenings, we drank beer and ordered takeout.

Without the distractions of work and daily life, I had more time to think. I shed so many tears that week at odd times. In my mind, I'd hear Daddy's voice or see his face, though the little things that were uniquely him were already beginning to fade.

Mostly I thought about the fact that ten months had passed and we were no closer to having a baby. Instead of feeling desperate, I began to feel despondent. Drew was sweet and patient. We knew the stress around Daddy's death hadn't helped our chances. I never shared my thoughts with anyone, but I was starting to feel like maybe it just wasn't meant to be.

Now we were on this remote little island, which we'd thought would be the ideal setting for getting pregnant. It was anything but. Between the sweltering heat and my lingering sadness, amorous nights just lost their appeal. Most nights I'd kiss Drew, roll over, and fall asleep with tears in my eyes.

Our week quickly came to a close, and we drove back to our comfortable bed. And air-conditioning.

"It feels like we've been camping out all week," I said as I unpacked my suitcase.

Drew shot me a side glance in agreement.

That night we fell into bed and passionately into each other's arms. Our longings—of loss, grief, the never-ending ache to be parents—were like flint to a flame.

Summer came to an end and life became hectic once more. Eleanor Nicholson had opened a new studio not far from our house, and I was teaching classes a few times a week. Our youth group geared up, and our women's Bible study started meeting once again. I missed my friends from the women's prison ministry. Still, God had spoken, and I'd obeyed.

In mid-September, I went for a routine checkup with Dr. Morgan, my ob-gyn. It had been almost a year since Drew and I had started trying to get pregnant, and I was anxious to see if everything was all right.

"How are you feeling?" said Dr. Morgan as he listened to my heart.

"Pretty good. A little tired."

I told him we'd gone backpacking over Labor Day, that I'd been more out of breath than usual but hadn't really been concerned. I'd experienced the ways in which grief seemed to manifest in my body since Daddy's death and assumed it was related to that.

My period was due the following Saturday. By that Wednesday, there was no sign of it starting. Despite the disappointing results I'd experienced in the past, I bought a home pregnancy test, just in case.

Anxious, I set everything out on the bathroom counter before going to bed that night. At the six the next morning, I woke up with adrenaline rushing through my veins. I walked to the bathroom, shut the door, and followed the directions on the box. Then I came back to bed to wait out the requisite thirty minutes.

Drew stirred.

"Well?" His voice was sleepy.

"Done. I promise I won't check it for thirty minutes."

I lay in the dark, preparing myself for the worst. At 6:29, however, I couldn't wait any longer. I hopped up and dashed to the bathroom.

The liquid in the test tube had turned from amethyst to a pale lilac. No doubt about it. I was pregnant.

I followed the beam of light from the bathroom to our bedroom and lay down beside Drew. "I can't believe it," he said, pulling me close.

"How did you know?" I asked, amazed by his perception.

"That smile of yours."

We lay in bed, wrapped in each other's arms and the warmth of our newfound joy. Tears streamed down my face. We were finally going to be parents.

As soon as it was light, I called Mama to give her the news.

She was overjoyed. "I'm just sorry your daddy won't be here to meet him. Or her."

"Me too," I said, experiencing a bittersweet moment of sorrow comingled with joy.

Next I called Horace, then a few of my closest friends. They were all full of questions: What was my due date? Had we thought about names? Did I have a nursery theme? There was so much to process. I was grateful to have seven and a half months before the baby arrived.

As I hung up the phone one last time, it occurred to me: this was the reason I'd felt I was supposed to quit the women's prison. I stopped to take it in. I thought back to that nagging feeling I'd had to say no to Linda. It was inexplicable at the time. Now I understood completely. God had orchestrated this—the baby, the timing. Drew and I had certainly done our part. But ultimately, it was God, not us, who was in control.

That afternoon we packed up our car and headed to Topsail Beach to spend the weekend with Drew's parents, who had rented a cottage there. The day couldn't have been more perfect. We cranked up the radio, rolled down the windows, and let the warm September breeze join our celebration. On the three-and-a-half-hour drive, we talked nonstop.

We imagined together what our baby would be like. What it would be like to trade diving trips for diapers. Then we moved on to practical matters. How we'd need to change the guest room into a nursery, and start buying baby stuff—a crib, stroller.

Finally, we got around to names. Over the past nine months, I'd distracted myself by researching baby names.

"I want a biblical name, of course," I said.

We both agreed that a name's meaning was important. We could think of numerous examples in the Bible where God had given someone a new name, something that they would come to live into. It was too soon to know the sex. Still, I sensed it was a girl. Maybe deep inside I believed it might be God's way of redeeming the loss of Lily.

"If it's a girl, I was thinking Elizabeth," I offered as we sped down a scenic road dotted with disheveled farmhouses and weathered oaks. I knew that in Hebrew, Elizabeth meant "set apart for God."

"I like it!" Drew said. "Would we call her Elizabeth? Or Liz?"

"Elizabeth," I said. "Liz sounds too grown-up."

"Have you thought about a boy's name? Just in case?"

I looked over and caught a wink.

"Maybe we could name him after Lawrence," he suggested.

Drew knew that nothing would make me happier. But Lawrence was long, and people might call him Larry. Maybe Christopher Lawrence? I'd always liked the name Chris.

"Or Marshall..." he offered. Drew's older brother was a Marshall.

"What about James Marshall?" I said. "That way we could use Daddy's name too." I was overwhelmed with joy.

Just two months earlier, I'd felt that God was punishing me—for my abortion, my promiscuity, the way I had lived my life with little thought of how he wanted me to live. Now everything seemed so perfect. This was mercy. *I'm finally pregnant.* I didn't want to let this moment pass unnoticed. I paused and drank it in like a glass of cool water on a hot day. God had answered our prayers. I was having a baby.

Thank you, Lord.

In late October, Drew and I drove to Atrium OB-GYN in Raleigh for my ten-week checkup. I was excited to have him along this time, since we hoped to find out the sex of our child.

As I lay on the table with my feet in the stirrups and Drew standing by my side, I felt a mix of excitement and anticipation. I hadn't had any problems other than a little bit of queasiness each morning, which I quelled with a few of the saltines I kept on my bedside table.

I looked over at the monitor as Dr. Morgan typed in our last name, the date, and the words "Baby Wagner." It still seemed so unreal. He squirted the ultrasound probe with cold jelly and placed it on my abdomen. He slid it down and around as I watched the blurred image on the black screen. Then he stopped and pressed it gently, and a small kidney-bean shape appeared.

"Hmm, there you go," he said, pleased.

Drew and I looked at each other, and then our eyes darted quickly back to the screen.

"It looks like you have yourselves a little girl," he said before we could even ask.

My heart almost leapt from my chest as I broke into a smile. "I knew it!" I said, looking at Drew, who was grinning too.

Dr. Morgan moved the probe again, first to the left, then to the right. Then up again.

"And there's another one," he said calmly.

"Another one?" I asked, incredulous.

"Yep! You're having twins!" he announced triumphantly, as if he'd had something to do with their conception.

I looked at Drew, whose mouth was gaping open. For an instant, time stood still as we took in this amazing news.

"Oh my gosh! Twins!"

Drew looked at me, speechless. Then his face relaxed and he reached over and kissed me. "Girl or boy?" he asked the doctor.

"Hard to tell . . . I think it's a girl."

Brittany, I thought, though Drew liked the name Hannah. We both did.

"But you may want to start thinking of boy names, just in case," Dr. Morgan cautioned.

"We already have," I told him.

Two babies. It was the best of all possible outcomes. And more miraculous than I could have imagined.

From the moment we discovered we were having twins, life changed irrevocably. The perfect house we'd bought a few years earlier would be adequate but cramped. We also discussed whether I'd be up to working with a twin pregnancy. I figured I'd find out as I got further along. I was healthy and wanted to keep writing until I didn't feel up to it. Drew, of course, was supportive. And then there was the baby equipment—doubled. Two beds, two sets of each outfit, a double stroller, and double the diapers. We knew one thing for sure: Having twins wasn't going to be cheap. But it certainly would be worth it.

"Drew!"

I'd just felt an intense cramp in my belly, one that caused me to reach across my swollen middle and brace myself. I was twenty-six weeks—halfway through my pregnancy—and everything had been fine. This was something new.

"Drew!" I called again, louder.

He rushed into our bedroom and found me sitting on the side of our bed, taking one deep breath after another.

"What's wrong?" he asked, his face pale with worry. He sat down and put his arm around me.

"I'm not sure. Fake labor pains? There's no way these babies are coming now."

"They can't be," he assured me. "You should call Dr. Morgan. Tell him what's going on."

I sat down on the bed, picked up the phone, and called the doctor's office. My twin pregnancy was automatically considered high-risk. The nurse I spoke with told me they would fit me in at two o'clock that afternoon.

I spent the rest of the morning in bed. The pain began to subside, but I was anxious, tuned in to every little twinge I felt. Around one thirty, Drew helped me into the car and drove me to my appointment.

"Sounds like Braxton Hicks, early labor pains," said Dr. Morgan. "We can put you on a medication to stop those. You'll also have to go on bed rest."

I looked at Drew. He was worried. "Bed rest?"

"Yes, complete bed rest. At home. We don't want those babies coming before thirty-seven weeks."

I'd spent the last two weeks reading a book on premature birth. The statistics were bleak. If the girls were born too early, they likely wouldn't survive. I was now twenty-six weeks. At thirty weeks, they'd have underdeveloped lungs and need to stay in the neonatal intensive care. Even then, it would be touch and go.

I did the math. It was now February 2. I hoped to make it full term, to forty. But even at thirty-seven, I still had twelve weeks to go. That was three months. What would I do with myself? How would I cope?

"Okay," I said, looking to Drew for reassurance. He would have to care for me, take on the grocery shopping and cleaning, and even get the nursery ready without my help. How would *he* cope?

I did as my doctor instructed and went to bed. A few days later, my optimism crumbled. I started worrying—about the kitchen floor and the blueberry stain on the tablecloth, now a day old. Who would look after those things? And what about our closets, the ones we'd meant to clean out? When would we ever find time once the twins arrived?

Then I remembered that we were in God's hands. He'd been there before the babies were conceived; why would He abandon us now? He was faithful, unchanging. Somehow, He would carry us through.

Mama came once a week for an overnight visit, and I was always relieved to see her walk through the door. She cleaned the house, ran errands, and kept me company. I had been a parent to my mother for several years, and it seemed that God had suddenly reversed our roles again. I needed a mother now, and yet I struggled with the guilt of having my aging mother wait on me when I was the one who should be caring for her.

Untethered

When Mama wasn't busy, she napped. Sometimes she'd complain about her back, and I knew she was worried that the cancer had returned. But through it all, she remained cheerful. I was grateful to have her there.

One night, as Mama finished up the dinner dishes, I called for her to come and read with me. She sat by my bed and we read for several hours, our silence broken only by an occasional comment or the ringing telephone. There was a sweet, much-needed peace between us. I felt the babies sensed it too.

As Mama rose to go to bed, I asked, "Do you want to feel the babies kick?"

She walked over, sat down, and tentatively placed her hand on my very large tummy.

"Here," I said, moving her hand to the appropriate spot.

She looked at me awkwardly.

"Did you feel that?" I asked.

"I think so." She hesitated. "I never remember my mama picking me up when I was a little girl. Just holding me in her arms."

My breath caught in my chest. I looked up, and our eyes met.

"Maybe that's why I was always so close to my daddy," she said.

That's when it all became clear. Why she'd made that comment all those years before, about Daddy loving me more than her. The comment that had pierced my heart. It had come out of a place of hurt, of woundedness. Now all I wanted was to take that hurt away. But that was impossible. All I could do was love her with whatever time we had left.

"Well," she said, "time for bed. I love you." She leaned over and pressed her face to mine.

"I love you too, Mama."

I was thirty-two and she was sixty-eight, and we had just broken new ground.

...

The medication worked for four weeks, but then the cramps starting coming every thirty minutes. Dr. Morgan didn't want to take a chance at my losing the babies, so he told me to come in. He'd check my cervix, make sure I wasn't dilated, then send me home.

After several hours of monitoring, he told me I'd need to wait out the next few months in the hospital.

"Hospital?" I said, feeling a mix of relief and alarm. Relief that I could be monitored, alarm that something might go terribly wrong.

"Don't forget you're high-risk," he said. "And with your premature labor, even more so. Every day you stay in bed gives those babies a better chance."

I knew he was right. Staying in bed seemed like such a small price to pay, but the prospect of lying in a hospital bed for seven weeks was daunting.

That afternoon, I settled into Room 1407 in the maternity ward of Rex Hospital, which was located just a couple of miles from our house. I was instructed to lie on my left side, which kept the contractions at bay. I was only allowed to sit up for meals, and to get up to go to the bathroom and shower. Whenever I did sit up, the contractions would start, so I would eat as quickly as possible, then lie back down on my side. There was a large window that looked out on a parking deck and a few flowering cherry trees. I watched as the trees began to bud, then burst into bloom.

My days started predawn, when a nurse would enter my room and turn on the lights to check my vital signs. I'd cooperate with my eyes half shut, then fall back asleep until breakfast. When I was bored, I'd watch TV. Mostly I read. C.S. Lewis's Space Trilogy and Madeleine L'Engle's Crosswicks Journals—fifteen books in all.

Sometimes I'd just lie there and stare out the window and reflect on my life up to this moment. For the most part, my life had been more flailing than faith. But then I'd met Drew and found my home. We'd traveled, shared work we both loved. We'd prayed and waited—not so patiently at times—for these babies. Now I was willing to do whatever it took to make sure they made it safely into this world.

As I turned my attention to preparing for motherhood, I thought a lot about Mama and the contentious relationship we'd had when I was younger. I'd felt I could never measure up, that I could never do enough to please her. I also knew I'd put her through hell. But when she was diagnosed with cancer, everything had changed. I'd realized I might lose her, and no matter how much we'd clashed in the past, I'd known it was time to set things right. So I'd tried harder. Become more patient and kind. I'd been there for her when she was sick. It was a start.

I was going to be a mother and I was going to be a good one. I believed with all my heart that these babies were a chance to redeem my relationship with Mama. I'd pour myself into these girls—make sure they always knew they were cherished and loved. That they'd been prayed for long before they were born. That there was nothing Drew and I wouldn't do for them. And that started right now, with bed rest.

As I rubbed my protruding belly and whispered their names, I began to fall in love. I wondered what they'd look like. Would they have Drew's lips? My blue eyes? Dr. Morgan had told me Elizabeth was already head-down in the birth canal. At twenty-eight weeks, she was ready to come out. *Focused.* Hannah was the one who moved in sweeping motions like a dolphin. I'd watch the tight skin across my belly rise and a bulge sweep from right to left. *Adventurous.* I couldn't wait to meet them and see if my predictions would come true.

As the weeks turned into a month, Drew started working on the nursery: painting the walls pink, ordering the crib and changing table we'd picked out before I'd gone into the hospital. It was hard not lending a hand. Something inside me desperately wanted to nest, but that was impossible. For now, Drew was doing his part, and I was here in the hospital doing mine. We were a good team.

My hospital room quickly became home. One night in March, Drew arrived with double dips of chocolate ice cream. He read Flannery O'Connor's *A Good Man Is Hard to Find* to me, and every now and then he'd lapse into Ms. O'Connor's southern dialect. As he read, I studied his face, memorizing each line and angle. I realized once again how precious he was, and just how deeply I loved him. I whispered a prayer of thanks for a gift so undeserved.

On a Saturday in April, some friends from church gathered around my bed and threw me a baby shower. Mama drove over to join us. Unwrapping matching pink outfits and hair bows made it all seem so real, and so worth what I was going through.

After everyone had gone, Mama bent over my bed to say goodbye, pressing her cheek to mine in a kiss.

"I hope I can be around to watch them grow up," she whispered. Her voice was wistful.

"You will," I whispered back.

Then she told me her tumors had reappeared. That she'd need a series of three-day hospital stays for chemo.

"Everything will be okay," I said, trying to cheer her. But this time, even I didn't believe it.

Near the end of April, when I'd made it to exactly thirty-five weeks, Dr. Morgan and Dr. Harden appeared at the foot of my bed. Their visits were one of the highlights of my otherwise monotonous days. They were excellent doctors who wanted to give my babies the best possible start. They were also funny and kind, and I sensed they liked me as much as I did them.

"We have good news," Dr. Morgan said. "You get to go home."

"Really?"

"Yep," said Dr. Harden. "We're hoping you can carry to thirty-seven weeks. But if you have the babies before then, they'll be fine."

"Thank you." A broad smile spread across my face. "I'll call Drew right now!"

"Just so you know," Dr. Harden said, giving Dr. Morgan a wink, "the two of us made a bet that you wouldn't make it to the parking lot."

I knew he was joking, but his comment stopped me cold. They thought I wouldn't even make it to the car? Much less home? Were my chances really that slim?

I understood that I was extremely pregnant. I'd added some ninety extra pounds to my formerly slender frame. I was huge. And I hadn't been on my feet for any length of time over the past three months. Maybe they were right. Still, I was desperate to get home and finish up the nursery. I wanted to line dresser drawers with scented paper and lovingly fill them with tiny pink outfits. Surely that wasn't too much to ask.

I did make it to the parking lot, and even to our house. Once again, I beat the odds.

On the first Tuesday in May, exactly two weeks after I'd left the hospital, my water broke. I had just finished sweeping our front porch, put the broom away, and walked into our bedroom. I felt something in my belly release, and I looked down and saw that I was standing in a pool of liquid. I immediately doubled over in horrible pain that reminded me of the afternoon of our brunch at Jack's when I'd been rushed to the hospital.

Now Drew wasn't home. And I needed to get to the emergency room.

I shuffled to the bathroom, grabbed a bath towel, walked back to our bedroom, and threw it down on the floor.

I called my doctor's office and they instructed me to come in. Drew had left an hour and a half earlier to meet a client for lunch at the Research Triangle Park, twenty minutes away. He'd told me he would only be at lunch for an hour, then come straight home. I looked at the clock. It was a few minutes after two. With that, my belly constricted in pain. I knew he was on his way home. Still, twenty minutes seemed like an eternity. I needed a plan.

I certainly couldn't drive myself. But I couldn't just stand there either.

I thought of my neighbor, Alice. She was a stay-at-home mom who was usually around during the day. Maybe she could help.

I dialed her number. No answer. I started to panic. The pain was getting worse, so I lay down on the bed and rolled onto my left side. If I'd learned one thing from all those months of bed rest, it was that lying on my left side would increase the blood flow to my uterus. *I sure could use that right now*, I thought.

A few minutes later, Drew walked through the door.

"Laura?" he called, as if he sensed something was wrong.

"In here! My water broke. Dr. Morgan wants me to come to his office right away."

As Drew helped me out the front door and down the steps, I saw Alice scurrying down the sidewalk, grinning ear to ear.

"Just breathe!" she cackled. "You'll be fine!"

I loved my neighbor. She'd been a good friend. But in that moment, I wanted to punch her out cold.

Six hours later, around nine o'clock, Dr. Morgan walked into my hospital room to check on me. I'd been having contractions off and on for about seven hours, and the pain and frequency were increasing.

"Busy night," he said. "I'm afraid we're going to have to take you down to the OR. The birthing rooms are all full. It's the only space available."

By now I was in so much pain, riding the wave of contractions, that I didn't care where I had these babies. I just wanted to have them *now*.

Before I knew it, I was being wheeled down the hall on a stretcher, Drew walking beside me. My feet were in the stirrups, my legs spread open, and a large white sheet barely covered my knees. As we passed nurses and doctors, I was keenly aware that the more private parts of me were on display for all the world to see.

For a brief second, my embarrassment eclipsed my pain. Then I was pushed into a large, tiled room with several observation windows. Three or four operating room nurses were there and helped the orderly get my stretcher in place.

A young nurse with strawberry-blond hair came over to me and smiled.

"We've never seen a twin birth! Would you mind if we watched?"

I gave her a half smile. I knew from months in the hospital that a multiple birth was a big deal. "Sure," I said, resigned. She seemed so excited. And the room was already buzzing with nurses and doctors tending to my high-risk delivery. What difference would two or three more bodies make?

I turned and saw Dr. Morgan scrubbing up and putting on his gloves. My belly tightened once more into a monstrous contraction as he checked my cervix.

"Ten centimeters," he said, smiling. "And she's crowning."

This was it. I took a long, deep breath as I'd been instructed to do in our Bradley classes.

"Okay!" he said. "I need you to push as hard as you can!"

I pushed and pushed harder. The pain came in waves, like the ocean rushing the shore. This seemed to be taking forever. Was anything even happening?

"Push! One more time!"

I bore down and pushed. The next moment, I heard crying.

"Here's Baby Number One!" For the first time in several hours, the pain momentarily stopped. I looked at Drew, whose face was a mix of exhaustion and joy. Then I looked at the bloody little bundle Dr. Morgan was holding in his hands. *Elizabeth.*

After he cut and tied the cord, a nurse wrapped her in a blanket and quickly whisked her away to be washed and weighed.

"You were amazing," said Drew. He pulled up his surgical mask and kissed me on the lips. This had been a journey. We'd made it. In that moment, I was sure I'd never loved him more.

The nurse who had taken Elizabeth appeared at my side and handed her to me. She was tiny, just under five pounds. I looked at her face, red and wrinkled and scrunched into a frown.

"She's beautiful," I said to Drew. And she was. In that moment, the world completely stopped. I was holding my daughter, our daughter, in my arms. The daughter I'd longed for and prayed for. She was truly an answer to prayer.

Dr. Morgan's voice broke through my reverie.

"Don't forget!" he said. "You've got another one in there!"

I laughed out loud. "I know!"

There was a sudden shuffling of bodies—nurses checking my monitor, adjusting my IV lines. A wave of pressure swept through my abdomen. I wanted more than anything to see this baby. As exhausted as I was, I was going to give this everything I had left.

I handed Elizabeth off to Drew and began pushing with all my might.

"Keep going! You can do it!" the nurses who'd asked to observe were cheering to my left. In some strange way, I was glad they were there.

"Just a few more pushes!" Dr. Morgan coaxed.

All at once there was a plop, and then another one, as Hannah slid into the world. There was another scurry of activity—tying and cutting the cord, a nurse wrapping her up and carrying her away.

"You did it!" Drew said, looking at me with so much tenderness I wanted to cry.

"*We* did it," I said.

Twelve minutes later, I was holding Hannah in my arms. She was larger than Elizabeth, six and a half pounds. Her face was round and serene. She was beautiful too. I stared at her for a few moments, not believing she was mine. Another nurse appeared and put Elizabeth in the crook of my empty arm.

In the midst of my joy, my thoughts turned to Daddy. Life and death had come full circle. The losses of the past thirty-two years—Lawrence, my first marriage, Lily, and Daddy—had carved a meandering river through my soul. Grief had had its way. And yet, in those dark and eroded places, God had been there. He'd brought light and hope. He'd given me a fresh start. With Drew. And now these two precious babies.

I looked into Drew's face, and into the faces of our newborn girls. Elizabeth opened one eye and peeked up at me, and, on cue, Hannah did the same.

"Hi, girls. I'm your mama."

And in their tiny little faces, I was sure I saw the trace of a smile.

Acknowledgments

Writing may be a solitary endeavor, but there are guides who show up along the way to challenge, encourage, and nurture you. They make your story better. I had the best companions a writer could ask for. I'm grateful.

Brooke Warner, you are an extraordinary coach, editor, publisher, and friend. This book would not exist without your wisdom, guidance, and encouragement. I'm forever indebted.

To my She Writes Press team: Shannon Green, my wonderful project manager; Krissa Lagos, my brilliant copy editor; Julie Metz, who nailed my cover on the first round; and to my She Writes sisters, a huge thanks.

To my publicity team at BookSparks—Crystal Patriarche, Tabitha Bailey, and Sabrina Kenoun—for launching my debut memoir into the world. Thank you for your hard work—and pixie dust.

I'm deeply grateful to Madeleine L'Engle, Jan Karon, and Ruth Bell Graham. You inspired a young writer, and you inspire me still.

A big thank you to Brené Brown, whose words have taught me to embrace my vulnerability. Owning and writing this story was "the ladder out of my shame hole."

To my early readers and those who wrote words of praise, I can't thank you enough: Marcie Alvis-Walker, Daniele Berman, Jen Brown, Heidi Bublitz, Robin Dawson, Echo Montgomery Garrett, Marianne Gingher, Amy Hackett, Rebecca Opdenaker Hinson,

Kim Johnston, Mary LaScala, Jonathan Merritt, Teresa Middleton, Michael Morris, Cheryl Sharp, and Rebecca Brewster Stevenson, your kindness and generosity made all the difference.

Kathy L. Murphy and Mandy Haynes, I'm proud to be a Pulpwood Queen. Thanks for the love.

My deepest gratitude to the friends and family who walked with me on this journey. You know who you are. I'm blessed.

Horace, I will never forget those predawn calls to review an early draft of my manuscript. Your insights were invaluable. It's really great having a Renaissance man and fellow writer for a brother.

Liz, Hannah, and Annie, being your mother is my magnum opus. I couldn't have done this without your encouragement (and hugs). Also Calin, Jeremy, and Hasten. I love you all.

Liz, when people ask me why I decided to write a memoir, I tell them that you once said, "Mum, you've had an interesting life. You should write about it." So I did.

To Stephen, for seeing me, and believing. Thank you for your love. I am so grateful to share this life with you. *Oof.*

~∂·ᴄ~

About the Author

Photo credit: Annie Timmons

Laura grew up in Raleigh, North Carolina, the daughter of a journalist and a teacher. She has been an advertising copywriter, newspaper columnist, staff writer for an international relief agency, travel writer, blogger, teacher, communications director for several nonprofits, and personal assistant to a *New York Times* best-selling author. Laura is passionate about her faith, books, travel, nature (especially the beach), social justice, and her family. She lives in Winston-Salem, North Carolina, with her husband, Stephen. To learn more, visit laurawhitfield.com.

SELECTED TITLES FROM SHE WRITES PRESS

She Writes Press is an independent publishing
company founded to serve women writers everywhere.
Visit us at www.shewritespress.com.

Fourteen: A Daughter's Memoir of Adventure, Sailing, and Survival by Leslie Johansen Nack. $16.95, 978-1-63152-941-2. A coming-of-age adventure story about a young girl who comes into her own power, fights back against abuse, becomes an accomplished sailor, and falls in love with the ocean and the natural world.

Hippie Chick: Coming of Age in the '60s by Ilene English. $16.95, 978-1-63152-586-5. After sixteen-year-old Ilene English, the youngest of six, finds her mother dead in the bathroom, she flies alone from New Jersey to San Francisco, embarking upon a journey that takes her through the earliest days of the counterculture, psychedelics, and free love, on into single parenthood, and eventually to a place of fully owning her own strengths and abilities.

Rethinking Possible: A Memoir of Resilience by Rebecca Faye Smith Galli. $16.95, 978-1-63152-220-8. After her brother's devastatingly young death tears her world apart, Becky Galli embarks upon a quest to recreate the sense of family she's lost—and learns about healing and the transformational power of love over loss along the way.

Change Maker: How My Brother's Death Woke Up My Life by Rebecca Austill-Clausen. $16.95, 978-1-63152-130-0. Rebecca Austill-Clausen was workaholic businesswoman with no prior psychic experience when she discovered that she could talk with her dead brother, not to mention multiple other spirits—and a whole new world opened up to her.

All Set for Black, Thanks: A New Look at Mourning by Miriam Weinstein. $16.95, 978-1-63152-109-6. A wry, irreverent take on how we mourn, how we remember, and how we keep our dead with us even as we (sort of) let them go.

Breaking Sad: What to Say After Loss, What Not to Say, and When to Just Show Up by Shelly Fisher and Jennifer Jones. $16.95, 978-1-63152-242-0. Real stories and real feedback regarding what should be said—and what should be kept to yourself—when you're navigating the conversation we are all so often too intimidated to start: the conversation about loss.